b.d.
5/75

75/5
EBN
R4.05

God in an age of atheism

GOD
in an age of
atheism

S. Paul Schilling

✌ abingdon press - nashville and new york

GOD IN AN AGE OF ATHEISM

Copyright © 1969 by Abingdon Press

All rights in this book are reserved.
No part of the book may be reproduced in any manner whatsoever without written permission of the publishers except brief quotations embodied in critical articles or reviews. For information address Abingdon Press, Nashville, Tennessee.

ISBN-0-687-15075-2
Library of Congress Catalog Card Number: 72-84713

Scripture quotations unless otherwise noted are from the Revised Standard Version of the Bible, copyrighted 1946 and 1952 by the Division of Christian Education, National Council of Churches, and are used by permission.

Excerpts from "Ernst Bloch: Philosopher of the Not-Yet" by S. Paul Schilling, copyright © 1967 Christian Century Foundation, are reprinted by permission from the November 15, 1967 issue of *The Christian Century*.

Excerpts from the author's review of Jürgen Moltmann, *Theology of Hope*, in *Interpretation*, 22 (1968), 480-83, are used by permission of *Interpretation*.

Quotations from the German news magazine *Der Spiegel*, No. 30, 1966, are used by permission.

SET UP, PRINTED, AND BOUND BY THE
PARTHENON PRESS, AT NASHVILLE,
TENNESSEE, UNITED STATES OF AMERICA

To
Robert and Janice Schilling
Paula and Bruce Foreman
beloved sons and daughters
by birth and marriage

preface

This book is mainly an outgrowth of research undertaken during sabbatical leave in Europe from June, 1966 to January, 1967. In the preceding months the "death-of-God" theology had registered its maximum impact in the United States. Though I did not then—as I do not now—believe that this movement signaled the approaching end of belief in God, the widespread attention accorded it indicated that it was symptomatic of an attitude much broader and deeper than itself. We are living through a time of doubt and unbelief more extensive and radical than anything experienced by the western world in the twentieth century. Those who assert that God has really died represent only one—and by no means the most important—of the varieties of contemporary atheism, which in turn are the most visible and pronounced expression of questions being asked by large numbers of thoughtful people, including many professing Christians.

It is therefore imperative that theology examine anew the meaning of the reality of God. This examination will be all the more significant and relevant if it can proceed in the context of a living encounter with atheistic thought at its best, as embodied in the large numbers of serious-minded persons who are committed to high human values, yet explicitly or implicitly deny all belief in a more-than-human God. Just what are they repudiating? What are the grounds for their rejection? To what degree have Christians themselves, by their traditionalism, their irrationalism, their lack of clarity in communication, or their failure to support profession with practice, contributed to the growth of such unbelief? I have explored questions like these, asking what meaning the answers arrived at might have for a sound Christian understanding of God.

For seven months Mrs. Schilling and I made our headquarters in Tübingen, Germany, drawn by the excellence of its Catholic and Protestant theological faculties and the quality of its university libraries. To extensive research in the pertinent literature we added personal consultations with about forty-five philosophers, theologians, pastors, and researchers in East and West Germany, Holland, Switzerland, and Czechoslovakia. Approximately one month was spent in Berlin (East and West), East Germany, and Prague. Especially valuable were frank, friendly discussions with seven Marxist thinkers. Informative also was participation in a conference of the *Paulus-Gesellschaft*, a predominantly Roman Catholic organization which has pioneered in promoting the expanding Marxist-Christian dialogue. Here I was privileged to present a paper on "Ideologie und christlicher Glaube" ("Ideology and Christian Faith").

During the months in Europe I concentrated chiefly on nineteenth-century and Marxist atheism. Since then, as before, I have devoted primary attention to other forms of atheism and to the works of English and French writers. The interpretations of the varieties of atheistic thought and the objections to theistic belief which are found in Part One of this volume emerged from this investigation. After the nature and bases of contemporary unbelief had become fairly clear, I turned to a reexamination of classical theism and consideration of various alternative conceptualizations, though always in the context of the atheistic critique. Thus the proposals made in Part Two are a direct response to the situation discussed in Part One.

The project was given specific focus and significantly advanced when I was invited to give the annual Lowell Institute Lectures in theology in Marsh Chapel of Boston University in the spring of 1968. Chapters I-IV of this book represent a revision and considerable expansion of these lectures.

My indebtedness to others is so great that I hesitate to mention particular persons and institutions. However, failure to do so would conceal the deep gratitude which I feel for valuable aid generously given. First of all acknowledgment should be made to Boston University for the sabbatical leave made possible by the School of Theology and for a research grant from the Graduate School. Thanks are due also to the University of Tübingen for making so freely available the full facilities of its excellent theological and philosophical libraries, and to the Lowell Institute for its lectureship invitation.

I am profoundly grateful to the many Europeans who graciously granted the interviews out of which came information and insights procurable in no other way; and especially to the Marxist thinkers for their hospitality, their warm friendliness, and their openness in discussion, which disclosed common interests beneath sharp differences and provided a stimulating adventure in understanding. Hans-Rudolf Müller-Schwefe, professor of practical theology at the University of Hamburg, who was himself working on the problem of atheism, was exceedingly helpful in personal conversations on several occasions, and in sharing bibliographies. Erich Kellner, director of the *Paulus-Gesellschaft,* made available the publications of his society and opened the way to participation in one of its semi-annual conferences.

I owe much to the many faculty colleagues, students, and friends who have shared their ideas, responded critically to tentative formulations, and suggested needed emphases. Nils Ehrenstrom, professor of ecumenics at the School of Theology, and Robert S. Cohen, chairman of the physics department in the Boston University Graduate School, have offered helpful guidance with respect to both persons and literature relevant to the investigation. Professor Catherine L. Gunsalus of West Virginia Wesleyan College and Gary Marks, doctoral candidate in systematic theology in Boston University, have rendered important assistance in research; and Miss Joyce Marieb, also a Ph.D. candidate in systematic theology at Boston University, has prepared the indexes.

Most of all I am grateful to my wife, who has participated in the research, typed several drafts of the manuscript, offered many constructive criticisms, both stylistic and substantive, and contributed immeasurably by her constant encouragement and support.

S. PAUL SCHILLING

Newton, Massachusetts

contents

introduction: UNDERSTANDING THE UNBELIEVER 13

part one: The Atheistic Critique

I. NINETEENTH-CENTURY SOURCES 23
    1. Ludwig Feuerbach 23
    2. Marxist-Leninist Atheism 26
        Karl Marx 26
        Friedrich Engels 29
        V. I. Lenin 32
    3. Friedrich Nietzsche 33

II. VARIETIES OF ATHEISTIC HUMANISM 40
    1. Freudian Psychoanalysis 40
    2. Marxism 51
        The Marxist Critique Today 51
        Ernst Bloch's Philosophy
          of the Not-Yet 58
    3. Existentialism 64
        The Self-definition of Man 65
        Atheism as Axiological Protest 71
        Responsible Humanism 76
    4. Scientific Humanism 79
        Nonreligious Naturalism 80
        Religious Humanism 85
    5. Linguistic Philosophy 90

6. "Christian Atheism"
   of the Death of God 100
   William Hamilton 102
   Thomas J. J. Altizer 105
   Richard L. Rubenstein 108
   Dorothee Sölle 111
   Herbert Braun 112

III. MAJOR BASES OF UNBELIEF 115

part two: Exploring Afresh the Meaning of God

IV. SIGNPOSTS 137

V. FINDINGS 191
   1. God as Being 194
   2. God as Creative Process 198
   3. God as Love 205
   4. God as Personal Life 209

Bibliography 217
Index of Persons 233
Index of Subjects 236

introduction: Understanding the Unbeliever

In the early summer of 1966 the following announcement, in the form of an obituary, appeared in the school paper of the Gerhard-Rohlfs-Gymnasium in Bremen, Germany, and was reprinted in the newsmagazine *Der Spiegel*:

Deceased After a Long Illness

God the Lord

As we hear, the war in Vietnam continues with unabated harshness, napalm bombs drop on the civilian population, Hitler-follower General Ky is further supported by America, more soldiers die daily.

As we read, men are starving continually in India, China, and Algeria, wheat is rotting in western grain-silos, church congregations take collections for a new section of their cemetery-fence.

As we see, in the kingdom of God ever more people are tortured, murdered, victimized by violence, stabbed, burned, or allowed to starve.

In our opinion, one conclusion is forced on everyone who thinks honestly: The God who once "over all things so wondrously reigned, whom my soul praised, who led me in green pastures," is absent, sick, on a journey, dead. A God who orders all for the best in Auschwitz, the Warsaw ghetto, Vietnam, and the Negro section of New York no longer exists. He has not finished his work. His position is open. He must be replaced. The future is open.

> In silent mourning,
>> Ingbert Lindemann, student of theology
>> Hermann Rademann, 13th grade
>> Wilfried Kuhlmann, student [1]

These words portray vividly, and probably accurately, both the atheism and the humanitarian rebelliousness which characterize multitudes of people in our time. Evidences of a deep erosion of faith in God—or in some reality which men have called God—can be seen on all sides. Whatever we may think of this occurrence, we dare not ignore it or pretend that it does not exist. It is present to some degree and at some times in many religious people, and in the church itself.

In the contemporary painting "The Return of the Prodigal Son," by Giorgio de Chirico, God appears as a lifeless white marble statue, and the returning boy as a robot without a face. In 1965, a collection of recent art of Christian significance was exhibited in various cities of West Germany entitled "Imago Dei Today."[2] Included were many works portraying the crucifixion, but only one dealing with the resurrection. Does this perhaps reflect, at least in part, the situation in our contemporary world? We are painfully conscious of the grim reality of suffering and death. Can we no longer comprehend or experience the meaning of victory or redemption? Is an awareness of the living presence of God a thing of the past?

It no longer taxes our credulity to believe in some of the characters of Greek mythology. Sisyphus, Theseus, and Prometheus, for example, have come convincingly to life in the existence of mid-twentieth-century man. Sisyphus was con-

---

[1] *Der Spiegel*, July 18, 1966.
[2] *Die Abschaffung Gottes; Imago Dei heute: Ausstellung des Evangelischen Forums.* Hamburg: Friedrich Wittig Verlag, n. d.

INTRODUCTION

demned to roll a huge stone up a steep hillside, only to have it escape him near the summit and hurtle to the bottom, whence he sought again to roll it to the top, repeating the sorry process ad infinitum. Sisyphus is our contemporary who is beset by the meaninglessness and absurdity of life. He strives for the ideal, but without hope, and alone. His question is not that of finding the highest meaning, but whether life has any meaning at all. He keeps struggling, but amid his repeated frustrations cries out, "What is it all for?"

In the same town with Sisyphus dwells Theseus, who like his ancient counterpart sets forth through a confusing labyrinth to find and slay the Minotaur, but even if successful must still find his way out. His plight was dramatically portrayed by the maze which was a major part of "Labyrinth," the fanciful exhibit of the National Film Board of Canada at Montreal's Expo 67. It contained no suggestion that the thread of Ariadne which saved Theseus is available to modern man. Theseus is our contemporary who thinks there is a meaning in life, but he doesn't know what it is or where to find it.

Strangely, in the same neighborhood is another character who manifests self-confidence and hope as well as courage. Prometheus, because he defied the gods by stealing fire from heaven, was chained to a lofty pinnacle where vultures continually devoured his liver, yet in heroic defiance he struggled for freedom. His namesake today rejects God or finds him irrelevant, but he believes profoundly in man and his ability, however great the odds against him, to break his bonds and fashion a world of justice and freedom for all.

Sisyphus and Theseus lack the confident assurance of Prometheus, but they agree with him in regarding man as wholly on his own in the universe, which if not hostile is indifferent to his needs and aspirations. There is no transcendent reality which cares about man, nothing beyond man himself which is concerned for his welfare. In short, there is no God.

In agreement with the judgment of the Second Vatican

Council, I assume that a Christian approach to these and related expressions of atheism rules out sweeping condemnation. Besides falling on deaf ears, negatively judgmental utterances overlook the sincerity, seriousness, and intelligence of the unbeliever, and the probability that his objections contain genuine truth. They also tend to align against one another, as antagonists, people who in a pluralistic, interdependent world need to learn to coexist if they are to exist at all. In our day we have seen the havoc wrought when blind anticommunism is abetted by emotional opposition to Marxist atheism. Furthermore, sensitive Christians cannot fail to identify themselves with unbelievers, in the awareness that both are sinners in need of God's forgiving love. All are alike included in "the ungodly" for whom Christ died. Or as Gustav Heinemann puts it, "Christ did not die against Karl Marx, but for us all." [3] If, therefore, we proclaim with understanding the good news we have received, we shall speak and act out of concern for the atheist rather than enmity toward him.

The alternative to condemnation, of course, is real dialogue. In the words of Bonhoeffer, "The Church must come out of its stagnation. We must move out again into the open air of intellectual discussion with the world, and risk saying controversial things." [4] "The world" today includes a great many atheists and agnostics. If we are to take them seriously we must really listen to them and try strenuously to understand what they are meaning. This requires the effort to follow their arguments step by step, and to find out what it is they are rejecting when they deny the reality of God. With pardonable tautology Martin Heidegger declares, "We pay attention to a thinker only as we think. This requires us to think

---

[3] Quoted by Friedrich Wilhelm Marquardt, " 'Solidarität mit den Gottlosen.' Zur Geschichte und Bedeutung eines Theologumenons," *Evangelische Theologie*, 20 (1960), 538.

[4] *Letters and Papers from Prison*, ed. Eberhard Bethge, rev. ed. (New York: The Macmillan Co., [1953] 1967), p. 208.

everything essential that is thought in his thought."[5]

If we adopt this attitude toward thoughtful people who question the reality of God, we can respond to them in two major ways. First, we may attempt to discover and clarify our differences, to expose the misunderstandings of the atheist, to refute his arguments, and to convince him of the superiority of the theistic position. The Christian dares not evade this kind of direct confrontation. He must heed the admonition of I Peter 3:15: "Always be prepared to make a defense to anyone who calls you to account for the hope that is in you." He can at least show that he does not fear open critical discussion, and he can win the respect of the other by demonstrating his concern for a reasonable faith. However, such debates are very likely to end at best in stalemate, and even our most skillful demolition of our opponent's arguments usually leaves him unconvinced and unconverted.

A second response which we may make to the atheist is that of using his criticisms in the task of rethinking and clarifying our own understanding of God. Obviously we can learn only negatively from the superficial, self-centered, self-sufficient idolator who wants no divine interference in his pursuit of comfort and pleasure. But the situation is vastly different with the man whose earnest search for truth leads to honest doubt or a definite rejection of religious faith. Simone Weil has observed: "There are two atheisms of which one is a purification of the notion of God."[6] The serious atheist who wrestles with ultimate questions is likely to contribute more to intelligent understanding of both God and man than the pious believer who placidly accepts prevailing views. The objections of the former may call attention to weaknesses and incongruities in notions of God long taken for granted. They may expose some false gods to which Christians themselves

[5] *Holzwege* (Frankfurt am Main: Vittorio Klostermann, 1950), p. 235.
[6] William Robert Miller (ed.), *The New Christianity* (New York: Delacorte Press, 1967), p. 267.

have given allegiance. They may bring to light facets of traditional theistic belief which believers have not related to expanding knowledge of the physical world, man, and society. They may disclose failures on the part of believers to communicate intelligibly to others what they mean by God. Or they may force believers to recognize that some of their own ideas have been vague, confused, or erroneous. There is therefore great value in listening carefully, though critically, to the atheists, and inquiring what their concerns may contribute positively to the improvement of our conceptions of God. It is this kind of inquiry which I propose to undertake, and in which I invite the reader's participation.

Obviously, we shall *not* attempt simply to scale down or tailor our belief in God to meet the specifications of the atheist. We shall not ask him what kind of God he will allow us to affirm! But we shall undertake a fresh look at the meaning of God in the light of—or in the darkness of!—the atheistic critique. The most crucial task facing Christian theology today is that of reconceiving the reality of God. It cannot be adequately performed without a clear awareness of the questions, doubts, objections, and rejections which characterize multitudes of thoughtful people. If there ever was a time when theology could be carried on in disregard of the skepticism of men and women outside the church—and others like them inside—that time is long since past.

To prepare the churches for the Fourth Assembly of the World Council of Churches held at Uppsala in July, 1968, the Council issued a study booklet, *All Things New*. The booklet—and to a considerable degree the Assembly itself—made an approach different from that usually made in such study guides: It began not with the church or even with the gospel, but with the world. It accepted with complete seriousness the secularization of our time, though without submerging the gospel in the process. This posture moved *The Chris-*

tian Century to comment hopefully: "Uppsala can sing a new song on unity if, following *All Things New,* it begins with the world rather than with itself." [7] It is essentially this approach which I am now proposing for Christian thought about God. Without downgrading other approaches, I am suggesting that just now there may be peculiar value in beginning with people outside the temple, those who doubt or deny God, and asking what they can contribute, by their very objections, to a clearer understanding of the divine reality. To listen attentively and receptively to the criticisms of honest and serious atheists can be for believers a new learning experience, and one which may open the way to a deeper and truer conception of God. Martin Buber once observed, "The atheist staring from his attic window is often nearer to God than the believer caught up in his own false image of God." [8]

In addition to the values already suggested, the procedure proposed promises two important fringe benefits. First, if it can be carried out forthrightly in local congregations among thoughtful laymen, it may stimulate a renewal of faith as well as of understanding. Recently I led an adult church school class in a three-month study of questions of belief and unbelief. Midway in the course a middle-aged woman told of the great release she felt when she saw openly written on the blackboard and heard frankly discussed objections which thoughtful people had raised to belief in God. Previously she had suppressed her doubts and avoided thinking about them or discussing them. The new experience of freedom helped her find a more mature faith.

Secondly, the attempt to rethink and restate the meaning of God in the light of the atheistic critique could prove to

[7] *The Christian Century,* 84 (1967), 1180.
[8] Quoted by Garret Barden, S.J. in his Introduction to Jean Lacroix's *The Meaning of Modern Atheism,* tr. Garret Barden (New York: The Macmillan Co., 1965), p. 12.

be one of the best ways of winning a hearing for Christian faith among atheists. Certainly it will be far more effective than a frontal attack on their ideas. Much atheism is implicit and indirect. The best answer to it may therefore also be indirect. Few experiences are likely to place faith in God in a more favorable light for the unbeliever than the discovery that his objections do not really apply to the beliefs of those whom in dialogue he has learned to know and respect.

Part One will endeavor to expound as objectively as possible the chief atheistic criticisms of theistic belief. Real understanding of atheism in the twentieth century requires an acquaintance with its main historical backgrounds and sources. In this connection it would be desirable to examine the arguments of the French and British materialists of the eighteenth century, largely dominated by the assumptions of the natural sciences (e.g., La Mettrie, Buffon, Robinet, Bonnet, Hartley, Priestley); the critical deism of Voltaire; the skeptical empiricism of Hume; and the positivism of Comte. However, the purpose of this volume will probably be best served if attention is limited to the views of the nineteenth-century atheists who have most directly influenced the major forms of atheism in our time. This brief survey, offered in Chapter I, will be followed in Chapter II by an investigation of six contemporary varieties of atheistic thought. To this will be added in Chapter III a summary of the main objections to belief in God which emerge, often held in common by representatives of different movements.

Part Two will utilize the atheistic critique in the effort to discover what the term God should mean for Christians today. Chapter IV will examine in some detail eight emphases which the atheistic objections indicate are needed if the meaning of the divine reality is to become intelligible today and communicable to unbelievers. Chapter V will attempt to derive from these proposals, and outline on the basis of them, a possible Christian conception of God.

part one

The Atheistic Critique

I. Nineteenth-Century Sources

1. LUDWIG FEUERBACH (1804-1872)

"The secret of theology," writes Ludwig Feuerbach, "is nothing else than anthropology."[1] What religion and theology call God or gods is a reflection of man's own characteristics, hence the real object of theological investigation is man himself. Reversing the idealism of his teacher Hegel, Feuerbach regarded nature instead of spirit as the ground of all being and focused attention on man rather than the Absolute. In both respects he foreshadowed the shape of much of the atheistic thought of the nineteenth and twentieth centuries.

According to Feuerbach, man's ideas of God have two closely related sources, intellectual and emotional. Intellectually, God is the objectification in an imaginary superhuman being of the higher characteristics of man himself. The individual finds in himself qualities capable of indefinite enhancement, but which he knows he can never bring to perfection; he therefore conceives them as realized in God. Thus he objectifies his own nature and makes it his God.[2] In portraying God as personal and incorporeal, man celebrates his desire for the supernaturalness, independence, unlimitedness, and immortality of his own personality. Similarly, the love of God for man is nothing other than man's own self-love deified.[3]

In religious belief, therefore, man unconsciously transposes human predicates to a divine subject. Feuerbach reverses this process, restoring the predicates, as he believes, to their right-

[1] *The Essence of Christianity* (London: John Chapman, 1854), p. 206.
[2] *Ibid.*, pp. 10-14.
[3] *Ibid.*, pp. 98, 104.

ful owner, the human species. True divinity belongs to the predicates, such as love, wisdom, and righteousness, not to the God imagined to possess them. A quality is not divine because God has it; rather, God is assumed to have it because it is in and for itself divine. Hence the real atheist is the person who denies the divine predicates in man, not he who refuses to project them into a supposed superhuman subject.[4]

An integral part of Feuerbach's critique of religion is his concept of alienation, which he takes over from Hegel but sharply revises. In inventing an objective God, man posits over against himself another being who as infinite, eternal, and perfectly good, wise, powerful, and holy is his opposite. Thus the religious man drives a wedge between the generic nature of man and the individual human being. Since man ascribes to God his own highest qualities, he can attribute to himself only the negative and limited ones. In effect he enriches God at the expense of man, and in the name of an illusory reality estranges from himself the best part of himself.[5]

The objectification which creates God in the image of man is for Feuerbach emotional as well as intellectual. Man's earthly existence is filled with pain, frustration, failure, anxiety, heart-breaking injustice, and the awareness of his own finitude and approaching death. But he longs for unlimited fulfillment, perfect happiness, and everlasting life. He therefore posits a God who will realize for him in another world the wishes which are thwarted on earth and who will overcome the evils which are so devastating here. But this God is nothing else than the illusory externalization of human hopes. The Love which satisfies our emotional wants "is himself the realized wish of the heart, the wish exalted to the certainty of

---

[4] *Ibid.*, pp. 14-21, 96 f.; *Vorläufige Thesen zur Reform der Philosophie, Sämtliche Werke*, ed. Wilhelm Bolin and Friedrich Jodl (Stuttgart: Fromann Verlag Günther Holzboog, 1960-64), II, 224, 236, 239.
[5] *The Essence of Christianity*, pp. 13-18, 32-37, 205.

its fulfillment, ... the certainty that the inmost wishes of the heart have objective validity and reality." "God is the nature of human feeling, unlimited, pure feeling, made objective."[6] In religion man turns away from inexorable nature and gives vent to his suppressed sighs. The God to whom he turns is "a tear of love, shed in the deepest concealment, over human misery."[7]

In the emotional aspect of religion Feuerbach finds the same reversal of subject and predicate which we have previously noted. An illustration is the Christian affirmation that God in love suffers for men. God, we say, is a sensitive, feeling God. Here suffering love is the predicate. In Feuerbach's view, however, it is actually the subject. What is really meant is that it is divine to suffer, that sensitivity and feeling are divine in nature. But in our need we transform the predicates into a personified subject. As feeling men we reach out in trust to a feeling God, imparting objective existence to traits of character which we cherish in ourselves and long to have eternally secured.[8]

The entire concern of Feuerbach's criticism of religion is to expose and reverse the false objectification which he finds in its history. At the close of Part One of his *Essence of Christianity* (1854) he declares that he has reduced "the supermundane, supernatural, and superhuman nature of God to the elements of human nature as its basic elements. . . . The beginning, middle, and end of religion is MAN."[9] With this achievement he no doubt felt that he had brought nearer to fulfillment the avowed aim of his lectures given at Heidelberg in 1848: to convert "the friends of God into the friends of man, believers into thinkers, worshipers into workers, candidates for the other world into students of this world, Chris-

---

[6] *Ibid.*, pp. 120, 134, 180 f.; cf. pp. 108 f.; *Das Wesen der Religion* (Leipzig: Alfred Kröner, 1923), pp. 340 f.
[7] *The Essence of Christianity*, p. 121.
[8] *Ibid.*, pp. 61-63.
[9] *Ibid.*, p. 183.

tians, who are on their own confession 'half-animal and half-angel,' into men—whole men." [10]

2. MARXIST-LENINIST ATHEISM

KARL MARX (1818-1883)

The starting point of Karl Marx's own critique of religion is that of Feuerbach. He shares Feuerbach's materialism, declaring with Friedrich Engels that "it is not consciousness that determines life, but life that determines consciousness." [11] He likewise accepts wholly Feuerbach's view that God is nothing other than the objectification of purely human traits. However, he finds Feuerbach's analysis too theoretical, separating man's thinking from his sensuous activity or practice; and too individualistic, failing to see that the essence of man is not an abstraction inherent in the isolated individual, or a mere genus, but the totality of men's social relations. Moreover, Marx does not stop, as does Feuerbach, with identifying the self-alienation which produces otherworldly religious belief; he goes on to offer an explanation of this alienation, which he finds in the self-cleavage and self-contradictoriness of human social life in the material world. This leads Marx to call for revolutionary action to remove the contradiction.[12] "The philosophers have only *interpreted* the world, in various ways; the point, however, is to *change* it." [13]

According to Marx, the inverted world-consciousness which is religion is produced by the world of social, economic, and political relations because that world in its present form is itself inverted—imperfect, unjust, and inhuman. Religion provides the "moral sanction," "solemn completion," and "universal ground for consolation and justification" of this society. "Religious distress is at the same time the *expression* of real

[10] *Das Wesen der Religion*, p. 341.
[11] Marx and Engels, "German Ideology," *On Religion* (Moscow: Foreign Languages Publishing House, 1957), pp. 74 f.
[12] Marx, "Theses on Feuerbach," *ibid.*, pp. 69-72.
[13] *Ibid*, p. 72.

distress and the *protest* against real distress. Religion is the sigh of the oppressed creature, the heart of a heartless world, just as it is the spirit of a spiritless situation. It is the *opium* of the people." [14]

Here it is worth noting that Marx's description of religion as opium is not nearly so central or so derogatory as is generally imagined. It occurs in the context of two other images: Religion is an expression of the suffering of oppressed people and a protest against this suffering. As such it serves the positive function of making endurable a life which otherwise could not be faced. Its narcotic effect consists in its encouraging the acceptance of "illusory happiness" instead of the "real happiness" on earth which is men's rightful heritage. It can deaden pain, but it cannot cure the disease; hence it needs to be abolished. Yet Marx's basic attack is directed less against the illusions of religion than against the *"condition which needs illusions.* The criticism of religion is therefore *in embryo the criticism of the vale of woe,* the *halo* of which is religion." Once philosophy has unmasked human self-alienation in its "saintly form" it must undertake to unmask also its "unholy forms"—law and politics.[15] Later Marx comes to see that law and the state, like religion, are themselves derived phenomena, part of the "superstructure" of society, dependent for fundamental change on the revolutionary transformation of the material and economic order.

Nevertheless, Marx sees religion as so closely bound up

[14] Marx, "Contribution to the Critique of Hegel's Philosophy of Right," *ibid.*, pp. 41 f. The term *opium* was first applied to religion by Bruno Bauer in 1841.

[15] *Ibid.*, p. 42. At the Congress of the Paulus-Gesellschaft held in Salzburg in 1965, Roger Garaudy pointed out that Marx's characterization of religion as the opium of the people should not be understood at all as a statement of the metaphysical nature of religion valid for all times and places, but rather as a description of the religion of a particular historical period in a definite geographical location. *Christentum und Marxismus— heute,* ed. Erich Kellner (Wien, Frankfurt, Zürich: Europa Verlag, 1966), p. 87. Garaudy is professor of philosophy at the University of Poitiers and director of the Center of Marxist Study and Research in Paris.

with the ills of society that the radical change needed includes its "resolute *positive* abolition." By *positive* here Marx means that the goal sought is less the denial of a superhuman God than the affirmation of man. "To be radical is to grasp the root of the matter. But for man the root is man himself. . . . The criticism of religion ends with the teaching that *man is the highest essence for man,* hence with the *categoric imperative to overthrow all relations* in which man is a debased, enslaved, abandoned, despicable essence." [16]

Marx's later discussions of religion are less polemical than those so far examined, but they offer the same basic interpretation in more refined form. In the opening chapter of *Capital* (1867), for example, he relates religious alienation to the mystery of "the fetishism of commodities." To the products of human labor in a manufacturing society are ascribed a kind of objective reality independent of their producers and a value which makes them exchangeable with other commodities. Thus what should be a relation between human beings becomes a relation between things. This fetishistic ascription of independent existence to the commodities which are the results of man's labor is analogous to religious alienation, in which the products of human thoughts and feelings are treated as objective beings which can enter into relations with men and women. However, this socio-economic fetishism also supports the continuation of religious alienation. Men whose social relations are largely controlled by the mysterious and inflexible laws governing the production and distribution of alien goods readily invent the existence of transcendent deities who in inscrutable ways control their destiny.[17]

Marx expects such religion to be overcome only through changes in the economic order which enable relationships between man and man, and man and nature, to become "intelligible" and "reasonable," that is, clearly discernible and

[16] *Ibid.,* p. 50.
[17] *Capital* (London: William Glaisher, 1920), I, 41-43.

rationally acceptable. "The life-process of society, which is based on the process of material production, does not strip off its mystical veil until it is treated as production by freely associated men, and is consciously regulated by them in accordance with a settled plan." [18] But in such a society "the religious reflexion of the real world . . . would disappear." The task of enlightened men is therefore not to fight religion but to create the kind of social order in which it will die out of itself, because the suffering wrought by irresistible, foreign, irrational, and unintelligible conditions of existence has been eradicated. In a truly "humane society" "religious inspiration" would be superfluous. Men would through their productive activity express their individualities, gain the satisfaction of meeting human needs, and see themselves as indispensable complements to one another, confirming and reflecting one another's existence in their thinking and their love. They would then have no need to seek the imaginary comforts of belief in God and a heavenly realm.[19] The social order here envisaged is not anti-religious, but simply a-religious.

FRIEDRICH ENGELS (1820-1895)

Like Marx, Friedrich Engels sees in religion "nothing but the fantastic reflection in men's minds of those external forces which control their daily life, a reflection in which the terrestrial forces assume the form of supernatural forces." [20] Early Christianity, he finds, was similar to the modern working-class movement, in that it appeared originally as "a movement of oppressed people, . . . of slaves and emancipated slaves, of poor people deprived of all rights, of peoples subjugated or dispersed by Rome." [21] In bourgeois society men are dominated by economic circumstances as though by an alien power; this situation calls forth the reflective action which

[18] *Ibid.*, p. 51.
[19] Marx and Engels, *Werke* (Berlin: Dietz Verlag, 1962), III, 546 f.
[20] "Anti-Dühring," *On Religion*, p. 146.
[21] "On the History of Early Christianity," *ibid.*, p. 313.

produces religious belief. Man proposes, while God disposes; but God is actually "the alien domination of the capitalist mode of production." However, when society frees itself from this bondage by taking over the ownership of the means of production and planning their use, that is, when men dispose as well as propose, religion will disappear, since the alien forces now reflected in it will no longer exist.[22] However, unlike Dühring and many twentieth-century Communist governments, Engels specifically opposes laws against churches and religious activities, on the ground that such restrictions will make religion a martyr and thus prolong its life. In the new social order, religion, if left alone, will die a natural death.[23]

Along with arguments like these which closely parallel the thought of Marx, Engels seeks to show the unscientific character of religion and its incongruity with a materialistic world view. When the socialist revolution failed to occur and a proletarian party with millions of members emerged, the strengthening of its class consciousness and sense of unity required the development of its own world view. This it found in dialectical materialism, to which Engels made notable contributions. Mingling elements taken from Hegel's dialectic, the materialistic evolutionary thought of Haeckel and others, and the three stages (theological, metaphysical, and scientific) of the positivist Auguste Comte, he arrives at a *Weltanschauung* which he regards as scientifically validated, and which allows no place for belief in God.

According to Engels, the mighty advances of natural science in the nineteenth century have made senseless and impossible the contradiction between man and nature, mind and matter, soul and body, which is assumed by Christianity.[24] At the same time, in our understanding of the natural order

[22] "Anti-Dühring," *ibid.*, pp. 147 f.
[23] *Ibid.*, p. 148.
[24] "Dialectics of Nature," *ibid.*, p. 187.

one fortress after another has capitulated to scientific explanation, until there is no longer any need for postulating a "Creator of heaven and earth." [25]

When we apply scientific analysis to the study of human history, we discover the key to understanding in the history of the development of labor.[26] Political decisions are in the last resort determined by "the development of the productive forces and relations of exchange." [27] At least in modern history all political struggles are class struggles, and in those aimed at emancipation it is economic freedom that is sought. Thus economic relations provide the decisive factor.[28] But what has this to do with religion? For Engels the answer is quite simple. At each stage of history religion serves the interests of some particular social class, though as a typical ideology it may be unconscious of this. Changes in religious beliefs and practices reflect changes in class relations. This circumstance now connotes the end of Christianity. It has grown incapable "of serving any progressive class as the ideological garb of its aspirations." Instead, it has become increasingly "the exclusive possession of the ruling classes," used by them "to keep the lower classes within bounds." But since religion has no rational foundation, when it loses its social function it will pass from the scene.[29]

Engels' confidence in the scientific nature of his world view provides an instructive preview of an assumption which appears regularly among Marxists in the twentieth century. The Marxist conception of history, he declares, "puts an end to philosophy in the realm of history, just as the dialectical conception of nature makes all natural philosophy both unnecessary and impossible. It is no longer a question anywhere of

---

[25] *Ibid.*, pp. 191 f.
[26] "Ludwig Feuerbach and the End of Classical German Philosophy," *ibid.*, p. 266.
[27] *Ibid.*, p. 258.
[28] *Ibid.*, p. 257.
[29] *Ibid.*, p. 264.

inventing interconnections out of our brain, but of discovering them in the facts."[30] Yet it is obvious that the process by which such connections are "discovered" makes extensive use of philosophical thought, and bears little resemblance to the method which formulates laws of phenomena only after proceeding rigorously from hypotheses through controlled experiment to objective verification.

V. I. LENIN (1870-1924)[31]

Lenin is much more polemical than his predecessors in his critique of religion. In a letter to Maxim Gorky in 1913, for example, he describes "any idea of any god at all" as "the most dangerous foulness, the most shameful 'infection.' A million *physical* sins, dirty tricks, acts of violence and infections are much more easily discovered by the crowd and therefore are much less dangerous, than the *subtle,* spiritual ideas of god, dressed up in the most attractive 'ideological' costumes."[32] The same emotional hatred appears in his reference to religion as a narcotic, where he makes a tiny but important change in Marx's phrase. Religion, asserts Lenin, "is opium for [Marx had said *of*] the people. Religion is a sort of spiritual booze, in which the slaves of capital drown their human image, their demand for a life more or less worthy of man."[33] For Lenin, religion is not as for Marx a drug created by the people themselves to make their misery endurable; it is, rather, intentionally concocted by the exploiting classes to produce in those who serve them a passive acceptance of their lot. Religion is above all a means of domination. All churches and religious

---

[30] *Ibid.,* p. 265.
[31] Though Lenin's life extends well into the twentieth century, his thought is considered here rather than under contemporary Marxism because his ideas have been incorporated in classic Marxist-Leninist doctrine to form the major historical and philosophical foundation of present-day Marxist atheism.
[32] *Collected Works* (Moscow: Foreign Language Book House; London: Lawrence and Wishart, 1960-66), XXXV, 122.
[33] *Ibid.,* X, 83 f.

organizations are primarily "instruments of bourgeois reaction that serve to defend exploitation and to befuddle the working class." [34] Therefore the struggle against religion is "the ABC of *all* materialism, and consequently of Marxism." [35]

Nevertheless, Lenin was realistic enough as a political tactician to adopt in practice essentially the position of Marx and Engels, who gave priority to the establishment of a socialist society and expected that in such an order religion would fall of its own weight. Thus Lenin can write that atheistic propaganda must be subordinated to the basic task of social democracy: "the development of the class struggle of the exploited *masses* against the exploiters." [36] With this in mind he counseled Party leaders to have due regard for the "religious prejudices" of workers, whose support might thereby be won for strikes and other forms of joint action. Aggressive propaganda in some circumstances might only divide atheistic and Christian workers, destroy the unity of the proletariat, and play into the hands of the priests. "Unity in this really revolutionary struggle of the oppressed class for the creation of a paradise on earth is more important to us than unity of proletarian opinion on paradise in heaven." [37]

3. FRIEDRICH NIETZSCHE (1844-1900)

In present-day theological discussion Nietzsche is most often cited as the major nineteenth-century source of death-of-God theology. However, his announcement of the death of God is not always related, as it needs to be, to his basic conception of religious belief and his philosophy as a whole.

The presupposition of all that Nietzsche says regarding the divine demise is his opinion, derived from Feuerbach, that God is only a projection into a supersensory realm of man's

[34] *Ibid.*, XV, 403; XXXV, 128.
[35] *Ibid.*, XV, 405.
[36] *Ibid.*, 406.
[37] *Ibid.*, XV, 406-9; X, 85-87.

own consciousness. For ordinary men religion provides "invaluable contentedness with their lot and condition, peace of heart, ennoblement of obedience, additional social happiness and sympathy, . . . something of justification of all the meanness, all the semi-poverty of their souls." It makes hardship endurable, "almost *turning* suffering *to account*, and in the end even hallowing and vindicating it." For "the strong and independent," those who rule, religion is a "means for overcoming resistance in the exercise of authority," thus binding rulers and subjects together. For men of "superior spirituality" it provides, for example through the contemplative orders, opportunity for more refined forms of government and escape from the noise, trouble, and filth of secular political life.[38] In all these manifestations man dichotomizes and degrades himself by ascribing his real greatness and strength to God and his weakness and meanness to himself.[39]

Nietzsche recognizes that the higher religions—he mentions especially Christianity and Buddhism—have in their concern for the suffering and oppressed performed "invaluable services." However, in so doing they have reversed all sound estimates of value, shattering the strong, breaking down "everything autonomous, manly, conquering, and imperious," and accomplishing the deterioration of man.[40] Christian morality is a slave morality. The equality of all men before God is a fraud. Concepts like the other world, the last judgment, and the soul and its immortality not only deny reality, but are means whereby the priest becomes and remains master. The ideals exalted by the church suck all the blood, love, and hope out of life, and "debase and pollute humanity." The cross is "the trade-mark of the most subterranean form of

[38] *Beyond Good and Evil: Prelude to a Philosophy of the Future*, tr. Helen Zimmern, par. 61; *Complete Works of Friedrich Nietzsche*, ed. Oscar Levy (New York: Russell & Russell, 1964), XII, 79-81; cf. *Thus Spake Zarathustra*, tr. Thomas Coleman (New York: Modern Library, n. d.), pp. 48 f.
[39] *The Will to Power*, par. 135; *Complete Works*, XIV, 113-15.
[40] *Beyond Good and Evil*, par. 62; *Complete Works*, XII, 83.

conspiracy that has ever existed,—against health, beauty, well-constitutedness, bravery, intellect, kindliness of soul, *against life itself.*" [41] As for God, the belief in "Divine Providence" is a "fatal belief," "the most *paralysing* for both the hand and the understanding that has ever existed." [42]

The task confronting enlightened men today is therefore the complete "transvaluation of all values." [43] Instead of hiding his head in celestial sands, man must learn to hold up his head, his "terrestrial head," and to affirm rather than deny himself. Instead of listening for the voice of an imaginary God, he should listen to the pure and upright voice of "the healthy body, perfect and square built," and affirm the powers and potentialities of man himself.[44] Here Nietzsche parts company with Feuerbach. For him release from the cramping influence of religious belief is net a matter of simple enlightenment, but of the positive assertion of the human will, the valiant struggle of man to become Superman.[45]

It is in this context that the oft-quoted fable of the "madman" is best interpreted. In *The Gay Science* Nietzsche tells of a madman who in broad daylight ran with a lantern to the marketplace crying repeatedly, "I seek God!" In response to the amused banter of the bystanders he went on:

Whither is God? . . . I shall tell you. *We have killed him*—you and I. All of us are his murderers. But how have we done this? How were we able to drink up the sea? . . . What did we do when we unchained this earth from its sun? Whither is it moving now? Whither are we moving now? Away from all suns? . . . Are we not straying as through an infinite nothing? Do we not feel the breath of empty space? Has it not become colder? Is not night and more night coming on all the while? Must not lanterns be lit in the morning? . . . God is dead. God remains dead. And we have killed

---

[41] *The Antichrist,* pars. 38, 62; *Complete Works,* XVI, 177, 231.
[42] *The Will to Power,* par. 243; *Complete Works,* XIV, 198.
[43] *The Antichrist,* par. 62; *Complete Works,* XVI, 231.
[44] *Thus Spake Zarathustra,* pp. 49 f.
[45] *Ibid.,* p. 92.

him. How shall we, the murderers of all murderers, comfort ourselves? What was holiest and most powerful of all that the world has yet owned has bled to death under our knives. Who will wipe this blood off us? . . . Is not the greatness of this deed too great for us? Must we not ourselves become gods simply to seem worthy of it? There has never been a greater deed; and he who will be born after us—for the sake of this deed he will be part of a higher history than hitherto.[46]

In short, men who now see the unreal and man-debasing nature of the God and the God-oriented values which they themselves have created have acted to replace them with true values which affirm and exalt man. Thus God is dead, and they have killed him. The awareness that the comfort of religious faith has been utterly destroyed and that man is on his own is a staggering one, and men cannot readily grasp or accept it. Thus the man who proclaims this truth is regarded as mad by the unenlightened men who hear him, even though they themselves have shared in the murder by accepting the new values while still professing the old. Further, when the madman notes their lack of comprehension he throws down his lantern and cries, "I come too early; my time has not come yet. This tremendous event is still on its way, still wandering —it has not yet reached the ears of man. . . . This deed is still more distant from them than the most distant stars—*and yet they have done it themselves.*" Even the churches, unknown to those who worship in them, are the tombs of God.[47] Yet the death of God means the liberation of man, who now for the first time is free to become himself, to develop fully all his capacities, to rule over his own life, and to assert without arbitrary restrictions his will to power.

The central element in Nietzsche's atheism, implicit in the foregoing, must now be made quite explicit. I refer to the

[46] *The Gay Science*, par. 125; Walter Kaufmann (ed.), *The Portable Nietzsche* (New York: Viking Press, 1965), pp. 95 f.
[47] *Ibid.*, p. 96.

nihilistic character of his teaching. In the judgment of Martin Heidegger, the term God for Nietzsche designates not only the Christian God, but also the supersensual world in general, the whole realm of ideas and ideals. Thus the death of God means for Nietzsche the end of Platonic metaphysics and the fulfillment of the fundamental tendency of two millennia of western history.[48] The supersensual world, formerly believed in, has lost all its power to impart connection and meaning to human life. It becomes only a transitory, unstable product of the sensual. But the latter denies its own nature by such a reduction of its opposite: The deposition of the supersensory thus sets aside the sensory also. As a result, the difference between the two disappears in the meaninglessness of a neither-nor. But then there remains nothing to which man can hold or toward which he can direct his life.[49] Hence the question of the madman: "Are we not straying as through an infinite nothing? . . . Is not night and more night coming on?" Man's only light is shed by the lanterns which he himself sets aglow. There are no enduring principles and no binding norms. Man has literally nowhere to turn but to himself.

Nihilism in this thoroughgoing sense is the complete devaluation or negation of values rather than their mere transvaluation. The murder of God by man means the liquidation by human thought of everything previously presumed to exist "in itself." The moral law, the authority of reason, God, progress, the greatest happiness of the greatest number, civilization, culture—these and other supposedly highest values lose their claim to human allegiance. The good, the true, and the beautiful are ideals which have no discoverable relation to the real world. There is simply no goal or ground of human existence, and no reply to the query, "Why?"[50] Nihilism means, writes Nietzsche, *"that the highest values are losing their*

[48] Martin Heidegger, "Nietzsches Wort 'Gott ist tot,'" *Holzwege*, pp. 196 f., 200.
[49] *Ibid.*, pp. 193, 199 f., 206 f.
[50] *Ibid.*, pp. 241 f., 201-5.

value. There is no bourne. There is no answer to the question: 'to what purpose?' " [51]

Values thus depend wholly on the point of view and the volition of the valuer—on their being regarded and willed as valuable. They have no worth in themselves, but attain value through being posited or affirmed as valuable by the will to power. Therefore the basic feature of all that claims reality or worth in human life is the will to power. Through it all values arise and all evaluation is carried out.[52]

Paradoxically, this conception of nihilism enables Nietzsche to view it positively as well as negatively, as the overcoming of itself. Thus the madman, in spite of his distress, can say of the murder of God, "There never was a greater deed." Through this act humanity enters a higher history than previously known, because in it the principle of all determination of values, the will to power, is experienced and accepted as constituting the reality of all that exists. Human self-consciousness wills itself as the fulfiller of the unconditioned will to power, and thereby finds its real essence. The nihilism involved in the devaluation of the highest values is overcome. Out of the wreckage of overthrown conceptions of being and value arises Superman. Superman is for Nietzsche not a particular example of man in whom the capacities and aims of ordinary man have been enormously enlarged and increased; he is, rather, the nature of modern humanity which now for the first time becomes free to fulfill itself. Superman is man who becomes man through the reality constituted by his own will to power.[53] Thus what it means to be human is lifted to a new dimension. Lordship over existence as such is transferred from a supposedly objective realm above man to the will of man defined as the will to power.[54] Significantly,

[51] *The Will to Power*, par. 2; *Complete Works*, XIV, 8.
[52] *The Will to Power*, pars. 583 A, 688, 689; *Complete Works*, XV, 82-84, 162-65.
[53] *Ibid.*, p. 232.
[54] *Ibid.*, pp. 235 f.

Nietzsche concludes the first part of *Thus Spake Zarathustra*, which appeared in 1883 one year after *The Gay Science*, with the words: "'Dead are all the Gods; now do we desire the Superman to live.'—Let this be our final will at the great noontide." [55]

---

[55] *Thus Spake Zarathustra*, p. 92.

II. Varieties of Atheistic Humanism

We are now ready to examine the major varieties of atheism which confront us in the seventh decade of our own century. I believe they can be accurately classified under six types, which we shall consider individually.

1. FREUDIAN PSYCHOANALYSIS

Like Feuerbach, Marx, and Nietzsche, Sigmund Freud (1856-1939) saw religion as a cultural phenomenon which can be best understood in terms of its origins. In his view, however, the determinative genetic influences are psychological rather than economic, social, or philosophical, and they center in the largely unconscious relation between father and son. In 1907, he speaks of religion in general as "a universal obsessional neurosis."[1] Several years later he describes the personal God of theistic belief as "psychologically nothing but a magnified father."[2]

In *Totem and Taboo* (1912) Freud traces the sources of religion, morality, and society itself to the Oedipus complex functioning in the human species. The book is an imaginative reconstruction rather than a scientific analysis, but Freud offers it as a serious explanation of the origins of society. With Darwin's conception of the primal horde as his starting point,

[1] "Obsessive Acts and Religious Practices," *Collected Papers*, authorized translation under the supervision of Joan Riviere (London: Hogarth Press and the Institute of Psycho-analysis, [1924-25] 1949-56), II, 34.
[2] Essay on Leonardo da Vinci, *Gesammelte Werke*, ed. Anna Freud et al. (London: Imago Publishing Co., 1942), VIII, 195; Ernest Jones, *The Life and Work of Sigmund Freud* (New York: Basic Books, 1953-57), III, 354.

Freud postulates a primeval event in which the sons, resenting their father's jealous prohibition of sexual relations with his females, united to slay and eat the father, accomplishing together what none of them would have dared to do singly. However, the sons' attitude toward their father was ambivalent, involving love and admiration as well as hate and resentment. Once the murder had been performed, the suppressed tender impulses asserted themselves. Overcome by guilt and remorse, the sons renounced the fruits of their deed and in an act of "subsequent obedience" reinstituted the original ban. The unconscious memory of the murder and its consequences is perpetuated in totemism. On special occasions the totem animal is ceremonially killed and eaten, but ordinarily the killing of the father substitute, the totem, is prohibited, and the ban on sexual relations with close tribal relatives remains in effect. Thus Freud traces to the sons' sense of guilt the two fundamental taboos of totemism. For him they correspond to the two repressed wishes of the Oedipus complex and the two crimes which above all others troubled primitive society: murder and incest.

Freud finds here also the origin of religious belief, since in time the totem was elevated to godhood, and the old ambivalent feelings toward the father survive in the worshiper's attitudes toward his god, combining fear and longing, defiant freedom and willing subjection.[3]

The totem religion had issued from the sense of guilt of the sons as an attempt to palliate this feeling and to conciliate the injured father through subsequent obedience. All later religions prove to be attempts to solve the same problem, varying only in accordance with the stage of culture in which they are attempted.[4]

In each instance the god is modeled after the father, and man's personal relation to his god depends on his relation to

[3] *Totem and Taboo*, tr. A. A. Brill (New York: New Republic, 1927), pp. 244-59 *et passim*.
[4] *Ibid.*, p. 252.

his physical father in the culture involved. "God is at bottom nothing but an exalted father." [5]

Some years later, in his "Psycho-analysis and Religious Origins," Freud sums up in more extreme form the views reached in *Totem and Taboo*. The psychoanalytic interpretation of the prehistoric and ethnological material, he writes, leads to

> an unexpectedly precise result: namely that God the Father once walked upon the earth in bodily form and exercised his sovereignty as chieftain of the primal human [sic] horde until his sons united to slay him. It emerges further that this crime of liberation and the reactions to it had as their result the appearance of the first social ties, the basic moral restrictions and the oldest form of religion, totemism. But the later religions too have the same content.[6]

In *Moses and Monotheism* (1937-39) Freud applies his theories specifically to Hebrew religion, and briefly to Christianity. In Freud's account Moses, who was an Egyptian rather than a Jew, acquired his belief in one exclusive God from the Egyptian tradition typified by Ikhnaton. Having converted his followers, the Jews in Egypt, to this faith, he was later killed by them. The murder heightened their sense of guilt. This deep guilt consciousness and the monotheism derived from Egypt have decisively influenced the character of Hebrew religion. According to Freud the murder of the prophet in monotheistic religions serves the same function as does the murder of the primitive father in totemism. The growth of monotheism is marked by the slow "return of the repressed." The idea of God as the highest Being emerges in four main stages, in which the totem animal is succeeded first by the human hero, then by gods, and finally by one God. Thus the grandeur of the primeval father is restored in the

[5] *Ibid.*, p. 256.
[6] *Collected Papers*, V, 96.

Law-giver on Mt. Sinai who requires absolute subjection to his holy will. The guilt associated with the primordial murder is replaced by guilt arising from sin against the Father-God and repressed hostility toward him. The result is ethical monotheism, which combines belief in one sole God with the moral asceticism implied in the duty to obey his righteous will.[7]

Freud finds his view of the origin of religion further reinforced by Christianity, with its doctrines of original sin and salvation through the sacrificial death of Jesus Christ. The primordial guilt is of course acknowledged only under the delusion of the glad tidings of deliverance. The fact of father-murder, the unmentionable crime, is not specified, being hidden in the notion of original sin. However, only murder could have required expiation by death. The connection between the delusion and historical truth is further established by the belief that the sacrificial victim was the Son of God. Thus Christianity manifests the ancient ambivalence in the father-son relation. Its central doctrine is

the reconciliation with God the Father, the expiation of the crime committed against him; but the other side of the relationship manifested itself in the Son, who had taken the guilt on his shoulders, becoming God himself beside the Father and in truth in place of the Father. Originally a Father religion, Christianity became a Son religion. The fate of having to displace the Father it could not escape.[8]

In a brief statement of this theory in *Totem and Taboo*, Freud sees the Christian eucharist as a revival of the old totem feast, in which the brothers now eat the flesh and blood of the son rather than the father; the sons thereby identify themselves with another son who represents them, and be-

[7] *Moses and Monotheism*, tr. Katherine Jones (New York: Alfred A. Knopf, 1939), pp. 208-12.
[8] *Ibid.*, pp. 213-15; see *Totem and Taboo*, pp. 268 f.

come holy themselves. Thus the Christian rite of communion is a late aftereffect of the primordial crime which both oppressed men and aroused their pride. "At bottom, however, it is a new setting aside of the father, a repetition of the crime that must be expiated." [9]

The most definitive statement of Freud's views is that contained in *The Future of an Illusion,* published in 1927. Here, too, God appears as a father-figure, but one to whom man turns not only in fear but trusting in his protection. Religious belief is an illusion, an unjustified wish-fulfillment growing out of the need of immature people to regard reality as harmonious with their wants. Man is painfully aware of his helplessness amid the dangers of nature and the evils of society itself, both individual and racial. Hence he returns unconsciously to his own childhood and that of the human race, and invents an all-powerful father who fulfills his most insistent needs and cherished desires. Thus emerges belief in a personal God, a superhuman Intelligence who orders everything to man's advantage. He rules benevolently over nature, guarantees the eventual obliteration of all the terrors and hardships of life, insures the ultimate establishment of righteousness in a moral world order, and prolongs man's earthly life eternally.[10]

All this is of course illusory. For Freud an illusion is not necessarily erroneous, that is, "unrealizable or incompatible with reality"; rather "we call a belief an illusion when wish-fulfillment is a prominent factor in its motivation, while disregarding its relations to reality, just as the illusion itself does."[11] It *could* be true, but there is no sound reason for believing that it is. Religious dogmas are not based on experience or careful reflection; instead they are "fulfillments of the

---

[9] *Totem and Taboo,* p. 269.
[10] *The Future of an Illusion,* tr. W. D. Robson-Scott (London: Hogarth Press, [1928] 1949), pp. 30, 32-34, 42, 52 f.
[11] *Ibid.,* pp. 54 f.

oldest, strongest and most insistent wishes of mankind; the secret of their strength is the strength of these wishes." [12]

The Logos which Freud calls his God allows the fulfillment only of those wishes "which external nature permits," and this only in the distant future for generations yet unborn. Hence religious beliefs should be given up.[13] The cosmos is far from being subject to human control. In events such as earthquakes, storms, floods, diseases, and death "nature rises up before us, sublime, pitiless, inexorable," indifferent to the desires of human beings. In such a world neurotics may seek escape in the consolations of religious illusion, but mature men will face reality as it is and chart their earthly course accordingly. Just as the child must leave his warm and comfortable home and venture into the hostile world, responsible men must surrender the belief that they are in the tender care of a loving providence, and unite to preserve mankind against the assaults of nature.[14]

Implicit in Freud's view of religion as illusion is his conviction that it is also dangerous. This is true in three respects. First, religious belief tends historically to ally itself with and hallow bad human institutions. Secondly, in discouraging or proscribing critical thought it impoverishes intelligence; restrictions on critical thinking in one area hinder the full development of reason in other spheres. Thirdly, religion threatens the foundations of morality. To ground ethical norms on the divine will risks the gradual destruction of moral values as belief in God declines. To avoid such dangers, man must learn to rely only on his own powers. Only when he has freed himself from threatening and protecting authority can he develop and use his capacities to the highest degree.[15]

We have noted that for Freud the acknowledgment that

[12] *Ibid.*, p. 52.
[13] *Ibid.*, p. 94.
[14] *Ibid.*, pp. 26 f., 57 f., 75-78, 85 f.
[15] *Ibid.*, pp. 66-74, 79 f.; Erich Fromm, *Psychoanalysis and Religion* (New Haven: Yale University Press, 1950), pp. 10-14.

religious beliefs are illusory does not in itself show them to be false. He explicitly states that some beliefs which fulfill human wishes may be true, and he asserts that his psychological examination of religion as illusion is not concerned with the question of the truth of religious doctrines.[16] "Of the reality value of most of them we cannot judge; yet as they cannot be proved, neither can they be refuted."[17] However, Freud makes plain that the illusoriness of religion renders its claims highly suspect: It is "very odd" that our traditional beliefs in God, a moral order, and a future life happen to coincide with what we ourselves would wish.[18] Elsewhere he is emphatic in expressing his personal rejection of any theistic interpretation of reality. In his imaginary conversation with a believer he asserts:

Your religious doctrines will have to be discarded. . . . You know why; in the long run nothing can withstand reason and experience, and the contradiction religion offers to both is only too palpable. Not even the purified religious ideas can escape this fate, so long as they still try to preserve anything of the consolation of religion. Certainly if you confine yourself to the belief in a higher spiritual being, whose qualities are indefinable and whose intentions cannot be discerned, then you are proof against the interference of science, but then you will also relinquish the interest of men.[19]

Similarly, in a letter to his Christian friend Oskar Pfister in 1929, Freud maintains that psychoanalysis "rests on the general scientific outlook, with which the religious outlook is incompatible." The essence of the latter is "the pious illusion of providence and a moral order, which are in conflict with reason."[20] Clearly Freud's own conclusion is that theistic

[16] *The Future of an Illusion*, pp. 52-54, 57.
[17] *Ibid.*, p. 55.
[18] *Ibid.*, pp. 57 f.
[19] *Ibid.*, p. 94.
[20] *Psychoanalysis and Faith. The Letters of Sigmund Freud and Oskar Pfister*, ed. Heinrich Meng and Ernst L. Freud, tr. Eric Mosbacher (New York: Basic Books, 1963), p. 129.

belief is not only illusory but erroneous, because he finds it irreconcilable with experience and reason as they are understood by psychoanalysis and the total scientific approach to reality.

Freud's conclusions on religion are shared by a large number of contemporary psychoanalysts. In view of the fundamental agreement between his ideas and those of his followers, there is no need for a separate exposition. However, it may be instructive to note a particular application of Freudianism made by his student Theodor Reik, and certain modifications offered by Erich Fromm at an early state of his thought.

Like Freud, Reik points out the unconscious motives and instinctual basis of some of the major articles of religious belief. However, he devotes special attention to investigating the genesis and psychic significance of dogma—the determinative beliefs of a religion—regarding it as basic.[21] He interprets religion essentially as a thought-system "comparable to the great illusory formations of neurosis and psychosis."[22] Following the method of his teacher, he discovers through investigations of psychopathological phenomena pervasive analogies between the obsessional actions of neurotic patients and the ritualistic activities of religious believers. Dogma he sees as an expression of compulsive thinking; ritual, as a manifestation of collective compulsive action.[23]

Illustrative of the close parallelism which Reik finds between the growth of dogma and obsessional neurosis are the conception of God itself and the rigidity with which religious belief comes to be held. (1) Like Freud, he holds that the idea of God has arisen out of the psychic conflicts generated by the ambivalent impulses of the son regarding the powerful

[21] *Dogma and Compulsion; Psychoanalytic Studies of Religion and Myths*, tr. Bernard Miall (New York: International Universities Press, 1951), pp. 11, 22.
[22] *Ibid.*, p. 88.
[23] *Ibid.*, p. 13.

father. The revolt, the patricide, and the resultant guilt reactions have elevated the primeval father to a divine status. The proofs of God's existence which are later carefully worked out are "intellectualizing overcompensations in respect of an insurrection against God." Such logic is "precisely like" the pseudo-logic which the obsessional neurotic uses to justify his belief in demons. In each case evidence is fabricated to support a belief already held.[24]

(2) Likewise, the insistence on submission and obedience in religious faith, with the suppression of all objections, is seen by Reik as correlative with the peculiarities of neurotic obsession. Salvation is portrayed as contingent on blind submission of the personal will to a stern God, "just as the peremptory superego and the instinctual id of the individual obsessional neurotic compel him to admit the most absurd ideas." In the classical New Testament trilogy of faith, hope, and love, primacy is initially given to love, but, as dogma grows and hardens, love is replaced by faith, and faith becomes rigid adherence to creedal assertions. This increase in compulsion is in theology as in neurosis an effort to compensate for doubt.[25]

Reik holds that the only scientific approach to religion, including the "Christian myths," is psychological investigation. He therefore rules out any philosophical or systematically theological inquiry into the truth of religious beliefs. He quotes with seeming approval the statement of Renan: "With God everything is possible, even that He should exist." [26] But clearly he finds no psychoanalytic evidence that would justify belief in the divine existence, and much to indicate that belief in God is nothing more than wish-fulfillment which has psychological value. "It does not greatly matter," he writes, "what illusion we choose in order to make life

[24] *Ibid.*, pp. 96 f.
[25] *Ibid.*, pp. 125-27.
[26] *Ibid.*, p. 153.

tolerable."[27] A similarly negative attitude is evident in his comment on the subject matter uncovered in the investigation of religion. Such study, like the study of all human history, "requires a conscientious submersion in a confused admixture of insanity, crime, and pettiness."[28] Obviously, such data do not lend much support to theistic faith, or to any affirmation of meaning or purpose in human existence.

Erich Fromm wrote his *The Dogma of Christ* in 1930, when he was a strict Freudian, though it was not published until 1955. Here he seeks to transcend Reik's psychologistic approach to religious ideas and practices by examining also the social and economic conditions of the people who accept them.[29] Yet his treatment is primarily psychological. His central concern is to trace the changes which occurred in belief in Jesus Christ during the first centuries of Christian history.

The earliest Christians, maintains Fromm, were poor, oppressed, and despairing people, with no prospect of a better earthly future, who projected into fantasy the hopes and longings for redress which had been denied them in reality. This fantasy centered in their adoptionist Christology, the faith that a man who suffered like them had been elevated to a god. By identification with him they might displace the ruling powers symbolized by god, emperor, and father, and establish themselves in their place.[30] Fromm finds the central significance of this belief in "the implied wish to overthrow the father-god or his earthly representatives." However, he lays less emphasis than Freud on the notion of a primordial murder: "The figure of the suffering Jesus originated primarily from the need for identification on the part of the suffering masses, and it was only secondarily determined by

[27] *Ibid.*, p. 14.
[28] *Ibid.*, p. 12.
[29] *The Dogma of Christ, and Other Essays on Religion, Psychology, and Culture*, tr. James Luther Adams (New York: Holt, Rinehart & Winston, 1963), pp. viii f., 41. Reik had been one of Fromm's teachers at the Psychoanalytic Institute in Berlin.
[30] *Ibid.*, pp. 41, 45, 49, 88.

the need for expiation for the crime of aggression against the father." [31]

With changes in the economic status and the social composition of the Christian community, the psychic attitude of the believers also underwent a change. The notion of a man becoming a god was transformed into that of a god becoming a man. Guilt came to be ascribed not to the rulers but to the suffering masses. Aggression was no longer aimed at the authorities, but at the sufferers themselves. Satisfaction was found not in the overthrow of the father, but "in the pardon and love which the father offers his submissive sons, and simultaneously in the regal, fatherly position which the suffering Jesus assumes while remaining the representative of the suffering masses. Jesus eventually became God without overthrowing God because he was always God." [32]

At this stage of his thought Fromm holds essentially the same view as Freud with regard to the truth of belief in a superhuman God. In succeeding years, however, he has stressed increasingly the positive human values to be found in the formulations and symbols of enlightened religion. The real problem of religion is the problem of man rather than that of God; what matters is the kinds of human experiences expressed by religious concepts and actions. At heart the conflict is not that between theistic belief and atheism, but "between a humanistic, religious attitude and an attitude which is equivalent to idolatry regardless of how this attitude is expressed—or disguised—in conscious thought." [33] Fromm finds this position harmonious with that of Freud himself. For Freud the aim of human development is the fulfillment of the ideals of "knowledge (reason, truth, logos), brotherly love, reduction of suffering, independence, and responsibility." These make up the ethical core of all great religions, and

[31] *Ibid.*, p. 89.
[32] *Ibid.*, p. 90.
[33] *Psychoanalysis and Religion*, pp. 113 f.

it is in the name of this ethical core that Freud criticizes theistic and supernatural belief because he finds it hindering the achievement of such aims.[34]

Since Fromm's own position, though psychoanalytically rooted, is essentially a nontheistic humanism, we shall have occasion to examine it further in connection with other examples of this type of thought.[35]

2. MARXISM

During the approximately six decades which have elapsed since the definitive formulation of Marxist-Leninist thought, its status in the world has radically changed. It is no longer a struggling minority position, but in one form or another the official social philosophy of governments ruling hundreds of millions of people. This changed situation has inevitably brought modifications in its critique, and especially in its practical treatment, of religious belief, though in fundamentals Marxist atheism remains much the same. In view of the range and complexity of the data, we shall need to be highly selective. After listing and illustrating the main characteristics of the mid-twentieth-century critique, we shall examine in particular the thought of Ernst Bloch, who represents contemporary Marxist atheism in its most penetrating form.

THE MARXIST CRITIQUE TODAY

1. Belief in God continues to be regarded by present-day Marxists as a false exteriorization of frustrated human hopes, an ideology which serves the economic interests of the ruling classes. Thinkers like Milan Machovec of Prague and Martin Robbe of East Berlin argue that religion arises out of the alienation experienced by men in certain historical circumstances, and that it reflects social content rather than ex-

[34] *Ibid.*, pp. 18 f.
[35] See below, pp. 88-90.

pressing objective truth.[36] Roger Garaudy reiterates that biblical religion in its understanding of God hypostasizes the unfulfilled expectations of men.[37] But the whole process is illusory. "For us atheists," writes Garaudy, "nothing is promised and no one is waiting." [38]

However, for the contemporary Marxist, Christian belief is not only erroneous; it is also frequently an instrument of exploitation and the preservation of an unjust status quo. In the Constantinian tradition, says Garaudy, the church has sanctified class domination and social inequality, regarding these as willed by God in judgment against human sin. It has successively offered justification for slavery, feudal serfdom, and the suppression of the proletariat.[39] Alliances between throne and altar in Lutheran Germany, between the Hapsburgs and the Catholic Church in Austria, and between Czarism and the Orthodox hierarchy in Russia have made the gospel a tool of nationalism, imperialism, and economic oppression. György Lukács of Budapest reaches somewhat similar conclusions regarding Christianity in the United States. The apologetic of American imperialism, he declares, has been energetically supported by the churches, especially Catholicism; indeed, "the propaganda of the Vatican is just as close to that of the Voice of America as the Banco di Santo Spirito is to Wall Street." In general the church and business have been as intimately connected as were capitalism and the Protestant sects at the time of their foundation. Such social circumstances, thinks Lukács, help to explain the alliance of the churches with American imperialism in the anticom-

[36] Machovec, *Marxismus und die dialektische Theologie* (Zürich: EVZ Verlag, 1965), pp. 156-58. Robbe, *Der Ursprung des Christentums* (Leipzig, Jena, Berlin: Urania-Verlag, 1967); and interview in East Berlin, Nov. 19, 1966.
[37] Erich Kellner (ed.), *Christentum und Marxismus—heute*, pp. 96, 108.
[38] *Ibid.*, p. 97; Garaudy, *From Anathema to Dialogue*, tr. Luke O'Neill (New York: Herder and Herder, 1966), p. 95.
[39] *Ibid.*, pp. 56, 99, 102, 123.

munist crusade of recent years.[40] With more sadness than anger, Martin Robbe told me of the shock he experienced recently in visiting a series of worship services in East Berlin, as he noted the passive attitudes expressed in prayers and hymns. He has been equally impressed by the lack of concern for changing society in the practice of Christians he has observed.

On the other hand, Marxist recognition of the contributions of Christianity to society has not been wholly absent in recent years. As early as 1936, Maurice Thorez paid tribute to the progressive role which Christianity has played at various times. He mentions its social service activities, its contribution to the human consciousness of solidarity, its effort to promote more just and peaceful human relations under feudalism, the genuineness of mutual concern within its religious communities, its creation of great cathedrals and other artistic works, and its service during the Middle Ages in the preservation of the great treasures of knowledge and art.[41] In a famous address at Bergamo in March, 1963, Palmiro Togliatti declared that the religious conscience does not necessarily oppose but may actually stimulate the building of socialism; he pointed out that certain moral values are shared by the Christian and Marxist conceptions of man and society. His theses were officially adopted by the Tenth Congress of the Italian Communist Party.[42] Nevertheless, most Marxists continue to regard Christianity as a tool of social reaction, and this judgment is a major ground of Marxist atheism.

2. Belief in God is seen by contemporary Marxists as inconsistent with both the methods and the results of modern science. The way to truth is the experimental investigation which seeks to discover and express in laws the uniformities of objective reality. Lev Hanzel of Bratislava offers three

[40] Lukács, *Die Zerstörung der Vernunft; der Weg des Irrationalismus von Schelling zu Hitler* (Berlin: Aufbau-Verlag, 1955), pp. 637, 641.
[41] Kellner, *Christentum und Marxismus—heute*, pp. 92 f.
[42] Garaudy, *From Anathema to Dialogue*, p. 118.

criteria characteristic of such inquiry: (a) it deals with definite, empirically verifiable objects; (b) its method makes possible the verification and demonstration of its conclusions; (c) it leads to an internally consistent and logically ordered system of knowledge. Religious belief, like the idealistic world views with which Marxists ordinarily identify it,[43] fails to meet these criteria.[44]

While agreeing on the nontheistic or atheistic implications of their avowed commitment to scientific method, Marxists occupy various places on the spectrum of unbelief. Some hold that natural science, since it demonstrates the complete uniformity of natural processes, leads consistently to a materialistic world view which excludes a religious interpretation of natural events.[45] Others maintain that all really meaningful questions are in principle capable of scientific answers, so that religious belief can function only where there are gaps in man's knowledge; as scientific progress steadily reduces these areas of ignorance, religion will become increasingly irrelevant.[46] Other writers go still further to insist that religion is irreconcilable with science, since it substitutes alleged divine revelation, a priori dogmas, and belief in miracle for empirically verifiable knowledge of objective reality.[47] Finally, some Marxists declare unequivocally that science denies the exis-

[43] For typical Marxist assumptions that Christianity is essentially a form of idealistic philosophy, see Olof Klohr, "Probleme des wissenschaftlichen Atheismus und der atheistischen Propaganda," *Deutsche Zeitschrift für Philosophie*, 12 (1964), 134 f.; Georg Klaus, *Jesuiten, Gott, Materie; Des Jesuitenpaters Wetter Revolte wider Vernunft und Wissenschaft* (Berlin: VEB Deutscher Verlag der Wissenschaften, 1957), p. 134; and F. W. Konstantinow (ed.), *Istoricesky materializm* (Historical Materialism), 2nd ed. (Moscow, 1954), p. 402 (quoted by Gustav A. Wetter, *Dialektischer und historischer Materialismus* [Frankfurt am Main: Fischer Bücherei, 1962], p. 265).

[44] Lev Hanzel, in Klohr (ed.), *Moderne Naturwissenschaft und Atheismus* (Berlin: VEB Deutscher Verlag der Wissenschaften, 1957), pp. 254, 267 f.

[45] Olof Klohr, *ibid.*, Preface, p. 9.

[46] Helmut Korch, *ibid.*, pp. 17, 21; cf. Lev Hanzel, *ibid.*, p. 257.

[47] Josef de Vries, in Kellner, *Christentum und Marximus–heute*, p. 50; Lev Hanzel, in Klohr, *op. cit.*, pp. 260 f.

tence of any transcendent, divine being, since such a being cannot be demonstrated on the basis of scientific evidence.[48] Thus in various ways atheism is seen as firmly grounded in the method of the natural sciences.[49]

It should be pointed out, however, that a minority of Marxists today—and probably a growing minority—no longer regard science as contradictory to religion. In the view of Roger Garaudy, for example, science helps to eliminate magic, superstition, and myth, but it does not affect what is basic in religious faith. The central debate between atheists and Christians is on the moral plane rather than the scientific.[50]

Integrally connected with and supportive of the Marxists' judgment that belief in God is unscientific is their charge that theology and the church have opposed free scientific research and hindered scientists in their pursuit of truth. Events like the condemnation of Copernicus and the persecution and enforced recantation of Galileo are frequently cited as typifying the basic anti-scientific character of Christian faith. Theologians, it is maintained, use the results of scientific inquiry when possible to support their dogmas, but otherwise attempt to stifle the open search for knowledge carried on by scientists.[51] It may be true, says Hans-Joachim Seidowski of East Berlin, that Christianity no longer operates in this fashion, but this is merely because it has lost the struggle and has no alternative. When, he asks, has religion voluntarily welcomed scientific teaching which seemed to contradict its dogmas, or taken the lead in initiating new scientific investigation? [52]

Marxists are as quick to use science to support their own materialism as to show the error of religious faith. All agree that Marx discovered that history proceeds according to uni-

[48] Lev Hanzel and Helmut Korch, in Klohr, *ibid.*, pp. 262 f., 16.
[49] Helmut Korch, *ibid.*, p. 24.
[50] *From Anathema to Dialogue*, pp. 107, 109.
[51] Georg Klaus, *Jesuiten, Gott, Materie; Des Jesuitenpaters Wetter Revolte wider Vernunft und Wissenschaft*, pp. 87 f., 166, 248. Klohr and Hanzel, in Klohr, *op. cit.*, pp. 14 f., 262 f.
[52] Interview in East Berlin, Nov. 14, 1966.

form and objective laws, so that his philosophy is basically scientific, whether or not all conclusions founded on it are right. But some of his present-day followers claim much more. Thus Georg Klaus maintains with Lenin that historical materialism is "an exact science, which correctly mirrors social events and serves as a lever to change them." Similarly, "dialectical materialism has on its side all the exact methods to which modern natural and social science owe their successes." For example, the materialistic hypothesis of the eternality of matter is supported by the fundamental physical principle of the indestructibility of matter.[53] Lev Hanzel goes so far as to maintain that "the results of modern science clearly prove the correctness of the Marxist conception of matter." [54] Such extreme claims have elicited the criticism by Christians and others that Marxism, far from being a strictly scientific theory, is really a world view and a faith merged with a partially scientific method. Thus Helmut Gollwitzer holds that communism transforms *methodic* a-theism, immanentism, and the this-worldly reference of science into dogmatic ontological atheism.[55] Marxists like Helmut Dressler of the Humboldt University in East Berlin, well aware of such criticism, admit the intrusion of the element of faith into some modern expressions of Marxism, but insist nevertheless that Marxism, es-

[53] Klaus, *op. cit.*, pp. 127, 165 f.
[54] In Klohr, *op. cit.*, p. 263.
[55] *Die marxistische Religionskritik und der christliche Glaube* (München, Hamburg: Siebenstern Taschenbuch Verlag, 1965). An especially glaring instance of this tendency in Marxist thought is provided by Olof Klohr, who lists five statements of Roman Catholicism regarding natural science, then the opposing propositions of "natural science and scientific philosophy." But Klohr neglects to indicate which of the latter stem from science and which from philosophy. Instead he assumes the complete congruity of the two, confusing scientific postulates with proven conclusions. Some of the contrasted affirmations are not contradictory at all, but complementary; for example, evolutionary development is treated as the opposite of God's creation of the world and man. Klohr, "Probleme des wissenschaftlichen Atheismus und der atheistischen Propaganda," *Deutsche Zeitschrift für Philosophie,* 12 (1964), 146 f.

pecially as represented by Marx himself, Engels, and Lenin, is "basically scientific."[56]

3. Rejection of belief in God is implicit in the fundamental humanism of Marxist thought. With its recognition of man as the highest expression of nature and its positive evaluation of all of man's earthly goods, Marxism asserts both his central importance and his responsibility to fulfill or "produce" himself through his own work. Thus Roger Garaudy espouses what he calls a "post-atheistic humanism," which leaves behind the negative quality of bourgeois atheism and accents the affirmation of man rather than the denial of God.[57]

Nevertheless, the denial of God remains genuine and emphatic; it is necessary to the full assertion of man. As Helmut Dressler puts it, in Marxism man is affirmed as the highest being, and God cannot be allowed to exist, for if he did he would replace man as the highest being.[58] To Marxists, belief in God as the omnipotent, sovereign Lord on whose power and grace man depends deprives man of the free initiative he should have in history.[59] By contrast, unbelief is a way of rescuing the honor of man. Thus, much Marxist atheism today is described by Johannes Baptist Metz as "postulatory" atheism: It is the condition or postulate of a positive humanism, the presupposition of a consistent and total stress on the primacy of man.[60] On this basis Helmut Gollwitzer declares that the ultimate roots of Marxist atheism are not theoretical or "scientific," but practical. Atheism is postulated because of a prior commitment. "God cannot be because his existence

[56] Interview, Nov. 8, 1966.
[57] In discussion at the Congress of the *Paulus-Gesellschaft* at Herrenchiemsee, 1966. *Neues Forum* (Vienna), 13 (June/July 1966), 329. See also, *From Anathema to Dialogue*, pp. 33, 109; and Marcel Reding, *Der politische Atheismus* (Graz: Verlag Styria, 1957), pp. 147 f., 160.
[58] Conversation in East Berlin, Nov. 8, 1966.
[59] *Initiative in History: A Christian-Marxist Exchange* (Cambridge, Mass.: Church Society for College Work, 1967), p. 4; Ernst Bloch, *Das Prinzip Hoffnung* (Frankfurt am Main: Suhrkamp Verlag, 1959), p. 1413.
[60] In Kellner, *Christentum und Marxismus—heute*, p. 114.

would exclude [man's] self-redemption." Hence theoretical argument, pro or con, though it cannot be avoided, tends to hide the existential ground of the decision.[61]

However, Christians should recognize that though Marxist humanism is man-centered, in its normative expressions it is not self-centered. Dynamic rather than mechanistic in its materialism, it seeks mainly to stress man's unavoidable responsibility for his own future, his obligation to supersede the given, and his role in history as a creator and initiator of the new. Thus according to Garaudy, Marxism accepts what Christianity has called a consciousness of the "superhuman in man," his capacity for the infinite, and transposes it into man's awareness of his incompleteness, his consciousness of his as yet unrealized possibilities, which he is summoned to fulfill in this concrete earthly order.[62] Man, says Julius Tomin of Prague, "should endeavor to realize the optimum of his life."[63]

ERNST BLOCH'S PHILOSOPHY OF THE NOT-YET

Ernst Bloch of Tübingen is unquestionably one of the profoundest European thinkers of the twentieth century. From the perspective of his philosophy of hope, he offers a critique of theistic belief which represents Marxist revolutionary humanism at its best. He therefore merits our special attention.

Bloch was born July 8, 1885, in Ludwigshafen, Germany, and has spent most of his life in Germany. However, driven by his concern for peace he moved to Switzerland in 1917. Returning after a few years, he emigrated again in 1933 because of the Nazi rise to power. From 1938 to 1947 he lived in the United States, chiefly in Cambridge, Massachusetts, and it was here that he wrote his two-volume *magnum opus*, *Das Prinzip Hoffnung* (*The Hope Principle*). In 1949 he

---

[61] *Die marxistische Religionskritik und der christliche Glaube*, p. 96.
[62] In Kellner, *Christentum und Marxismus—heute*, p. 77.
[63] Conversation in Prague, Nov. 26, 1966.

became a professor of philosophy at the University of Leipzig in East Germany. By the mid-fifties, however, he was deeply disappointed by developments in Marxist thought and political life and, because of his critical writings, lost favor in dominant Marxist circles. Honored by his colleagues on his seventieth birthday in 1955, he was castigated as a revisionist in a symposium two years later. In 1961 he accepted a call to the University of Tübingen in West Germany, where as guest professor he enjoys a position of great honor and widening influence.

With piercing insight, and with learning reminiscent of Aristotle, Thomas Aquinas, and Hegel, but without tight systematization, Bloch has for fifty years philosophized about the whole range of human experience. His seventeen published books and his more than a hundred articles discuss not only epistemology, metaphysics, and anthropology, but theology, social and political theory, history, international relations, literature, drama, art, poetry, and music.

Both the major direction of Bloch's thought and one of its chief points of contact with Christian theology are indicated in his second book, *Thomas Münzer as Theologian of the Revolution* (1921). The fact that he chose the radical Protestant Münzer as the subject of a highly appreciative study is itself significant, as is the citation, opposite the Table of Contents, of the Pauline passage: "And those who deal with the world as though they had no dealings with it. For the form of this world is passing away" (I Cor. 7:31). In Bloch's interpretation, of course, these words do not entail world denial, but a joyous acceptance of change and openness to the unknown future in which human hopes and values may be more fully realized.

Three interrelated motifs appear again and again in Bloch's writings: front, the new, and matter. To understand what he means by them is to discover also his criticism of, his indebtedness to, and his possible significance for, Christian thought.

1. *Front.* The nature of reality is to move forward. "The real is process"; it proceeds on a moving, changing front from the unfinished past toward a future which is possible but not yet fully determined. The "front" is at every present the most advanced segment of time where we find ourselves living and acting. The point at which every reality begins to break forth is the *not*, the experience of lack or of hunger for something which is *not-yet*, but which through striving may become real. The "true genesis is not at the beginning but at the end," since the awareness of not-having is always determined by the having toward which the not-having aims. Latency for something and tendency toward something are rooted in the nature of things. Hence man is always on the way, participating in a dangerous expedition, a risky pilgrimage in which he is summoned to transcend every present, but without the guarantee of a transcendent reality already complete. Man's highest good is the kingdom of freedom pointed to by the biblical symbols of the Exodus and the kingdom of God. This goal is in the last analysis real and possible because it is potential in the world process itself. Yet it is not certain of attainment, and men must work for it in active hope.[64]

2. *The New.* The not-yet is fully temporal and therefore involves true newness. It lies ever before us as a still possible novelty (*Novum*) which is genuinely future in that it has never before occurred. Humanity is on the way toward its "homeland," which Bloch unabashedly calls Utopia. In his thought the term connotes not a final ideal realm, but a direction which he finds variously expressed in philosophy, litera-

---

[64] *Das Prinzip Hoffnung*, pp. 225, 16-18, 1629, 1625, 284 f., 1566; *Philosophische Grundfragen; Zur Ontologie des Noch-Nicht-Seins* (Frankfurt am Main: Suhrkamp Verlag, 1961), pp. 8 f., 25, 39 f.; *Tübinger Einleitung in die Philosophie*, I (Frankfurt am Main: Suhrkamp Verlag, 1963), 176; *Dokumente der Paulus-Gesellschaft*, ed. Erich Kellner, XII, 118.

ture, and life as that which alone endures, happiness, freedom, nonalienation, the golden age, the land where milk and honey flow, the eternal feminine, the trumpet signal in *Fidelio*, and the Christlikeness of the day of resurrection. Most of all it is the new heaven and the new earth proclaimed by the prophets and the New Testament writers, who were more interested in salvation than in creation. The meaning of time, the future, and real newness is best typified not by the winged Greek gods of time like Nike and Hermes, but by Jahweh, who in the burning bush defines his name to Moses as "I will be who I will be" (a more accurate translation than the traditional "I am who I am" in Exod. 3:14). Time is not endless extension into a future which accomplishes what was already foreordained; it is rather the *kairos* of John the Baptist and Thomas Münzer, the creative or "filled" time which brings into being the truly new.[65]

3. *Matter.* That which ferments in the not and is born in the not-yet, the ground of all unfixed possibilities which makes possible the new, is "matter." However, Bloch emphatically rejects all mechanistic notions of matter as dead, changeless stuff. The Jacobs of theology have robbed matter of its birthright as firstborn; thus matter has become an Esau! The birthright is restored by dialectical materialism, which is a marriage of the idealistic and materialistic traditions. Here matter is conceived dynamically and qualitatively, as the ground of possibility of an advancing, open-ended process. As its cognate *mater* suggests, matter is the ultimate source of all objectively real possibilities, the substratum of the movement and novelty of existence. It is the fruitful womb from which man's future and its own are born. From its creativity spring both the changing activities of inorganic nature and all the values sought by men in society. Its character is such that man cannot live by bread alone, but will raise, in the classless

[65] *Philosophische Grundfragen*, pp. 25 f., 31; *Das Prinzip Hoffnung*, pp. 1626 f.; *Tübinger Einleitung in die Philosophie*, I, 185.

society even more than now, questions of the whither and the why. Its potentialities are limitless and never exhausted.[66] In Bloch's view the revolutionary change implied by all three motifs occurs through the joint activity of socialized man and nature, which are inseparable. The total world process provides the necessary objective basis for the realization of the possible, but man must contribute the subjective factor which alone can translate possibility into reality. Free people working in an open environment—this is the formula for the humanization of nature and pilgrimage toward our homeland. "The Archimedean point [in history] is for Marxism the working man, . . . the relation of man to man and to nature." In this relation Prometheus, not only as a rebel and embezzler but also as a symbol of changeability, is the most eminent saint in the philosophical calendar![67]

Bloch's thought is thus a massive projection of a philosophy of hope, the foci of which are the human subject who hopes and the cosmos which makes hope "hopeable." "Only the horizon of the future, with the horizon of the past as vestibule, gives to reality its true dimension." The world is in the process of becoming, and it is knowing, working man who opens the doors through which the not-yet emerges to become real.[68]

Bloch's eschatological orientation leads him to criticize both Marxism and religion. In his view present-day Marxist orthodoxy is inadequately dialectical; it is mechanistic and necessitarian rather than dynamic, allowing little room for movement toward the new. It is dogmatic, rigid, bound by belief in inflexible law. It fails to recognize the distinctive place of man in nature. Finally, it overlooks the part played by a wide range

[66] *Philosophische Grundfragen*, pp. 27-33; *Das Prinzip Hoffnung*, pp. 1577, 1627 f.; *Dokumente der Paulus-Gesellschaft*, XII, 100, 112, 117 f.
[67] *Das Prinzip Hoffnung*, pp. 303, 333 f., 287 f., 1629; *Tübinger Einleitung in die Philosophie*, II, 178 f; *Geist der Utopie* (Frankfurt am Main: Suhrkamp Verlag, [1923] 1964), p. 347.
[68] *Das Prinzip Hoffnung*, pp. 8, 5 f., 332, 16.

of values in history, where the ideational superstructure often assumes primacy by activating the physical substructure, rather than vice versa.

In theism, including much Christianity, Bloch is repelled by the belief in God as the most real or most perfect being, the fixed, enthroned absolute who requires and guarantees the fulfillment of his arbitrary will; as well as by the corresponding view of men as subjects of God who, lacking independent initiative, are summoned to unquestioning trust and obedience. Such religion is indeed futuristic, projecting into heaven the consummation of presently thwarted human hopes, but the outcome is already determined; thus there is no place for genuine movement forward, no really open future, and no genuinely transcending hope. At the same time, traditional Christianity has acquiesced in social injustice and resisted change, casting its lot with the capitalistic materialism which it calls Christian while failing to see the deeply Christian impulse in the dialectical materialism which seeks a classless society.[69]

In relation to such static theism, asserts Bloch, Nietzsche's word that "God is dead" is true. The deity imagined as a timeless absolute sovereign of an already finished world is nonexistent. Actually, the Bible itself when demythologized points in the opposite direction. The faith it proclaims centers in motifs like exodus, kingdom, a new heaven and a new earth, and "hope that does not disappoint us" (Rom. 5:5). In its deepest dimension it is a book of rebellion. Jesus himself was a rebel who was true to his convictions until death but did not will this death, hoping that the chalice would not have to be drunk. His words and deeds represent a complete departure from a closed conception of being. Therefore, says Bloch, "only an atheist can be a good Christian," and the Romans were quite right—though unaware of the meaning

[69] *Das Prinzip Hoffnung*, pp. 1524 f., 1625, 1527, 1529; *Erbschaft dieser Zeit* (Frankfurt am Main: Suhrkamp Verlag, [1935] 1962), pp. 160, 406-8.

—when they called the first Christians atheists. The atheist is no Antichrist; he is rather positively dedicated to the "utopian" view of man and his world and to the kingdom of freedom which is largely missing from ordinary religious belief.

No anthropological criticism of religion takes away the Christian hope; it only removes from this hope that which would cancel it as hope: the hypostasized mythology of its fulfillment in the God who has already settled everything. Nor is atheism nihilistic; in de-divinized nature there remains a reality of which religious projection is a false interpretation, but which is not fabricated by man. This is the active ground of the new, that which beckons us from ahead and toward which our human purposes are directed. The "field" vacated by the departure of the gods remains; it is the field of infinite possibilities, and men must decide by their action whether it will be filled with heaven or with hell.[70]

The question may be fairly raised as to whether Bloch's world view is accurately described as atheistic. Critics have pointed out that he credits to matter, or the world process, powers and activities which much Christian theism ascribes to God. In so doing is he not to some degree simply redefining God, remaining basically a theist in spite of himself? The fact remains that he regards himself as an atheist, and his self-estimate must be taken seriously. Understanding will be advanced if Christians examine carefully the kind of theism he rejects, his reasons for this rejection, and the dynamic conception of reality which commands his positive allegiance.

3. EXISTENTIALISM

In Dostoyevsky's *The Brothers Karamazov*, Mitya is in prison, charged with the murder of his father. Aware of his

[70] *Tübinger Einleitung in die Philosophie*, II, 175 f.; *Das Prinzip Hoffnung*, pp. 17, 240, 1490 f., 1524, 1527 f., 1529-34; Theodor Heim, "Blochs Atheismus," *Ernst Bloch zu ehren; Beiträge zu seinem Werk*, ed. Siegfried Unseld (Frankfurt am Main: Suhrkamp Verlag, 1965), pp. 158, 173-75.

innocence, in a conversation with his brother Alyosha he tells of the new sense of joy in his sheer existence which has come to him in prison. Then he continues:

It's God that's worrying me. . . . What if He doesn't exist? . . . If He doesn't exist, man is the chief of the earth, of the universe. Magnificent! Only how is he going to be good without God? That's the question. . . . For whom is man going to love then? To whom will he be thankful? To whom will he sing the hymn? . . . Rakitin says that one can love humanity without God. Well, only a snivelling idiot can maintain that. I can't understand it.[71]

Twentieth-century existentialists have faced all the questions raised by Mitya and accepted unhesitatingly the humanistic implications of the atheism he ponders. If God doesn't exist, then man is indeed the source as well as the object of all good—a view which may produce both dread and a sense of deliverance, a consciousness of both limitation and freedom. For thinkers like Jean-Paul Sartre and Albert Camus, rejection of belief in God follows equally from the priority of existence over essence and from the scope and intensity of meaningless human suffering.

The Self-definition of Man

According to Sartre, the starting point of all thought about reality is the subjectivity or self-consciousness of the individual. "First of all, man exists, turns up, appears on the scene," and only afterward can he be conceptually defined. "Thrust" into existence, he begins with no fixed or given human nature; rather he makes himself what he becomes by his free decisions and actions from moment to moment, and he is nothing other than this.[72]

[71] Fyodor Dostoyevsky, *The Brothers Karamazov*, tr. Constance Garnett (New York: Modern Library, n. d.), p. 628.
[72] Jean-Paul Sartre, *Existentialism*, tr. Bernard Frechtman (New York: Philosophical Library, 1947), pp. 18, 20, 42 f. This work was originally a lecture delivered in Paris in 1945, and later published as *L'existentialisme est un humanisme*.

This means that values too are the creation of man, having no reality apart from the willing subject. "Life has no meaning *a priori*. . . . It's up to you to give it a meaning, and value is nothing else than the meaning that you choose." The structure of the values chosen arises through the individual alone, and corresponds to nothing whatever in a supposedly objective order.[73] In Sartre's play *The Wall*, Pablo, a freedom fighter in the Spanish Civil War, is given the choice between being executed or having his life spared on condition that he reveal the whereabouts of Ramon Gris, another freedom fighter. There is no reason why he should shield Gris, with whom he has broken off friendship, and whose life has no more value than his own. In fact, for Pablo no life has any value, and nothing has the slightest meaning any longer. Yet though he knows that Gris is concealed in the house of a cousin, he decides he would rather die than disclose the secret. His sole concern is that he might die "respectably," not in fear. As a joke he informs his captors that the other is hiding in the cemetery, and awaits death as soon as his lie has been discovered. In the meantime, however, Ramon Gris quarrels with his cousin and flees to the cemetery, where he is promptly taken captive. When Pablo learns why he has not been shot, his head whirls and he laughs until the tears come—a reaction expressing at once his own relief at escaping death and the bizarre meaninglessness of man's supposedly ethical choices.[74]

Actually, however, man's awareness of himself as the sole determiner of his values is no laughing matter; on the contrary, it involves him in anguish and forlornness. Since he exists in relation to other men, his choices affect their lives, and he is thus in the position of making laws for them as well as for himself. Each man becomes the basis of value in the

[73] *Ibid.*, p. 58; Sartre, *Being and Nothingness*, tr. Hazel E. Barnes (New York: Citadel Press, 1965), p. 38.
[74] Sartre, *Le mur* (Paris: Gallimard, 1939).

world without being really the foundation of his own being, which is altogether contingent. Conscious of the depth of his responsibility, he experiences dread, which is increased by his haunting realization that he might be mistaken in his choices. Sartre follows Kierkegaard in contemplating the possible anguish of Abraham in asking, "Is it really an angel who has ordered me to sacrifice my son, and am I really Abraham? What proof do I have?" [75]

Another consequence of the complete contingency of being is human forlornness. Another way of saying that there is no a priori good which ought to be chosen is to admit that there is no infinite, perfect consciousness which could conceive the good. Men are alone in the cosmos. But if God does not exist, Ivan Karamazov is right in declaring that "everything is permitted." Hence man is forlorn, with nothing to cling to, either within or without.[76]

It is difficult to give a consistent account of the relation in Sartre's thought between his affirmation of human freedom and his denial of the existence of God. In some passages, as already noted, he argues from the absence of God and any objective structure in reality to the actuality of man's freedom. Man cannot choose whether to be free or not. He *is* his freedom. His freedom is implied in the universal contingency of being, and thereby in the "absurdity" of being. This choice of being is absurd not because it is irrational but because "there has never been any possibility of not choosing oneself." But since this awareness produces anxiety and forsakenness, it is no occassion for unbridled rejoicing. Sartre can even speak of our being "condemned to be free." [77]

On the other hand, a major motivation for Sartre's atheism is his conviction that the existence of God would jeopardize human freedom. If God existed man could not be the source

[75] *Existentialism,* p. 24; *Being and Nothingness,* p. 455.
[76] *Existentialism,* p. 27; *Being and Nothingness,* pp. 37-40.
[77] *Existentialism,* p. 28; *Les mouches* (Paris: Gallimard, 1943), III, 2; *Being and Nothingness,* p. 455.

of meaning and value. If values are given in advance of human choices, men cannot be wholly free. The believer yields to the "spirit of seriousness" which Sartre emphatically repudiates because it leads to

> an ethics which is ashamed of itself and does not dare speak its name. It has obscured all its goals in order to free itself from anguish. Man pursues being blindly by hiding from himself the free project which is this pursuit. He makes himself such that he is waited *for* by all the tasks placed along his way. Objects are mute demands, and he is nothing in himself but the passive obedience to these demands.[78]

Whatever may be for Sartre the basic causal relation between the reality of freedom and the unreality of God, it is clear that he asserts both in close connection with each other. The combination is an essential characteristic of Sartrian atheism. Where all existence is contingent, "God" is a redundant and contradictory hypothesis. To assert his existence is merely to add to the groundless reality of the world another groundless reality. He can be neither the cause of himself nor the necessary being of traditional theology. If self-caused, he would have to exist as cause before he could cause himself. "Necessary being" would mean a being whose possibility implied existence; however, this is only a form of the ontological argument which attempts unjustifiably to move from the order of knowledge to the order of being. We can indeed think of possibility as "an ontological structure of the real. Then it belongs to certain beings as *their* possibility; it is the possibility which they are.... In this case being sustains its own possibilities in being; it is their foundation." But "the necessity of being can not then be denied from its possibility." Thus even God himself, "if he exists, is contingent." [79]

In view of this thoroughgoing contingency, human exis-

---

[78] *Being and Nothingness*, p. 544; cf. pp. 37, 39; *La nausée* (Paris: Gallimard, 1938), pp. 107 ff.
[79] *Being and Nothingness*, pp. 56 f.

tence is absurd, not only in the sense that its choices are non-rational, but in the full sense of complete irrationality, meaninglessness, and futility. Roquetin, the protagonist of Sartre's novel *Nausea*, sees all human beings and all physical things as superfluous; none of us has the slightest reason for being there. The "long dead snake" which in imagination he sees at his feet becomes for him the symbol of the absurdity of existence and the key to his own nausea. In one moment he experiences "the absolute: the absolute or the absurd." [80] "I know perfectly well that it was the World in all its nakedness which was suddenly revealing itself, and I choked with fury at that huge absurd being." [81] In the "horrible ecstasy" of this experience Roquetin perceives that "the essential thing is contingency. . . . By definition, existence is not necessary. To exist is simply *to be there;* what exists appears, lets itself be *encountered.*" This contingency cannot be overcome or dissipated by the invention of a necessary Being; "it is absolute, and, consequently perfect gratuitousness. Everything is gratuitous, that park, this town, and myself." [82]

In spite of man's meaningless situation, Sartre sees no point in a resort to suicide. Suicide too is "an absurdity which causes my life to be submerged in the absurd." [83] "It is absurd that we are born; it is absurd that we die." [84]

The senselessness of man's life is also the dominant motif of the writings of Albert Camus. His novel *The Plague* is not only a vivid and sensitive day-by-day account of the terrifying, numbing impact of the bubonic plague on the life of a North African city; it is also a portrayal of Camus's conception of human existence as a whole. Thus near the end of the book Dr. Rieux asks, "What does that mean—'plague'? Just life,

---

[80] *La nausée,* pp. 163 f.
[81] *Ibid.,* p. 170.
[82] *Ibid.,* p. 166.
[83] *Being and Nothingness,* p. 516.
[84] *Ibid.,* p. 523.

no more than that." [85] Earlier he declares in commenting on the constant danger of infection, "What's natural is the microbe. All the rest—health, integrity, purity (if you like)—is a product of the human will." [86]

The central meaning of the entire work of Camus is contained in his interpretation of the myth of Sisyphus. "Sisyphus is the absurd hero. He *is*, as much through his passions as through his torture. His scorn of the gods, his hatred of death, and his passion for life won him that unspeakable penalty in which the whole being is exerted toward accomplishing nothing. This is the price that must be paid for the passions of this earth." [87]

Most of the main characters in *The Plague* become "absurd heroes" in this sense. Rambert's repeatedly fruitless attempts to leave Oran to join his beloved in Paris, his playing his only phonograph record ten times a day, the weary, endlessly repeated efforts of the inhabitants to combat the plague by ineffective measures, their little victories which never last—all convey Camus's perception of existence. "Since the order of this world is shaped by death," the best course is to refuse to believe in God and "struggle with all our might against death, without raising our eyes toward the heaven where he sits in silence." But our victories never last, and culminate in "never-ending defeat." [88]

Yet there is tragic heroism in our existence. Though conscious of the futility of his action, Sisyphus returns again and again to the foot of the mountain. In so doing he becomes

---

[85] *The Plague*, tr. Stuart Gilbert (New York: Modern Library, 1948), pp. 276 f. I am aware that some critics regard as erroneous any identification of Camus with existentialism. For present purposes this question can be left open. However, with respect to the reality of God Camus takes basically the same position as Sartre and other atheistic existentialists. It therefore seems quite sound to interpret his views in this context.
[86] *Ibid.*, p. 229.
[87] *The Myth of Sisyphus, and Other Essays*, tr. Justin O'Brien (New York: Vintage Books, 1959), p. 89.
[88] *The Plague*, pp. 147 f., 117 f.

"superior to his fate. He is stronger than his rock. . . . The lucidity that was to constitute his torture at the same time crowns his victory. There is no fate that cannot be surmounted by scorn."[89] With such an attitude man may even experience a measure of happiness. He is facing his situation and performing his tasks, making his own decisions and acting on them in his own strength. Sisyphus and not the universe is "the master of his days." He "teaches the higher fidelity that negates the gods and raises rocks."[90]

ATHEISM AS AXIOLOGICAL PROTEST

The defiance of Sisyphus calls dramatic attention to an aspect of existentialist atheism which merits closer examination—the rejection of God in the name of the values sought by men condemned to suffering and mortality. In *The Brothers Karamazov* Ivan protests vehemently against a world in which innocent human beings, including helpless children, suffer hideous cruelties at the hands of those who hold power over them, even parents. Ivan cannot understand how such a world can be the creation of a good God, or how a just Creator could permit such suffering or fail to use his power in behalf of the victims. The evidence, Ivan thinks, points to indifference rather than concern at the heart of the universe. He cries out for justice, but sees injustice rampant and unavenged. For him it is unconvincing to seek refuge in the hope of an ultimate harmony when all who suffer now will find peace and joy. "I renounce the higher harmony altogether. It's not worth the tears of that one tortured child who beat itself on the breast with its little fist and prayed . . . with its unexpiated tears to 'dear, kind God'!"[91]

In Camus's *The Plague* Dr. Rieux betrays the same angry rebelliousness following the agonizing death of a child. When

---
[89] *The Myth of Sisyphus*, pp. 89 f.
[90] *Ibid.*, p. 91.
[91] Pp. 247-55.

the priest observes that such an event is revolting because we cannot understand it, but suggests that "perhaps we should love what we cannot understand," the doctor replies, "No, Father, I've a very different idea of love. And until my dying day I shall refuse to love a scheme of things in which children are put to torture." [92]

In this spirit Camus writes of the "metaphysical revolt" of our time, which is a revolt of man against the conditions of his life—creation itself—but also a search for order and for clarity and unity of thought. "Metaphysical rebellion is a claim, motivated by the concept of a complete unity, against the suffering of life and death and a protest against the human condition both for its incompleteness, thanks to death, and its wastefulness, thanks to evil." Man rebels simultaneously against his "mass death sentence" and against "the power that compels him to live in this condition." Hence he is a blasphemer rather than an atheist in the usual sense: He denounces God "as the father of death and as the supreme outrage." At least at first, he "defies more than he denies." [93] However, if God is conceived as a reality worthy of worship and trustful commitment, Camus's rebel, who obviously finds no evidence for such a reality, takes an essentially atheistic position.

Such atheism is clearly expressed in the thought of Maurice Merleau-Ponty. To believe in a creator, he maintains, we must either deny the reality of evil or accept a God who upholds a cosmos in which man is sacrificed. But evil is patently real, indicating that the world has not been thought through and that there is no absolute who conceived it.[94]

A variation of this theme appears in Sartre's argument from the difficulty man experiences when he tries to do the good.

[92] Pp. 196 f.
[93] *The Rebel: An Essay on Man in Revolt,* tr. Anthony Bower (New York: Vintage Books, 1957), pp. 24, 25.
[94] *Sens et Non-Sens* (Paris: Gallimard, 1948), pp. 192 f.; *Éloge de la philosophie* (Paris: Gallimard, 1953), pp. 64 f.

Everything man does is a mixture of good and evil. Even when he tries to act according to love for others he gets "soiled hands," arousing antagonism and causing suffering in those he tries to help. Hence it is impossible for man to do the right. But this rules out any divine will or law, for if a divine law existed it would be possible for man to do the good by obeying it.[95]

In *The Devil and the Good Lord,* Sartre also voices protests similar to those of Camus's characters. Goetz, who had claimed conversion from evil to good, finally admits that he alone was the source of the orders he had pretended to receive:

I alone, priest; you are right, I alone, I supplicated, I demanded a sign, I sent messages to Heaven, no reply. Heaven ignored my very name. Each minute I wondered what I could BE in the eyes of God. Now I know the answer: nothing. God does not see me, God does not hear me, God does not know me. You see this emptiness over our heads? That is God. You see this gap in the door? It is God. You see that hole in the ground? That is God again. Silence is God. Absence is God. God is the loneliness of man. There was no one but myself; I alone decided on Evil; and I alone invented good. It was I who cheated, I who worked miracles, I who accused myself today, I alone who can absolve myself; I, man. If God exists, man is nothing; if man exists . . . .

Man, of course, does exist, the sole determiner of good and evil. So Goetz continues: "Heinrich, I am going to tell you a colossal joke: God doesn't exist. He doesn't exist. Joy, tears of joy. Halleluiah! . . . I have delivered us. No more Heaven, no more Hell; nothing but earth." [96]

Hilda, Goetz's latest lover, is equally convinced of the emptiness of life, but her response is one of bitterness and anger

[95] *Saint Genêt* (Paris: Gallimard, 1952), p. 29; *The Devil and the Good Lord* (New York: Vintage Books, 1962), Acts II and III; *Les mains sales* (Paris: Gallimard, 1948).
[96] *The Devil and the Good Lord,* III, 10, pp. 141 f.

rather than joy in deliverance. Catherine has died in agonizing loneliness after being driven away by Goetz, whom she truly loved even though he ruined her life. Urged to pray for her pardon, Hilda exclaims,

> Implore Thy pardon! What hast Thou to forgive us? Thou art the one who shouldst ask our forgiveness! I do not know what Thou hast in store for me, and I did not even know that girl, but if Thou dost condemn her, I shall refuse to enter heaven. Dost Thou believe a thousand years of Paradise would make me forget the terror in her eyes? ... I am on the side of humanity. Thou hast the power to let me die without confession and summon me suddenly before Thy bar of judgment; but we shall then see who shall judge the other.[97]

Just as passionate as the revolt of Sartre and Camus against God in the name of man is their indignation against the church, both for its traditional interpretation of evil and for its frequent indifference to human misery. Early in *The Devil and the Good Lord,* Heinrich, the priest, by sheer will asserts his belief that everything happens according to the will of God, "even to the death of a little child, and that all is good. I believe because it is absurd!"[98] But such credulity proves unequal to the reality of suffering, and before the end of the play Heinrich renounces his faith. In *The Plague* Father Paneloux portrays the disaster as an omnipotent God's chastisement of men for their wickedness, and calls on his congregation to repent. Later, after he has witnessed the horrible death of a small boy, his explanation of history falls to pieces, and eventually he himself dies, not of the plague but because his world has collapsed.[99]

It is clear that theological interpretations like these have provided an important ground for existentialist atheism. The same may be said of the ethical deficiencies of believers,

[97] *Ibid.,* II, 6, pp. 93 f.
[98] *Ibid.,* I, 1, pp. 10, 13.
[99] Pp. 189-211.

particularly when related to lack of concern in the presence of human wretchedness and exploitation. In *The Brothers Karamazov* the Grand Inquisitor speaks of "correcting" the work of Christ, the Prisoner, by making decisions precisely opposite to those of Jesus in his temptations.[100] Founding his work on miracle, mystery, and authority, the Inquisitor takes away from men the discomfort of having to decide for themselves, demanding and securing obedience in return for the promise of bread and eternal security. Hypocritically he claims that in this way he makes men happy, while he and other rulers accept the unhappiness of taking on themselves the curse of the knowledge of good and evil. Though the accomplices of the Grand Inquisitor are called "the clever people," Alyosha and Ivan agree that their only "secret" is the atheism which hides behind their pious pretense. "Your Inquisitor does not believe in God, that's his secret!" Thus does Dostoyevsky express his estimate of the crass authoritarian materialism of the official Russian church of his day.

With the sadness of disappointed hopes, Camus speaks frankly to a group of Benedictine monks regarding the failure of their church to lift its voice against injustice amid the horrors of the fourth and fifth decades of the twentieth century. Millions of unbelievers, he declares, listened in vain for an unmistakable condemnation of totalitarian tyranny by Rome or the Christian church. It is no answer to claim that papal encyclicals provide this condemnation, for the language of such statements is so ambiguous that it is simply not heard. A church which contents itself with the abstractions of encyclicals is itself deserving of condemnation. The world expects Christians to free themselves from abstraction and confront specifically the blood-drenched countenance of our present history. "The unification which we need is one of men who are determined to speak a clear language and to take sides with their own persons. When a Spanish bishop blesses

[100] P. 269; cf. pp. 259-72.

political executions he is no longer a bishop or a Christian, not even a man; he is then a dog, just as much as he who from the lofty standpoint of an ideology orders the execution." Is there nothing in the beliefs of Christians, asks Camus, which could move them to join the struggle for justice? If Christianity answers with words only, persists in compromises, and repudiates the virtue of resistance and rebellion which marked it long ago, then "Christians will live, but Christianity will die." [101]

RESPONSIBLE HUMANISM

"Can one be a saint without God?" asks Tarrou in Camus's *The Plague*.[102] Though the question is not directly answered by Dr. Rieux, it is answered with at least a partial affirmative by the commitment of many existentialists to the purely human values which make claims on them. As Sartre asserts in the title of his definitive essay, *existentialism is a humanism*. Indeed, Sartre finds man's existence characterized by a kind of self-transcendence, a "passing-beyond" himself. Man exists as he projects or loses himself outside himself in pursuing transcendent goals. Man's only universe is one of human subjectivity, but subjectivity here refers to everything human, not only to the individual.

This connection between transcendency, as a constituent element of man—not in the sense that God is transcendent, but in the sense of passing beyond—and subjectivity, in the sense that man is not closed in on himself but is always present in a human universe, is what we call existentialist humanism. Humanism, because we remind man that there is no law-maker other than himself, and that in his forlornness he will decide by himself; because we point out that man will fulfill himself as man, not in turning

---

[101] Camus, "Der Ungläubige und die Christen," *Fragen der Zeit* (Hamburg: Rowohlt Verlag, 1960), pp. 74 f., 78.
[102] P. 230.

toward himself, but in seeking outside of himself a goal which is just this liberation, just this particular fulfillment.[103]

Existentialist humanism sees each man as responsible for his own existence—for what he is and becomes. However, this responsibility extends beyond his own individuality to include all men. Sartre's declaration that man chooses himself means not only that every man chooses himself, but that in so doing he chooses all men. Every action which creates the man I want to be simultaneously creates an image of man as I think he should be. What I choose is always what I regard as good, but nothing can be good for me if it is not good for all.[104]

Sartre reaches the same conclusion through his existential modification of Descartes's famous *cogito ergo sum*. The situation into which we are thrown is a social situation in which our lives are involved with others. The *I* which thinks and exists is not a strictly individual *I*; the reality it discovers includes others no less than itself. "Through the *I think* we reach our own self in the presence of others, and the others are just as real to us as our own self. Thus, the man who becomes aware of himself through the *cogito* also perceives all others, and he perceives them as the condition of his own existence." [105]

The assertion of freedom likewise implies an obligation of the individual to other persons. Honest men, says Sartre, seek freedom as such, freedom for freedom's sake, as the basis for all values. Real freedom, however, is always sought in particular circumstances, in relation to concrete goals. We therefore discover that our freedom depends on that of others, and theirs on ours.

Of course, freedom as the definition of man does not depend on others, but as soon as there is involvement, I am obliged to want others to have freedom at the same time that I want my own

[103] *Existentialism*, pp. 59 f.
[104] *Ibid.*, p. 20.
[105] *Ibid.*, p. 44.

freedom. I can take freedom as my goal only if I take that of others as a goal as well. Consequently, when, in all honesty, I've recognized that man is a being in whom existence precedes essence, that he is a free being who, in various circumstances, can want only his freedom, I have at the same time recognized that I can want only the freedom of others.[106]

Human interdependence is further reinforced by suffering and the rebellion it evokes. All men are confronted by evil and death, and from the depths of their being they cry out for justice. In this protest suffering is seen to be a collective experience. Overwhelmed by "the strangeness of things," we realize that this feeling is shared by all men. Thus in our trials rebellion performs the same function as the *cogito* in the sphere of thought: it provides the first evidence. But this evidence draws the individual out of his solitariness. According to Camus, "It founds its first value on the whole human race. I rebel—therefore we exist." [107]

Moreover, the rebel is moved to loving concern for his fellow sufferers. "Those who find no rest in God or in history are condemned to live for those who, like themselves, cannot live: in fact, for the humiliated." [108] Thus Tarrou loses his peace when he realizes that we all have the plague, and that "we can't stir a finger in this world without the risk of bringing death to somebody." The only answer is for each man to do what he can to alleviate suffering. If men cannot be saved, at least we can so act as to do them the least possible harm, and perhaps occasionally even some good. On this basis Tarrou resolves "to have no truck with anything which, directly or indirectly, for good reasons or for bad, brings death to anyone or justifies others' putting him to death." [109] Here also is the ground for Camus's own active opposition to capital

[106] *Ibid.*, pp. 54 f.
[107] *The Rebel*, p. 22; cf. p. 303.
[108] *Ibid.*, p. 271.
[109] *The Plague*, pp. 228 f.

punishment. He rejects Christian hope in eternal life and a future kingdom as only a postponed and unfounded answer to presently experienced evil. However, his socially responsible, this-worldly humanism manifests a concern for suffering men which is comparable to that of authentic Christian faith, yet which is conspicuously absent in many who profess that faith.

4. SCIENTIFIC HUMANISM

It is often assumed that the decisive struggle for the minds of men today is that being waged between Christianity and communism. Differing sharply with this verdict are many representatives of another position who, though atheistic in outlook, reject Marxism just as vigorously as they do Christian belief. The basic opposition, writes Margaret Knight of Aberdeen, is between religious dogma and science. Though Christianity and communism are rivals, they are both dogmatic systems, and opposed to the mythical thinking of both is the empirical search for truth of scientific humanism. By *scientific*, Knight means the method which, instead of clinging to unchangeable dogmas, proceeds by hypotheses based on observation and constantly checked and revised in the light of newly discovered facts. *Humanism* designates a belief concerned with men and their earthly lives, not with supernatural beings and another world; its goal is the unfolding of all the capacities of men and women for their welfare, happiness, and mental and aesthetic fulfillment.[110] Implicitly and often explicitly atheistic, this point of view is without question typical of multitudes of thoughtful people today. Sometimes it is militantly upheld; more frequently, as in the case of Gerhard Szczesny of Munich, it is advanced as a positive and superior alternative to Christian belief by critically minded Westerners with varied interests who are committed to human enlightenment but have moved outside the conceptual world of Chris-

[110] Margaret Knight, "Erziehung ohne Religion," *Club Voltaire I*, ed. Gerhard Szczesny (München: Szczesny Verlag, 1963), pp. 57 f.

tian faith. Some are completely secular in their naturalistic humanism; others, like Julian Huxley, espouse a nontheistic religious humanism. Both forms demand our attention.

NONRELIGIOUS NATURALISM

Secularistic naturalistic humanists offer four major considerations in support of their atheism: (1) the opposition between scientific method and religious belief; (2) the extent of human suffering; (3) the negative effect of religious belief on the struggle for human justice; and (4) the tendency of theistic belief to diminish human responsibility.

1. According to the scientific humanist, man attains truth to the degree that he follows the method of the natural sciences, which move from empirical observation through hypothesis and controlled experiment to verification and the formulation of laws commanding universal assent. This procedure assumes that hypotheses are tentative until they are validated by objective tests, and its conclusions are always subject to revision. Yet it is has enormously increased man's knowledge of his world and given him an almost incredible mastery over nature. In so doing it has made understandable vast areas long shrouded in mystery and demonstrated the natural causation of many phenomena once attributed to divine action. Thus God becomes increasingly unnecessary and worthless as an explanatory principle.

Not only does science thus undermine a traditional basis for belief in God; it also offers nothing in its place. A method which takes as its model the investigation of sense data finds nothing intelligible in man's response in faith and commitment to the total reality which confronts him. There is no scientific evidence for "a metaphysically postulated supreme being which transcends conceivability and experienceability," which supposedly produces and sustains this world and the people who inhabit it.[111] The scientific evidence, thinks Gerhard Szczesny, indicates that there is nothing beyond the physical order. From an immanent source the world develops as a universal continuum, an interconnected causal process. Humanity itself is thus an occurrence within nature, though the highest form of existence we know.[112]

To this argument some naturalistic humanists add the charge that theistic belief hinders the advance of science and its liberating effects. Thus Max Bense asserts that the full development of human capacities demands the uninhibited use of reason, but belief in a transcendent supreme being substitutes subjective faith for critical thinking about the objective world, thereby renouncing or seriously limiting reason.[113] In similar vein, Morris R. Cohen contrasts the passionate loyalty to traditional beliefs with the insatiable curiosity and desire for logical consistency which he regards as characteristic of religion and science respectively. "Religious truth is absolute and its possession makes everything else unimportant. Hence religion never preaches the duty of critical thought, of searching or investigating supposed facts." [114]

If the religious believer seeks to answer this charge by pointing to the relative peace now prevailing between science and religion, or to a widely agreed upon division of labor which for some removes the source of the conflict, the naturalist is likely to attribute this simply to repeated defeats of religion and victorious advances of science. For example, Barbara Wootton insists that "if the natural sciences are no longer in conflict with religion, it is because religion no longer dares to

[111] Max Bense, "Warum man Atheist sein muss," *Club Voltaire I*, ed. Gerhard Szczesny, p. 67.
[112] *The Future of Unbelief*, tr. Edward B. Garside (London: Heinemann, 1962), pp. 145, 149.
[113] *Ibid.*, pp. 69-71.
[114] "The Dark Side of Religion," *Religion from Tolstoy to Camus*, ed. Walter Kaufmann (New York: Harper & Brothers, 1961), pp. 283, 285.

say anything about the behaviour of natural phenomena, having always been proved wrong when it did so." [115]

2. Among naturalistic humanists the problem of suffering is a relatively secondary ground of atheism, yet for some it plays an important part. Bertrand Russell, for example, finds that the evil in the world contradicts Christian belief.[116] Walter Kaufmann reaches similar conclusions. Popular theism, he declares, maintains not only that God is just, but that he is infinitely merciful, loving, and perfect. Then why is there so much suffering? "The theism preached from thousands of pulpits and credited by millions of believers is disproved by Auschwitz and a billion lesser evils." Nor does it help to take refuge in a doctrine of immortality or resurrection. If an omnipotent God can give Anne Frank eternal happiness in heaven, why must he allow her, after long months of anxious hiding, to fall victim to the Nazis and be killed? [117]

The fact that religious faith survives in spite of such glaring evils is seen by Szczesny as a sign of its weakness rather than its strength. The desire for a feeling of security impedes the critical thought which would be needed to search for new answers to ultimate questions. "In the face of modern crises and catastrophes the security afforded by a venerable and firmly built structure of belief makes Christianity, as a whole, taboo and hinders open critical analysis of it." [118] A similar attitude is reflected in the thought of Kingsley Martin when he declares, "The chief enemies of humanism are those who hold that revealed religion is a necessity, whether or not it is objectively true." [119]

---

[115] *Testament of Social Science* (London: Allen; New York: Norton, 1950), p. 111 (British ed.).
[116] *Why I Am Not a Christian* (New York: Simon and Schuster, 1957), pp. 13, 20.
[117] *The Faith of a Heretic* (Garden City, N.Y.: Doubleday & Co., 1961), pp. 149, 151 f., 160.
[118] *The Future of Unbelief*, p. 12.
[119] Harold John Blackham (ed.), *Objections to Humanism* (London: Constable, 1963), p. 82.

3. Some naturalistic humanists are almost as extreme as the Marxists in reproaching Christian believers for failure to support the struggle for social justice. Morris R. Cohen accuses Christianity of having been in general

> on the side of the powerful classes who have supported it—royalists in France, landowners in England, the *cientifico* or exploiting class in Mexico, etc. Here and there some religious leader or group has shown sympathy with the oppressed; but the Church as a whole has property interests which affiliate it with those in power.[120]

Gerhard Szczesny presents a similar indictment, citing the scant support by the churches of efforts to outlaw child labor in the nineteenth century and the tendency of the churches to view the difference between rich and poor as divinely ordained and valid for all time. Christians, he writes, place before men not model lives, but model talk.[121] Further, "the notion that earthly existence in itself has no meaning, but is no more than a preparatory testing ground for the eternal life, necessarily fails to lend support to man's personal and social sense of responsibility." [122]

An even more serious indictment lodged against religious belief is the sorry record of persecution and violence in the name of orthodoxy. Christianity, declares Arnulf Överland, is the gospel of peace and love, "but wars of religion, burnings of heretics, and trials of witches have cost the lives of millions of human beings." [123] Citing similar violations of the professed belief in a loving and merciful God, Morris R. Cohen maintains that "cruel persecution and intolerance are not

---

[120] *Religion from Tolstoy to Camus,* p. 291.
[121] The original German has a vivid play on words which is difficult to preserve in translation: "Die Christen sind keine Vorbilder, sondern Vorredner."
[122] *The Future of Belief,* p. 197; Günther Backhaus, *Atheismus eine Selbsttäuschung?* (München: Ernst Reinhardt, 1962), pp. 17 f.
[123] "Drei Artikel des Unglaubens," *Club Voltaire I,* ed. Gerhard Szczesny, p. 51.

accidents, but grow out of the very essence of religion, namely, its absolute claims." The claim by any faith to possess the absolute truth supernaturally revealed by God leads logically to opposition to other religions as sinful errors. Hence although religions sometimes speak eloquently of human brotherhood, historically they have divided humanity into sects, often pitting one against the other. In contrast, science unites men into one community concerned with the enlightenment of all.[124]

4. Implicit in all three of the humanist arguments so far discussed is a further consideration which now needs to be explicated. Like theoretical Marxism, scientific humanism is atheistic because of its positive concern for the fullest and freest development of man on the earth. It sees theistic belief as shifting to God the responsibility which properly belongs to man, and to another and illusory realm the accomplishments which should be sought in this world. Belief in God must therefore be superseded by acceptance of full human responsibility. Man is totally and solely responsible for himself and his world.[125]

From this perspective atheistic humanism attacks the ethics no less than the world views of religious believers. It regards Christian existence, for example, as heteronomously rather than autonomously grounded, and sees the Christian ethical life as vitiated by the church's imposition of static moral prescriptions linked to future rewards and punishments. In the words of Gerhard Szczesny, "All moral systems which deny that a sound basis for human behavior is found in man himself, and which undertake to propagate the view that human

[124] *Religion from Tolstoy to Camus*, pp. 188 f.
[125] Margaret Knight, "Erziehung ohne Religion," *Club Voltaire I*, ed. Gerhard Szczesny, pp. 57 f.; Wilhelm F. Kasch, *Atheistischer Humanismus und christliche Existenz in der Gegenwart* (Tübingen: J. C. B. Mohr [Paul Siebeck], 1964), pp. 6, 9 f.; Jean Lacroix, *The Meaning of Modern Atheism*, tr. Garret Barden, S.J. (New York: The Macmillan Co., 1965), p. 28; Max Bense, *Club Voltaire I*, p. 67.

behavior can be effectively induced only by transcendental regulation, are actually lending support to immorality."[126]

RELIGIOUS HUMANISM

Among contemporary humanists who reject belief in a superhuman God on scientific grounds are some who in spite of their atheism find truth and value in a broadly religious interpretation of experience. A distinguished representative of this position is Julian Huxley, whose nontheistic evolutionary naturalism we shall now briefly examine, with limited reference to somewhat similar positions.

Like other scientific naturalists, Huxley is committed to "the progressive method of observation and hypothesis, followed by the checking of hypothesis by fresh observation."[127] This method leaves no place for "the god hypothesis" in the interpretation of nature. Indeed, such a hypothesis often bars the way to a better and truer interpretation. In objectifying and personifying qualities which are actually in man as a part of nature, it introduces a basic cleavage into reality and obscures its fundamental unity. Huxley finds that such a dualism between natural and supernatural is excluded by the sciences. The discoveries of astronomy, physiology, biology, and psychology necessitate "a naturalistic hypothesis, in which there is no room for the supernatural, and the spiritual forces at work in the cosmos are seen as a part of nature just as much as the material forces."[128]

The notion of a supernatural divine being is according to Huxley a rationalization which was perhaps inevitable at more primitive levels of human culture, but which has outlived the usefulness it once had. The world came into being through evolution rather than creation. Man, having emerged

[126] *The Future of Unbelief*, p. 191; cf. pp. 100, 217 f.
[127] *Religion Without Revelation*, rev. ed. (New York: Harper & Brothers, [1927] 1957), p. 50.
[128] *Ibid.*, pp. 6-7, 14, 38-41, 58, 209 f.; Huxley (ed.), *The Humanist Frame* (New York: Harper & Brothers, 1961), p. 40.

to dominance, is "the sole agent for the future evolution of this planet." Moreover, in coping with life he must rely on his own unaided efforts. "Operationally, God is beginning to resemble not a ruler, but the last fading smile of a cosmic Cheshire cat." [129]

Huxley finds additional support for his atheistic position in several other considerations which resemble those cited by humanists already mentioned. Belief in a God who is all-wise, all-powerful, and all-good is incompatible with the harsh reality of evil—the ignorance, disorder, strife, and physical and mental suffering which are so devastating to human well-being. Belief in the absoluteness of God, who therefore provides unassailable authority for moral commandments, doctrinal correctness, and claims to revelation and inspiration, is a serious obstacle to moral, intellectual, and religious progress. The same absolutistic belief, linked with ignorance of modern psychological understanding of unconscious motivation, allows fanatical moralists and power-hungry politicians to identify their subjective feelings with the will of an objective God, with disastrous results in the lives of those over whom they wield authority.[130]

For the rejected belief in a supernatural God, Huxley substitutes confidence in the "vast untapped possibilities" of the evolutionary process, which reach their highest level in man. This confidence he believes to be grounded in knowledge. The "world-stuff" which composes the cosmos, when organized as it is in the human brain, can carry on mental as well as physical activities. The result has been the appearance of man with all his capacities for qualitative richness of experience. He is the highest form of life thus far produced on earth, and the only organism capable of further advance. Hence he has the high destiny of using the mental and spiritual forces

[129] *The Humanist Frame*, pp. 17-19, 14; *Religion Without Revelation*, pp. 18, 58.
[130] *Religion Without Revelation*, pp. 39-41, 48; *The Humanist Frame*, p. 40.

which operate within him—not outside him—to become the instrument of new progress. "My faith," writes Huxley, "is in the possibilities of man." Man is not central in the universe, but he has "immense significance," for it is peculiarly in him that the possibilities of existence are increasingly realized. Belief in this ever-growing fulfillment of potentialities is the central concept of evolutionary humanism.[131]

A similar orientation appears in the thought of Gustav Wyneken, who replaces Christian belief with concern for the totality of man's intellectual and cultural life, while allowing Christianity a place as one possible form of this life. Our goal should be "the elevation, coronation, and enlivening of our biological-social and rational existence through the freely creative power of man." However, this activity occurs within the physical world, and a possible future religion must be no longer historically conditioned, but rooted in our knowledge and experience of nature.[132]

J. P. van Praag, chairman of the International Humanist and Ethical Union, likewise stresses the creative possibilities of man, the being that realizes itself only by transcending itself. Human existence is to be conceived as "human deployment, a deployment which aims at true humanity." Since man's relationships are cosmic as well as natural and social, his life may be said to have "religious" meaning. Humanism is "a conviction of life by which man with the totality of his faculties is connected with the totality of his conditions of existence." [133]

Though religious implications are clearly present in the humanism of Wyneken and van Praag, they are much more developed in the new religion proposed by Julian Huxley.

[131] *Ibid.*, pp. 217, 214, 220, 239, 18, 235-37, 47 f.; Huxley, *Essays of a Humanist* (London: Chatto and Windus, 1964), pp. 114 f.
[132] Wyneken, *Abschied vom Christentum* (München: Szczesny Verlag, 1963), pp. 254 f.
[133] Van Praag, *Humanism* (Utrecht: International Humanist and Ethical Union, 1957), pp. 18-21.

In his view religious experiences can no longer be interpreted in terms of relations between man and a personal God or a supernatural realm. Nevertheless, it is impossible to explain away experiences like those of an awareness of transcendent power, communion with a higher reality, a sense of sacredness, or a consciousness of inner peace in spite of distress. Such occurrences are real, and of great importance. They point to forces which transcend our private selves, whether in external nature or in our social environment. "They are the outcome of human minds in their strange commerce with outer reality and in the still stranger and often unconscious internal struggle between their components." Our task is therefore to reinterpret them in evolutionary terms and in accord with scientific knowledge now available.[134]

The religion of the future will be a way of life grounded in our apprehension of a sacredness in existence, our attitude of reverence, awe, and wonder in relation to those aspects of existence which have to do primarily with human destiny. Destiny confronts us in such events as birth, falling in love, sickness, suffering, death; our own ideals and shortcomings; our questions about what is valuable and enduring; and perhaps most truly in our awareness of unrealized possibilities, guilt, and imperfection.[135] Thus nontheistic, humanistic religion will be concerned with the deepest aspects of our day-by-day relationships in the here-and-now. Huxley suggests that it might be thought of as "applied spiritual ecology." The relations important to it are those of mankind with external nature and those of individuals with one another and with their communities.[136]

A variation of the religious humanism typified by Huxley is found in the mature thought of Erich Fromm, which is both psychoanalytically and socially oriented. According to

---

[134] *Religion Without Revelation,* pp. 44-46, 60, 223; *Essays of a Humanist,* pp. 109 f.
[135] *Religion Without Revelation,* pp. 9 f., 24 f., 42 f., 62.
[136] *Ibid.,* p. 43; *Essays of a Humanist,* p. 108.

Fromm the important religious issue confronting man is not that of belief or disbelief in God, but that of the presence or absence of certain human value commitments, of which theistic belief may be one expression.

The problem of religion is not the problem of God but the problem of man; religious formulations and religious symbols are attempts to give expression to certain kinds of human experience. What matters is the nature of these experiences. The symbol system is only the cue from which we can infer the underlying human reality.[137]

At heart belief in God signifies devotion to the fulfillment of the highest human potentialities: personal wholeness, love and participation in work as a meaningful activity, ultimate concern for spiritual rather than materialistic values—truth, love, and justice. The founders of all the great religions were one in regarding the supreme aim of life as "concern with man's soul and the unfolding of his powers of love and reason." Likewise, on the negative side genuine unbelief is not verbalized rejection of the symbol "God," but idolatries like the deification of the state, race, the machine, or economic success. Such attitudes "threaten the most precious spiritual possessions of man." Hence the real danger confronting us is not the death of God but the death of man.[138]

The crucial question, therefore, is whether man "lives love and thinks truth. If he does so the belief systems he uses will be secondary. If he does not they are of no importance." Many professed believers in God exhibit human attitudes indicating idol worship or faithlessness, while many avowed atheists manifest in concrete action the love and brotherliness which reflect real faith and a deeply religious spirit. If we center attention on the acceptance or denial of "God" we deal with the shell rather than the kernel of the problem, and hinder

[137] *Psychoanalysis and Religion*, p. 113.
[138] *The Dogma of Christ*, pp. 101 f.; *Psychoanalysis and Religion*, pp. 99, 118 f.

the development of the attitude which is truly religious because it is humanistic.[139]

Fromm's position makes unmistakably clear the essential characteristic which all scientific and philosophical humanists, whether religious or secular, have in common—a fundamental belief in the oneness, improvability, and ethical-social responsibility of man, coupled with a conviction that the fulfillment of his possibilities depends on man's own efforts.[140] Such humanism is without doubt the working presupposition or practical mood of multitudes of persons in Europe and America today, whatever beliefs they may verbally profess. The sharp difference between this orientation and that of the Christian theist on the ultimate reference of man's life should not obscure their important agreements or the possibility and urgent need of active cooperation in common tasks.

5. LINGUISTIC PHILOSOPHY

A specialized twentieth-century expression of scientific method which has had atheistic implications for some thinkers is linguistic analysis, at present the dominant movement in Anglo-Saxon philosophy. This movement assumes various forms, but all follow a method of inquiry which centers in the analysis of the meaning and use of language and the bearing of this analysis on basic philosophical questions. The use of linguistic analysis as a tool does not commit the user to any particular metaphysics. Some philosophers and theologians find the analysis of language an avenue to clear and meaningful discourse concerning God. However, for other thinkers the application of the methods of natural science to the logic of language has led to conclusions which if not atheistic are clearly nontheistic. It is these conclusions and

---

[139] *Psychoanalysis and Religion*, pp. 9, 113 f.; cf. *Socialist Humanism*, ed. Erich Fromm (Garden City, N.Y.: Doubleday & Co., Anchor Books, 1966), pp. 11 f.
[140] *Socialist Humanism*, pp. vii, xii.

the arguments used in reaching them which now concern us.

Logical positivism, vigorously upheld in such works as Ludwig Wittgenstein's *Tractatus Logico-Philosophicus* (1922) and Alfred J. Ayer's *Language, Truth and Logic* (1935), maintained that only those propositions are factually meaningful which can be verified according to the canons of sense perception. Karl Popper later sought to make the criterion more precise by adding empirical falsifiability to verifiability: The only meaningful statements are those whose possible falsity can be determined by empirical observation. According to these principles, only two classes of sentences are meaningful: (1) those which are purely analytic, in which the predicate concept is logically implicit in the subject concept, as in ordinary definitions of terms, the propositions of formal logic and mathematics, or the tautologous assertion that a husband has a wife; and (2) those which are subject to verification or falsification through sensory investigation, such as the statement that it is now snowing. Only the second type of sentence is factually significant or entitled to be regarded as saying anything about the real world.

For the logical positivist, judgments of value are obviously devoid of literal significance. They may more or less accurately express the attitude or belief of the person who makes them, but they say nothing which can be scientifically tested regarding any objective state of affairs: They are "simply expressions of emotion which can be neither true nor false." [141] For example, says Ayer, the declaration that a particular act of stealing or stealing in general is wrong has no factual meaning, since it cannot be shown to be either true or false. It expresses only the speaker's sentiment of moral disapproval. Another man may feel differently about stealing, but neither can, strictly speaking, contradict the other, since neither is

[141] Alfred J. Ayer, *Language, Truth and Logic* (New York: Dover Publications, n. d.), pp. 102 f.

asserting a genuine proposition. Ethical judgments are as unverifiable as cries of pain or words of command; they do not say anything which belongs in the category of truth and falsehood. They have no definable meaning and no objective validity whatever.[142] Hence a science or system of ethics is impossible. As a branch of knowledge ethics can be no more than a department of psychology or sociology.[143]

Similarly excluded by the verification principle from the forum of significant discussion are practically all the questions of Christian theology, including that of the reality of God. Statements about God cannot be either verified or falsified by any reference to sense experience. They yield information, it is claimed, only about the thinking or believing human subject, and they tell nothing about the object believed in.[144]

With these presuppositions Alfred J. Ayer argues that the existence of a God can be neither demonstrated nor shown to be probable. Only a priori propositions can be logically certain. However, they are certain only because they are tautologous, and from tautological statements only further tautologies can be deduced. Hence there is no possibility of inferring the existence of a God from any a priori statement. But neither can a divine existence be shown to be probable, since probability can be argued only from empirical propositions. Assertions concerning God are not empirically meaningful, but metaphysical; hence they cannot be regarded as either true or false, probable or improbable.[145]

Within this context Ayer maintains also that the argument for God from religious experience is "altogether fallacious." We can verify the factuality of the experience, but not its

---

[142] *Ibid.*, pp. 107-9, 22.
[143] *Ibid.*, p. 112.
[144] Max Bense, "Warum man Atheist sein muss," *Club Voltaire I*, ed. Gerhard Szczesny, pp. 68 f.; C. B. Martin, "A Religious Way of Knowing," *New Essays in Philosophical Theology*, ed. Antony Flew and Alasdair MacIntyre (New York: The Macmillan Co., 1955), p. 95.
[145] *Language, Truth and Logic*, pp. 114-19.

referent, whereas in sense perception both the experience and its referent can be verified. The fact that people have religious experiences is psychologically interesting, but it in no way implies the reality of religious knowledge. Such experiences are emotive, not cognitive, and do not issue in verifiable propositions.[146]

The same point is illustrated by Wittgenstein's comparison of Michelangelo's painting of the creation of Adam with a picture of a tropical plant. "There is a technique of comparison between picture and plant," but there is no way of comparing God in the painting with the real God. If we say to another person, "I can show you only the picture, but not the real thing," we do not clearly communicate, since we have not taught the other "the technique of using this picture." Wittgenstein also points out that the pictures of God sometimes used in the religious education of children do not have the same "consequences" as pictures of aunts. In the former we are never shown the original presumably portrayed by the picture, whereas the picture of an aunt may be compared, at least on some occasions, with the living relative herself.[147] This absence of empirical verifiability makes meaningful religious assertion impossible.

Closely related to the problem of verification is that of the ambiguity of religious and theological terms. The early Wittgenstein insisted that what can be said at all can be clearly said, and the concluding proposition of his *Tractatus* affirms: "Whereof one cannot speak, thereon one must be silent." [148] Precision is notably absent in religious discourse. When a believer talks of a Judgment Day we do not know what he may mean. When he asserts that such a day will occur and

---

[146] *Ibid.*, pp. 119 f.
[147] Ludwig Wittgenstein, *Lectures and Conversations on Aesthetics, Psychology and Religious Belief*, ed. Cyril Barrett (Oxford: Basil Blackwell & Mott, 1966), pp. 59, 63.
[148] *Tractatus Logico-Philosophicus*, tr. C. K. Ogden (London: Kegan Paul, 1922), p. 189.

an atheist declares it will not, do they mean the same by the terms they use? Indeed, it is not even clear what our criterion is for the meaning of the term "the same." Talk of a Last Judgment is on an entirely different plane from talk of a bus on the street. When we talk of chairs and doors our meaning is quite definite, but when we speak of death or a spiritual existence varied and changing meanings are involved, and clear communication breaks down.[149]

What can be said precisely about God? Those who speak of his existence do not mean the same thing that they mean when they speak of the existence of persons or objects encountered in ordinary life. Likewise, terms like being-itself, love, and spirit when applied to God are not used in any ordinary sense. Since the term "God" and the words applied to him are so equivocal, statements about God cannot be judged either true or false. God-talk is simply meaningless.

The difficulty is compounded when the emotional overtones associated with the act of believing in God are considered. Belief or unbelief with respect to God often entails a value judgment not usually involved in these terms. It is regarded as "good" to believe in him. Not to believe is thought to be somehow "bad." But ordinarily if I do not believe in the existence of something no one thinks there is anything "wrong" with my position.[150] This intrusion of affective elements makes judgment concerning truth and error all the more inaccurate.

Linguistic philosophers are now less inclined than formerly to assert, on the basis of the verification principle, the complete meaninglessness of statements concerned with religious belief. In recent years logical positivism has largely given way to logical empiricism or logical analysis. Behavioristic theories of language have been discarded or modified. Theological language is no longer categorically ruled out as nonsense.

[149] *Lectures and Conversations,* pp. 53, 58, 65.
[150] *Ibid.,* pp. 59 f.

A leading influence in this direction has been the work of the later Wittgenstein, notably his recognition of a multiplicity of "language-games"—different ways of using words and sentences.[151] Thus a "blunder" is a blunder only in a "particular system" or game but not in another. "Belief" may have quite different connotations in different relationships.[152] In ordinary life the term suggests a certain tentativeness or lack of assurance, as when we say that we "only believe" —rather than know—that something is true. But to believe in God in the fullest sense implies deep conviction producing commitment of one's life.

It is now widely acknowledged that language may fill a variety of roles, depending on subject-matter, context, or other factors. The verification principle is too narrow to apply to all. Analysts therefore look for the meaning of language in the way it gets used. Each language is seen to have its own logic, and this logic must be critically investigated to discover whether it is coherent or defective as it is used.

The plurality of languages is the first of five ways in which John Macquarrie finds linguistic philosophers now moving toward a more favorable estimate of theological language and religious belief. The other four are: a growing distrust of the reduction of all language to that used in physics, and a corresponding acceptance of the validity of person-language; a recognition of the diversity and complexity of conceptions of meaning, which are not exhausted in a neat division of significance into descriptive and emotive; an acknowledgment that some levels of experience may be better illuminated by in-

[151] *Philosophical Investigations* (Oxford: Basil Blackwell & Mott, [1953] 1958), pp. 6, 11-12, 47, 52 f., 100. Wittgenstein's use of the term "language-games" springs from the fact that the activities called games are of such diverse kinds that they cannot be accurately described by any common definition. They exhibit striking differences as well as similarities. Likewise, forms of language differ so notably from one another, in spite of their similarities, that they cannot be reduced to any one form without serious distortion.

[152] *Lectures and Conversations*, pp. 59 f.

direct, oblique, or symbolic language than by direct empirical description; and a tendency to relate language to the concrete, existential discourse situation out of which it arises. Because of developments like these, real dialogue grounded in mutual respect is now proving to be possible between logical analysts and theologians who seriously attempt to understand linguistic philosophy.[153]

Nevertheless, logical empiricists remain for the most part unwilling to grant to theological statements any cognitive or metaphysical validity. Even those who are friendly toward religion are reluctant to admit the possibility that talk about God may refer to some transcendent, more-than-human reality. They concede that theological language can be meaningful, but not that it tells anything about ultimate reality. In short, they remain to a considerable degree positivistic. No doubt the absence of any generally recognized method of verifying or falsifying theological propositions has much to do with this position.

For many contemporary empiricists, therefore, the only alternative to atheism or agnosticism is a view of religion which separates it from any claim to knowledge of God or a supersensible order. Various interpretations of theological language have sought to pursue this alternative. Such language may be understood in moral terms, so that assertions concerning God are regarded as expressing ethical intentions. It may be interpreted personally or existentially, as reflecting the individual's sense of finitude, guilt, and mortality. It may be seen as the expression of a basic attitude toward the world and a recognition of the value of such an attitude for the personal and social life of humanity. It may be treated as a form of poetry which contributes toward the formation of human character but has no reference to any transcendent norms or divine purpose. Historic theism may find truth in all these

---

[153] John Maquarrie, *God-Talk; An Examination of the Language and Logic of Theology* (New York: Harper & Row, 1967), pp. 111-19.

conceptions of the function of religious and theological language. However, on the central issue of reference to a divine reality other and more than man they represent a radical departure from theistic faith.

It should be pointed out that neither logical positivists nor the more moderate logical empiricists are strictly speaking atheists. The former do not deny the existence or reality of God, but maintain simply that, since propositions concerning God convey no clear meaning, he cannot be either affirmed or denied. Alfred J. Ayer, for example, explicitly dissociates his view of religious assertions from those held by atheists and agnostics. The agnostic regards "the existence of a god as a possibility in which there is no good reason either to believe or disbelieve," and the atheist maintains that "it is at least probable that no god exists." For Ayer, however, "all utterances about the nature of God are nonsensical"—a view which he finds "incompatible" with the other two positions. The atheist's assertion that no god exists is just as nonsensical as the theist's affirmation, since only significant propositions can be significantly contradicted. The agnostic does not deny that the question of the existence of a transcendent god is a significant question, and he assumes that one of the two possible answers is true, while maintaining that in the absence of convincing evidence on either side we should withhold commitment. But this whole way of thinking is ruled out if the alternatives in question do not express genuine propositions at all.[154]

Therefore, writes Ayer,

we offer the theist the same comfort as we gave the moralist. His assertions cannot possibly be valid, but they cannot be invalid either. As he says nothing at all about the world, he cannot justly be accused of saying anything false, or anything for which he has insufficient grounds. It is only when the theist claims that in

[154] *Language, Truth and Logic*, pp. 115 f.

asserting the existence of a transcendent god he is expressing a genuine proposition that we are entitled to disagree with him.[155]

For the same reasons Ayer concludes that "there is no logical ground for antagonism between religion and natural science." Since theistic utterances are not real propositions, "they cannot stand in any logical relation to the propositions of science." On the issue of truth and falsehood, therefore, there is no opposition between the theist and the natural scientist. The only real basis for antagonism is the fact that the scientific attitude tends to undermine religious awe by encouraging men to believe that they can through knowledge control natural phenomena and to some degree control their own destiny.[156]

In spite of Ayer's protestations of neutrality, it is hard to escape the conviction that in logical positivism the scales are weighted against the theist. "If 'god' is a metaphysical term," writes Ayer, "then it cannot be even probable that a god exists." The reason, of course, is that the assertion of a god's existence cannot be either true or false.[157] To be consistent, Ayer should say also, "It cannot be even probable that a god does not exist." This he does not do. However, he does conclude his discussion of the possibility of religious knowledge —again citing the absence of "literal significance" in theistic assertions—with the statement: "The point which we wish to establish is that there cannot be any transcendent truths of religion." [158] The total impression left by his treatment of theological propositions is that since they are not valid, they are for all practical purposes invalid. Certainly small "comfort" is offered and little respect shown when the theist is assured that his utterances do not contradict science, simply because they have nothing to do with truth!

[155] *Ibid.*, p. 116.
[156] *Ibid.*, p. 117.
[157] *Ibid.*, p. 115.
[158] *Ibid.*, pp. 117 f.

In principle, the positivistic linguistic analyst holds that God can be neither affirmed nor denied. However, in effect this involves refusing to acknowledge any divine reality and opposing as unjustifiable the position of those who do. Therefore, although theoretically the positivist should reject atheism no less than theism, in fact he argues vigorously against the claims of the latter and says little about the former. The net result is that he is much closer to those who deny God than to those who affirm him.[159]

In some respects the same may be fairly said of the logical empiricists who now recognize meaning in religious language. In their various reinterpretations they have demonstrated genuine understanding and appreciation of some of the basic concerns of religious faith. However, their denial of any transcendent reference or cognitive validity to theological statements is basically a nontheistic position. The conceptions of religion which they advance are expressly designed to preserve certain positive values of religious faith unencumbered by belief in any ultimate reality to which the name "God" might be given.

This combination of an atheistic tendency with a positive evaluation of religion is well illustrated by the thought of Paul M. van Buren. Following his early espousal of a Barthian view of God as the transcendent Other disclosed only in Jesus Christ, van Buren was led by his close study of Oxford analytic philosophy to accept a modified form of the verification principle, and thus to repudiate his earlier use of theological language. Using linguistic analysis as a tool to discover "the secular meaning of the gospel," he rejects as equally meaningless the language of classical Christianity, which makes God an object, and the non-objectifying language of existentialist

---

[159] In some instances, however, the absence of universally acceptable evidence leads to explicitly atheistic conclusions. Norwood Russell Hanson, for example, states that since the data and arguments offered in support of the divine existence are "wholly deficient, I do not *believe in* God." "What I Don't Believe," *Continuum,* 5 (1967), 103.

theology. The trouble lies in the word "God" itself, to which no clear meaning can be assigned. There is thus no place for talk of God. The same is true of any other term which presumably denotes the "transcendent." However, the language of faith may speak intelligibly to our time if it is related to "men's experience of each other and of things."

Van Buren therefore interprets the gospel wholly in historical and ethical terms. Christian faith connotes a way of life in which the Christian can become free for his neighbor, a man for others, released for a life of reconciliation. The norm of this "perspective" is the events which center in Easter—the disciples' experience of being set free by Jesus. Jesus' freedom becomes contagious. The Christian's witness to the world consists in expressing, describing, and commending this historical perspective on the world, other people, and himself. This is the meaning of the declaration, "Jesus is Lord." If we understand Christology in completely nonmetaphysical terms, van Buren's position might be accurately described as a christological atheism. To critics who, missing a transcendent God, call for more than a historical dimension, he replies, "What would that 'more' be?" There is no "empirical linguistic anchorage" for a "more." Both faith and theology must proceed without God.[160]

6. "CHRISTIAN ATHEISM" OF THE DEATH OF GOD

Clearly distinguishable from the varieties of atheism thus far considered is the very recent but widely publicized movement which proclaims the death of God. Like most of the other types, it is anthropomorphic and this-worldly in focus. However, its chief representatives regard their views as Christian in spite of, or even because of, their atheistic import.

[160] Van Buren, *The Secular Meaning of the Gospel* (New York: The Macmillan Co.; London: SCM Press, 1963), pp. (in Brit. ed.) 1-3, 8, 68, 99-101, 109 f., 120-26, 134, 141 f., 149, 155 f., 178-83, 191, 195-200.

Powerfully impressed by the anti-metaphysical mood of our secular, technological culture and so-called modern man's declining sense of a transcendent God, these thinkers have responded with a theology of radical immanentism.

Twentieth-century death-of-God thought originated in the United States, and its most vocal advocates are Americans, though its roots may be traced in the growing empiricism, secularism, and skepticism of European culture in the nineteenth century. Hegel calls attention to the "infinite pain," "the feeling on which the religion of modern times is founded, the feeling that God himself is dead." [161] In interpreting the death of Christ, Hegel cites the hymn of Johann Rist and asserts that the declaration, "God has died, God himself is dead," is both "the highest expression of the divine idea" and "a shocking, terrifying conception which confronts us with the deepest abyss of estrangement." [162] Hegel, of course, is not denying God, but rather affirming the dialectical character of the divine existence. But when, some decades later, Nietzsche has his madman announce, "God is dead!" he is undoubtedly voicing his own nihilism.

Twentieth-century exponents of death-of-God theology are not nihilistic, but they accept and expound in closely related ways what they regard as the liberating truth of Nietzsche's judgment. The two best-known representatives of this movement, both of whom work within a Christian perspective, are William Hamilton and Thomas J. J. Altizer. Death-of-God thought is also to be found in contemporary Judaism, as ex-

[161] G. W. F. Hegel, *Erste Druckschriften. Sämtliche Werke*, ed. Georg Lasson, I (Leipzig: Felix Meiner, 1928), 344. *Phänomenologie des Geistes. Sämtliche Werke*, II, 523, 545.

[162] G. W. F. Hegel, *Die absolute Religion. Sämtliche Werke*, XIV (Leipzig: Felix Meiner, 1929), 157 f. Rist's exact words are, "O great distress, God himself is dead!" ("O grosse Not! Gott selbst ist tot!") They open the second stanza of the hymn which begins, "O sadness, O sorrow of the heart." In current editions of the *Evangelisches Kirchengesangbuch* the latter part of the line has been modified to read: "God's Son lies dead!" ("Gottes Sohn liegt tot!")

emplified in the position of Rabbi Richard L. Rubenstein, director of the B'nai B'rith Hillel Foundation at the University of Pittsburgh and Carnegie Institute of Technology. In some ways akin to these thinkers is the recent thought of two German theologians, Dorothee Sölle of Bonn, and Herbert Braun, Professor of New Testament at the University of Mainz. Brief examination of the views of these five scholars should provide an accurate picture of the central characteristics and scope of the type of thought which they represent.

WILLIAM HAMILTON

Hamilton has nowhere developed his conception systematically. It is present implicitly in his *The New Essence of Christianity*,[163] and explicitly in a number of loosely related articles. He relies considerably on autobiographical references, interpretations of Greek and Shakespearean drama and other literary works, and poetic and metaphorical language to convey his ideas. When the fragments are brought together a fairly definite picture emerges, although it is not always clear whether the death of God designates an objective occurrence or a human experience of the loss of a relation to a divine reality which once was real.

In any event, Hamilton explicitly disavows the traditional atheism which maintains that God does not exist and never has existed. "There was once a God," he writes, "to whom adoration, praise and trust were appropriate, possible and even necessary, but . . . there is now no such God." [164] "Death of God" is a metaphor, but one which accurately describes "something that is happening to a particular group of modern Western Christians today." [165] "The confidence with which

[163] New York: Association Press, 1961.
[164] "The Death of God," *Playboy*, August, 1966, p. 84.
[165] "The Shape of a Radical Theology," *The Christian Century*, 82 (1965), 1220.

we thought we could speak of God is gone." Instead has come a sense of having lost God himself.[166]

Moreover, what has happened is not simply a temporary eclipse, disappearance, absence, or silence. "We mean 'death,'" and the death metaphor portrays an irretrievable loss. "We do not expect the return of the Christian God, open or disguised."[167]

The death of God might be called a drama in three acts. It occurred first in the Incarnation, culminating in the death of Christ on the cross; next, in the widespread collapse of faith in the nineteenth century; and now, in contemporary man's experience of the divine unreality. Qualitatively, the phenomenon of God's death is also marked by three main characteristics. First, it involves a breakdown in the conception of a God who is a meeter of human needs and a solver of human problems. Secondly, it reflects the impossibility for modern man of reconciling the reality of suffering with the power and goodness of God. Thirdly, it expresses man's heightened sense of his ability, realizable through modern science and technology, to control nature for his own ends.[168] This theology does not ignore or deny the mysterious, the holy, or even the transcendent in human life, but it cannot give the name God to such experiences. Rather it seeks to find and celebrate them amid the demands and choices of ordinary life in the world.[169]

To believe in God's death is by no means a purely negative experience. On the contrary, it is profoundly affirmative. Hamilton "stakes out his claim" to be Christian by replacing faith in God with devotion to Jesus and loving service to the

[166] "The Death-of-God Theologies Today," Thomas J. J. Altizer and William Hamilton, *Radical Theology and the Death of God* (Indianapolis: Bobbs-Merrill, 1966), pp. 41, 46 f.
[167] "The Death of God," p. 84; "The Shape of a Radical Theology," p. 1221.
[168] "The Death of God," pp. 137 f.
[169] *Ibid.*, pp. 138 f.

human community in his name. Enough is known of Jesus in the New Testament record that he can provide a positive focus for Christian faith and life. Thus the Christian is he who is "bound to Jesus, obedient to him, and obedient as he was obedient."[170] If Hamilton is asked why he makes such a commitment when he cannot accept Jesus' God, he replies simply that he has made a free choice:

Jesus is the one to whom I repair, the one before whom I stand, the one whose way with others is also to be my way because there is something there, in his words, his life, his way with others, his death, that I do not find elsewhere. I am drawn, and I have given my allegiance.[171]

Such obedience to Jesus drives the Christian into the world and moves him to love for the neighbor. Here Hamilton is strongly influenced by Bonhoeffer, though he transmutes Bonhoeffer's "religionless Christianity" into godless Christianity. The death-of-God Protestant, asserts Hamilton, does not move, as in traditional Christian ethics, from God to neighbor, or from faith to love, loving others in response to the love of God; rather he moves to the neighbor in the world of work, technology, money, politics, and sex out of his awareness of the absence of God. He seeks to find Jesus in his neighbor and to "become Jesus" at every point of his brother's need.[172]

Hamilton's theology might well be called a declaration of human independence. With the means now at our disposal we can in confidence face our concrete tasks as worldly men who need neither religion nor God. Yet he can also describe the whole experience of the death of God, and in part our ethical existence, as a time of "waiting for God." Moreover, although he has described the loss of God as irretrievable, he speaks of praying for God's return, and descending into the

[170] "The Shape of a Radical Theology," p. 1221.
[171] Ibid.
[172] "The Death-of-God Theology," pp. 331, 342-44.

darkness of doubt so that "something may emerge on the other side." Our very godlessness "is partly a search for a language and a style by which we might be enabled to stand before Him once again, delighting in His presence." [173]

THOMAS J. J. ALTIZER

The most complete and systematic statement of the meaning of the death of God is that of Thomas J. J. Altizer. He holds that we need today a radically new theological method, which requires first of all a forthright acknowledgment of the death of God and the end of the cognitive meanings and moral values associated with the God of Christendom; "all traditional theological thinking is now irrelevant." [174] Altizer's answer to this need is an original synthesis of elements derived from Nietzsche, Hegel, William Blake, and Mircea Eliade.

For Altizer as for Hamilton, to say that God is dead does not mean simply that modern man can no longer believe in God, that God is silent or in eclipse, or that he has withdrawn from history or creation. It means rather to affirm the occurrence of "a historical event," "final and irrevocable." God has actually "died in *our* time, in *our* history, in *our* existence," and therefore is "not present in the Word of faith." [175]

Playing an influential role in Altizer's thinking is the ancient symbol of the coincidence of opposites, which is exemplified in various forms by Chinese Taoism, two schools of Mahayana Buddhism, Indian Yoga, alchemy, and Nicholas Cusanus' conception of God. According to this principle reality at its deepest level is dialectical, combining contraries in underlying unity. We therefore understand it best when we

[173] *Ibid.*, pp. 334, 341-43, 336.
[174] Altizer, *Mircea Eliade and the Dialectic of the Sacred* (Philadelphia: Westminster Press, 1963), pp. 13, 20.
[175] Altizer, *The Gospel of Christian Atheism* (Philadelphia: Westminster Press, 1966), pp. 103, 107; "Creative Negation in Theology," *The Christian Century*, 82 (1965), 866; *Mircea Eliade* . . . , p. 13.

think dialectically, recognizing the paradoxical relation between opposites—being and nonbeing, eternity and time, nature and man, sacred and profane, and so on—and perceiving the self-negating activity by which they move toward ultimate reconciliation.[176]

Altizer interprets the Christian doctrine of the Incarnation in these terms, finding in the Pauline doctrine of the *kenosis* (Phil. 2:7-8) an especially fitting symbol. The death of God denotes the self-annihilation or self-negation of God, in which Being becomes "its own Other," "sacrifices" itself, or becomes the opposite of its own original identity.[177] This occurred primally when God emptied or incarnated himself in Christ. He "died as God in Jesus Christ in order to embody Himself redemptively in the world." The transcendent Source and Ground of all existence emptied himself of his sovereignty and transcendence and became man in Jesus Christ, in such a way as to make possible his final reconciliation with the world. The passion and death of Christ in particular opened the way to the ultimate "transformation and transfiguration of all things"—the coming of the kingdom of God.[178] The Christian Word is an incarnate Word, real only as it becomes one with human flesh.[179]

The process of God's self-annihilation which began in Jesus is not completed in him; it involves a metamorphosis which "is only gradually and progressively realized in history, as God's original self-negation becomes actualized throughout the total range of human experience." Through this descent of the Word into concrete human history in all its fullness, the primordial God empties himself of his original life and

---

[176] *Mircea Eliade* . . . , pp. 81-104, 114.

[177] *The Gospel of Christian Atheism*, pp. 106 f., 71.

[178] *Ibid.*, pp. 105 f., 111; *the Altizer-Montgomery dialogue* (Chicago: Inter-Varsity Press, 1967), pp. 8-10. The latter work is a transcription of a discussion between Altizer and John W. Montgomery at the University of Chicago on Feb. 24, 1967.

[179] "Creative Negation in Theology," p. 866.

power and steadily recedes into "an empty and alien other," "a lifeless nothingness." The process moves continually forward toward an eschatological goal.[180]

Here the traditional theological distinction between the sacred and the profane, "the other world" and "this world," is overcome. The sacred moves into or becomes "coincident" with the profane, not by canceling but by transforming it. "The most radical expression of profane existence will coincide with the highest expression of the sacred." In Christ's new and repeated manifestation he does not descend from "above," but is *"wholly* and *fully* incarnate in our midst."[181] The Incarnation is thus a recurring reality. The forward path of the sacred into the profane leads through the present. "The center is everywhere, eternity begins in every now."[182] God's original death becomes in our history "a movement into the total body of humanity." The incarnate Word is not to be identified with "the exalted Christ who is present in the images and cultus of the Church." It becomes instead "the Jesus who is actually and fully incarnate in every human hand and face." In this perspective we see that Christ is always present in the moment immediately before us. Once we recognize this, "we can truly love the world and can embrace even its pain and darkness as an epiphany of the body of Christ." The "dark night" of profane existence is really our way to "the Christ who is Alpha and Omega, Beginning and End, Darkness and Light—Darkness and Light at once!"[183]

It is this continuing Incarnation, thinks Altizer, which is announced in the Christian gospel. It is good news precisely because it involves Christ without God. The Christian proclaims an event which annihilates the power of transcendent Spirit and liberates man from his suppressive subordination to

[180] *The Gospel of Christian Atheism,* pp. 107-9, 103.
[181] *Mircea Eliade* . . . , pp. 17 f.
[182] *Ibid.,* p. 200. Here Altizer makes use of a modified form of Nietzsche's doctrine of eternal recurrence.
[183] *The Gospel of Christian Atheism,* pp. 155 f., 109 f., 71, 18.

the distant, almighty Creator.[184] The Christian therefore acclaims rather than bewails the death of God. He can see even the darkness and chaos which confront him as a partial consummation of the movement originated by God in Christ. Further, his liberation from any kind of alien power, transcendent ground, awesome mystery, or ultimate norm releases him for fullness of life in the world here and now.[185] Thus Altizer provides a new instance of what Samuel H. Miller has described as "exultant atheism," which exhibits some of the characteristics often associated with religious belief itself.[186]

According to Altizer, this triumphant experience of liberation is open only to the Christian. Every open-eyed man today knows that God is absent, but the Christian alone knows that God is dead, since he alone knows the reality of the Incarnation which brings to an end the primordial reality of God. "Only the Christian has died in Christ to the transcendent realm of the sacred," being thus enabled to live in "the fully incarnate body of Christ." [187] It would be quite false, therefore, to suppose that atheism is excluded by Christian faith; on the contrary, an incarnational faith implies and requires the atheism of the death of God.

RICHARD L. RUBENSTEIN

In at least partial contradiction of Altizer's statement that only Christians can know the death of God, the American Jewish theologian Richard L. Rubenstein has declared his essential agreement with the style of religious thought typified by Hamilton and Altizer. He is not willing to assert that God is dead, since no man can know this. However, he does feel

[184] *Ibid.*, pp. 107, 100 f.
[185] *the Altizer-Montgomery dialogue*, p. 17.
[186] Miller, *The Dilemma of Modern Belief* (New York: Harper & Row, 1963), p. 41.
[187] *The Gospel of Christian Atheism*, pp. 111, 102; *Mircea Eliade . . .* , p. 18; "Creative Negation in Theology," p. 866.

compelled to say, as a statement about man and his culture, that "we live in the time of the 'death of God.'" He has tried to avoid using the term "death-of-God theology," because of its inadequacy and its Christian connections. Nevertheless, he finds it inescapable, as "the only way of expressing the void which confronts man where once God stood." The thread uniting earth with heaven has been broken. Our human values, norms, and choices no longer have any vertical reference to a transcendent source. We stand alone "in a cold, silent, unfeeling cosmos, unaided by any purposeful power beyond our own resources." [188]

Rubenstein has felt forced to this bleak conclusion by the agonizing suffering of the Jewish people under the Nazi regime during World War II, culminating in the murder of six million Jews. The holocaust represented by the death camp at Auschwitz makes impossible any belief in a God who guides the destiny of his people and cares for their welfare. Traditional Jewish theology regards nature and history as ultimately controlled by an omnipotent God for his beneficent ends. It therefore interprets catastrophes as instruments of God in the punishment or discipline of his chosen but sinful people. However, to hold this view consistently the believer must regard Hitler and his Elite Guard as instruments of the divine will. "The most demonic, antihuman explosion in all history" must be seen as "a meaningful expression of God's purposes." This interpretation is so repugnant to Rubenstein that he turns his back decisively on traditional Jewish theism: "How can Jews believe in an omnipotent, beneficent God after Auschwitz?" [189]

Rubenstein rejects classical theism also because he finds it irreconcilable with human freedom. Following Tillich, he

[188] Rubenstein, *After Auschwitz; Radical Theology and Contemporary Judaism* (Indianapolis: Bobbs-Merrill, 1966), pp. 151 f., 224 f.
[189] *Ibid.*, pp. 153, 204; cf. pp. 52-56, 58; Rubenstein, "Judaism and the Death of God," *Playboy*, July, 1967, pp. 70, 131.

holds that a personal God who controls the cosmos and the activities of men undermines human moral autonomy and makes impossible the unfettered self-fulfillment of man.[190] Strangely, he appears not to consider a third alternative to the choice between an all-determining God and no God: the possibility of a God who creates man for responsible freedom within a dependable order. Such a conception, which is certainly not without support in the Old Testament, would also make it unnecessary to regard Hitler's massacre of the Jews as the will of God. But Rubenstein does not examine this possibility. In fact, he is in the anomalous position of denying God because at Auschwitz he did not curb the very freedom which Rubenstein insists God should allow to men!

Rubenstein still finds a legitimate place for the term God, when it is reinterpreted. He has renounced all belief in vertical transcendence or in the God who was "the ultimate actor in history." But he believes in "God, the Holy Nothingness known to mystics of all ages, out of which we have come and to which we shall return. . . . In the final analysis omnipotent Nothingness is the Lord of all creation." But in the indifferent cosmos which we inhabit such a God offers only dissolution and death as our ultimate destiny.[191]

This makes all the more important the preservation of the religious community and its structure, order, and tradition. Precisely because our human condition is unredeemed and hopeless, we need the priestly ministry of religion. It provides "a ritual and mythic structure" which enable us to share and celebrate the crises of good and evil, life and death. Hence for the foreseeable future churches and synagogues will remain irreplaceable institutions. Just as Christians in a time of the death of God continue to confess allegiance to the gospel of Christ, so Jewish theologians affirm the indispensa-

[190] *After Auschwitz*, p. 87.
[191] *Ibid.*, pp. 154, 205.

bility of the Torah.[192] Judaism "is the way we Jews share our lives in an unfeeling and silent cosmos. It is the flickering candle we have lighted in the dark to enlighten and warm us."[193]

Dorothee Sölle

In German theology today the nearest approach to death-of-God thought as so far examined is the work of the lay theologian Dorothee Sölle. Her christological emphasis bears a close relation to the views of Hamilton and Altizer, and for her too the death of God is a concrete event in the past two centuries of European history. However, the event has occurred in men, not objectively, and it connotes the hiddenness or absence of God rather than his permanent departure. The term "death of God" implies neither atheism nor theism; rather it expresses theologically man's psycho-social experience of the end of all immediate certainty, and the "infinite pain" (referred to by Hegel) and sense of loss which have resulted. To us God is no longer ontologically or metaphysically real.[194]

In her book *Christ the Representative*, after examining the meaning of representation in general and in the history of theology in particular, Sölle uses the word to express the central role of Jesus Christ. Like man, God is irreplaceable but representable, and in our post-metaphysical age he must be represented by another.[195] The only God recognizable in our time is the one who permits himself to be provisionally represented in Jesus Christ. Christ does not replace the dead God but represents the living God among men. Likewise, he does not replace us but represents us before God. By suffering

[192] *Ibid.*, pp. 154, 205 f., 263; "Judaism and the Death of God," pp. 74, 130-32.
[193] *After Auschwitz*, p. 225.
[194] Sölle, *Christ the Representative: An Essay in Theology after the "Death of God,"* tr. David Lewis (Philadelphia: Fortress Press, 1967), pp. 10-12, 137, 140 f.
[195] *Ibid.*, pp. 50, 56.

and dying for and with us he also represents us among men. We in turn are called upon to represent God in the world, to "play God for one another" in a time when he is no longer directly present.[196]

The same ethical concern, the same sensitivity to human suffering, and the same disbelief in God as serene, omnipotent Ruler which we have found in many atheists are clearly present in Sölle. Likewise apparent in her thought is the influence of Bonhoeffer already noted in American death-of-God thinkers. She speaks of God as being mocked, tortured, gassed, and defeated in the world, and calls on Christians to participate "in the sufferings of God in Christ." [197] In this faith, she adds,

they know that God is helpless and needs help. When the time was fulfilled, God had done something for us for long enough. He put himself at risk, made himself dependent upon us, identified himself with the non-identical. From now on, it is high time for us to do something for him.[198]

HERBERT BRAUN

Although Braun does not proclaim the death of God, he interprets the word *God* in a manner which has manifest affinities with the views of the death-of-God thinkers. In Bultmannian fashion he understands God not as an objectified metaphysical reality existing for himself, but wholly in terms of human relationships. According to the central witness of the New Testament, the Christian encounters God as the whence of his intimately connected experiences of "I may" and "I ought," his sense of being both "taken care of" and "obligated." But this double awareness comes to him not from something in the cosmos beyond him, but from his fellowman. To this human whence, we give the name God. He is present

[196] *Ibid.*, pp. 142-44, 128, 139 f.
[197] *Ibid.*, p. 151.
[198] *Ibid.*, pp. 151 f.

"where I am placed under obligation, where I am engaged ... in unconditional 'I may' and 'I ought.'" Thus God is "a definite type of relation with one's fellowman."[199]

For Braun, therefore, God is the predicate of the action and interaction of human subjects. In a debate with Helmut Gollwitzer at Mainz on February 13, 1964, he insisted that we know God as subject only through his predicates. Where loving takes place, there is God. He who abides in love abides in God (I John 4:16). But apparently Braun is reluctant to convert the proposition and affirm without qualification that God is love. In the dialogue Gollwitzer expressed his view that it is not enough to say, "This occurrence is itself God"; we should rather assert, "It is God who himself so loves and initiates this event." This formulation Braun rejected as too objective and mythical.[200]

Braun does not regard his position as atheistic. "The atheist misses *man*." Indeed, Braun wonders whether the atheist really exists, since every relation of a man with his fellowman involves something of the interaction between the "I may" and the "I ought" of New Testament faith.[201] With respect to this event the atheistic position appears insignificant, while a theistic world view is likewise vacuous.[202]

Leaving aside now the thought of Herbert Braun, we may observe in summary that the thoroughgoing death-of-God theologies represent an absolute immanentism which abolishes all transcendence. To live consciously in the twentieth century is to experience the negation of the sacred by the secular

---

[199] Braun, "The Problem of a New Testament Theology," *Journal for Theology and Church*, I; *The Bultmann School of Biblical Interpretation: New Directions?* Ed. Robert W. Funk (Tübingen: J. C. B. Mohr [Paul Siebeck]; New York: Harper & Row, 1965), pp. 182 f.; Braun, *Gesammelte Studien zum Neuen Testament und seiner Umwelt* (Tübingen: J. C. B. Mohr [Paul Siebeck], 1962), pp. 295-98, 341.
[200] *Post Bultmann locutum*, I, ed. Horst Symanowski (Hamburg-Bergstedt: Herbert Reich-Evangelischer Verlag, 1965), pp. 11, 15, 30-33.
[201] "The Problem of a New Testament Theology," p. 183.
[202] *Gesammelte Studien* ..., p. 298.

and profane, "the collapse of any meaning or reality lying beyond the newly discovered immanence of modern man." [203] Obviously we confront here an example of a tendency which is inherent in almost all varieties of atheism. It is assumed that if this world is to be taken seriously, every other reality must be denied. God must die in order that man may live. The fact that professing Christians now share this assumption indicates unmistakably how far they have departed from a tradition which, as generally understood, has declared that man without God cannot be fully man.

---

[203] Altizer, *The Gospel of Christian Atheism*, pp. 154, 22.

III. Major Bases of Unbelief

Our survey of the major varieties of atheism has disclosed considerable similarity in the grounds cited for rejection of belief in God. Some of the same motifs appear repeatedly in different contexts. We shall understand the atheistic critique more clearly if we now examine these recurring emphases in systematic fashion.

Seven main considerations may be readily identified. As they are elaborated, the reader will no doubt think of weaknesses—some of them serious—in the arguments offered. The atheistic case is not so strong as it may appear when presented without rebuttal. We should therefore hear it critically as well as receptively. Nevertheless, our primary purpose will be to listen and to learn. As suggested earlier, the vigor, directness, and partial cogency of the atheistic reasoning should force us to deal forthrightly with the problems raised and to resist every temptation to evade them. If we respond in this attitude we are likely to experience a heightening of our own understanding. Therefore, our concern will be not to rush to the defense of the faith with counterarguments, but to lay foundations for later reexamination of what we mean by the reality of God.

1. Belief in God is rejected by many as untrue on the ground that *it can be explained as an objectification of purely human ideals, wishes, longings, or needs*. It originates in the psychological, sociological, or anthropological structure of man himself, which affords no basis for assertions concerning a reality beyond man to which his hopes supposedly refer. A precursor of this objection appeared already in the eighteenth

century in David Hume, who rejected the argument for God from the order of the world, insisting that the order claimed depends purely on man's arrangement of what he finds. The assertion of order and uniformity in nature, said Hume, represents a value judgment of man arising out of his experience of causal relations, and cannot be predicated of nature itself or attributed to a divine mind.[1]

In the nineteenth and twentieth centuries the notion of projection implicit in Hume is explicated, broadened, and emphasized. Thus Feuerbach explains God as a reflection of the highest characteristics of the human species, the ascription to God of the qualities in man himself which man regards as divine, and the objectification in a higher realm of the wishes for perfect happiness and fulfillment which are thwarted by the pains, failures, and anxieties of his mortal existence.

For Nietzsche, too, God is only a projection into a supersensory realm of man's own consciousness, an exteriorization of unfulfilled hopes which helps him to be contented with his present lot and makes his suffering endurable. Human self-estrangement is involved also, since man dichotomizes and degrades himself by ascribing his strength and greatness to God and his weakness and meanness to himself. Further, men afflicted with this low self-estimate are easy prey for the strong, independent, ruling classes, who use religious belief to stifle opposition and buttress their authority.

Marx and his followers attribute religious belief to the self-alienation which is inherent in class-oriented social and economic relations. Suffering from unrelieved injustice and exploitation, men invent another world in which these evils are overcome. Belief in God is the *expression* of real distress, a *protest* against distress, and *consolation* amid distress. It springs from a situation of frustration and oppression which needs delusion to make it bearable, and it is encouraged by

---

[1] *Dialogues Concerning Natural Religion, Hume: Selections*, ed. Charles W. Hendel, Jr. (New York: Charles Scribner's Sons, 1927), pp. 306 f.

the ruling classes whose economic interests it serves. But it is false, and men need to be freed from it.

In our time the classic form of the genetic explanation of religious belief as wish-fulfillment is found in the psychoanalytic theories of Freud and others. According to this view a universal father complex leads to the personification of extrahuman forces as a divine father or a paternalistic ruler. Just as the infant, terrified by its helplessness, clings to its father for protection, so men who are chronologically adult, aware of their weakness in the face of the danger, mystery, finitude, and mortality of life, find in the belief in a powerful universal father relief from the conflicts which began in childhood. Religious beliefs are thus not the result of rational reflection, but fulfillments of the most ancient and persistent wishes of men, and in this sense illusory. Religion is a kind of "obsessional neurosis of humanity." An illusion in Freud's use of the term could be true, and he does not specifically brand religion as false. But clearly for him the motive of self-interest which produces religious belief is so strong as to render it highly suspect. As he puts it, it would be "very nice" if the universe were created by a benevolent God who providentially rules a moral world order and gives man a future life, "but at the same time it is very odd that this is all just as we should wish it ourselves." [2]

In general, those who treat religion as wish-fulfillment growing out of psychological or social factors regard it as a delusion as well as an illusion in Freud's sense. I cannot resist pointing out that we have here a flagrant instance of the fallacy of origins—asserting the falsity of a proposition or opinion because the process of its growth from lowly beginnings can be traced. Such a description tells nothing whatever about the truth of any judgment. Yet many people today dismiss belief in God as untrue because it has arisen in response to deep-seated longings of the human heart.

[2] *The Future of an Illusion*, p. 58.

2. A second major ground for the rejection of theistic faith is the judgment, stressed particularly by Marxists and scientific humanists, that *such faith is in one way or another inconsistent with scientific method and the scientific view of reality.* This argument takes four main forms.

a. The most trustworthy method of attaining truth—if not indeed the only dependable one—is that followed by the natural sciences. On the basis of empirical observation, the investigator forms hypotheses, verifies, rejects, or modifies them by controlled experiment, and in the light of the evidence thus gained formulates laws which command universal acceptance. Hypotheses are held tentatively until they are objectively tested and confirmed, and conclusions are always open to revision. Yet this procedure has resulted in a vast expansion in man's knowledge and control of the natural order, pushed back the horizon of mystery, and demonstrated the natural causation of phenomena long attributed to divine agency. Thus God has been rendered increasingly unnecessary and useless as a principle of explanation. Religion can function only where gaps remain in man's knowledge; since in principle all questions with real meaning are capable of scientific answers, belief in God will decrease in relevance as science steadily diminishes human ignorance.

b. Furthermore, it is maintained, such a hypothesis often stands in the way of a sound explanation. It objectifies and personifies qualities which are really in man as a part of nature, thus introducing a false dualism into reality and obscuring its essential unity. The assumption of a supernatural order above the natural is irreconcilable with science, since it substitutes alleged divine revelation, a priori dogmas, and belief in miraculous divine intervention for empirically verifiable knowledge of objective reality. The discoveries of astronomy, physics, biology, physiology, and psychology demonstrate the validity of the naturalistic hypothesis and leave no room for divine agency.

c. Moreover, there is no objective evidence, in a sense acceptable to the sciences, for the metaphysical postulate of a supreme being which allegedly creates and sustains this world and its inhabitants. Naturally a method of knowing which finds its definitive model in the investigation of sense data finds nothing intelligible in man's response in faith to the total reality which confronts him. The Christian claim, writes Gustav Wyneken, is without foundation; the existence of God cannot be demonstrated in either nature or history, but can only be presupposed. If we adhere to the scientific evidence, we shall conclude that there is no reality beyond the order of nature. The world is an interconnected causal process which contains within itself the source and ground of its development. Man himself, the highest form of existence we know, has emerged from and within nature.[3]

d. To arguments like these, many Marxists and naturalistic humanists add a fourth, more pragmatic in nature. Theology and the church, it is charged, have historically opposed free scientific research and hindered the pursuit of truth for its own sake. Being relatively little concerned with the realm of time and space and much concerned to defend a system of dogmas regarding man's eternal salvation, Christianity has been suspicious of inquiries which might upset its supposedly revealed truths. Hence the objective, truth-seeking investigations of scientists like Copernicus, Galileo, and Darwin have often been opposed and denounced by the churches—convincing demonstration, say the Marxists, of the inherently antiscientific character of Christian faith.

Morris R. Cohen contends that in the struggles of Christianity against modern astronomy, geology, and biology, as well as against the scientific treatment of biblical history, "the old adherents of religion did not want to know the truth," but only their own particular faith.[4] In a different but related

[3] *Abschied vom Christentum*, pp. 246 f.
[4] "Drei Artikel des Unglaubens," *Club Voltaire I*, ed. Gerhard Szczesny, p. 50.

context, Arnulf Överland, after citing Freud's reminder of the "depressing contrast" between the alert, eager intelligence of a healthy child and the intellectual weakness of the average adult, ascribes to religious education a significant share in the guilt for this increasing dullness and narrow-mindedness. According to Överland's observation, the believer is not supposed to think, but to believe! [5]

If the Christian tries to counter such charges by insisting that Christians today regularly support rather than inhibit free scientific investigation, or by calling attention to the widely accepted division of labor which for many removes a major source of conflict between science and religion, the naturalist is likely to remain unimpressed. For example, the Marxist Hans-Joachim Seidowski attributes the change simply to Christianity's grudging recognition that it has lost the struggle. He insists that religion has never willingly accepted scientific views which seemed to contravene its dogmas or played a leading role in initiating scientific inquiry.[6]

3. The attempt to apply scientific precision to men's use of language leads to a third objection to belief in God—the fact that *the term "God" lacks clear, univocal meaning which can be unambiguously communicated.* Even unsophisticated minds have experienced this difficulty. Horst Symanowski, industrial minister in Mainz-Kastel, tells of a factory worker who says to his fellow worker, who is also a pastor: "Don't say 'God.' That means nothing to me. When you say 'coffee,' I see before me a color, perceive at the same time a smell, and have already with the sound of the word a taste on my tongue. With the word 'God' I don't notice anything. Therefore better not say it at all." [7]

[5] "The Dark Side of Religion," *Religion from Tolstoy to Camus*, ed. Walter Kaufmann, pp. 285, 45.
[6] Interview in East Berlin, Nov. 14, 1966.
[7] Foreword to *Post Bultmann locutum*, I, ed. Horst Symanowski, 7.

The criticism has been stated in more refined manner by the logical positivists and other linguistic philosophers, in two main ways. First, it is held that, since all statements to be meaningful must be verifiable or falsifiable in terms of sense perception, the question of God is excluded from significant discussion. Secondly, it is maintained that the word "God" has so many different connotations that the reality of whatever it may denote can be neither affirmed nor denied. Walter Kaufmann finds a vast variety of meanings in reference to the deeds and words of God appearing in the different biblical writings, the works of Jewish and Christian mystics, the church fathers, and theologians and philosophers through the centuries. Since the word "God" is so clearly not univocal, and since the terms applied to him are not intended to mean what they generally mean, Kaufmann concludes that "most *statements about God are essentially ambiguous.* They cannot be called true or false. Interpretations of them are usually ingenious or trivial or heretical—and often all three. The propositions themselves defy translation." [8]

With regard to the love of God, the ambiguity appears especially in connection with human suffering. Some linguistic analysts have complained that sophisticated theists tend to refuse to admit that any conceivable empirical fact could "count against" their assertions. In Basil Mitchell's parable of the Stranger, for example, in time of war in an occupied country a member of the resistance continues to trust the Stranger as "on our side" even though the latter is sometimes seen delivering patriots to the hostile power. No negative evidence can shake the conviction of the believer that even the ravages of disease and the premature death of dear ones are somehow consistent with the love of God. In such instances what does it really mean to maintain that God "loves" us? Albert Camus in *The Plague* poses the same prob-

[8] *Critique of Religion and Philosophy* (New York: Harper & Brothers, 1958), pp. 129 f.

lem. Confronting the agony of a dying child, Father Paneloux attempts to maintain his belief in divine love by regarding it as beyond our understanding. However, Dr. Rieux insists that love in either God or man is inconsistent with acquiescence in the suffering of the one loved.

Some logical analysts today have departed from a strict application of the verification principle, and recognize the legitimacy in different contexts of different forms of language. Likewise, philosophers of religion sympathetic to linguistic analysis have sought in various ways to preserve noncognitive significance for theological statements. The proposals of R. B. Braithwaite, R. M. Hare, and Paul M. van Buren come readily to mind. Yet all these interpretations involve a reduction of what is signified, so that theological statements are no longer regarded as assertions about any independent reality, but are seen as valid expressions of a human attitude, perspective, or volitional posture. As such they convey discoverable meaning, and on their own level they are worthy of respect, but they have no cognitive connotation. They transmit no knowledge whatever concerning a more-than-human God.

4. A particularly vigorous thrust of the atheistic attack springs from the conviction that *theistic faith is irreconcilable with the extent and intensity of human suffering.* Probably most of those who deny any divine reality today do so more because of the existential impact of the pain and injustice endured by innocent people than because of any theoretical world view, though the two influences often reinforce each other.

In November, 1966 in Prague I asked Milan Machovec, a Marxist philosopher, what were the major grounds for his atheist position; he cited first of all "the depth of evil in the world. I can't combine faith in God with Auschwitz." He mentioned a mother being forced into the gas chambers with her two children, the seventy thousand Jews taken by the

Nazis from Amsterdam alone, and similar horrors, with no divine intervention or sign of providence. His conclusion was simple: "Either there is no God, or I don't belong to him."

Richard L. Rubenstein, the Jewish rabbi, reaches a similar verdict: After Auschwitz Jews can no longer believe in a good and all-powerful God who rules in history. "The thread uniting God and man, heaven and earth, has been broken." In an indifferent, purposeless cosmos, we have no beneficent divine power to turn to, and nothing to rely on but our own resources.[9]

The stark reality of human suffering, unaccompanied by any concrete evidence of cosmic concern or opposition, also contributes heavily to the atheism of the existentialists, sometimes arousing their bitter protest. Thus Maurice Merleau-Ponty argues that to believe in a creator we must either treat evil as unreal or admit that God in sustaining the cosmos allows men to be sacrificed. However, the overwhelming reality of evil leaves us only the latter alternative. Hence we must conclude that the world has not been thought through, and that no absolute could have conceived it.[10] Alluding to a famous passage in Dostoyevsky, Albert Camus comments that the Grand Inquisitors offer men the bread of this earth without freedom.

"Come down from the cross and we will believe in you," their police agents are already crying on Golgotha. But He did not come down and, even, at the most tortured moment of His agony, He protested to God at having been forsaken. There are, thus, no longer any proofs, but faith and the mystery that the rebels reject and at which the Grand Inquisitors scoff. Everything is permitted and centuries of crime are prepared in that cataclysmic moment. From Paul to Stalin, the popes who have chosen Caesar have prepared the way for Caesars who quickly learn to despise popes.

[9] Rubenstein, *After Auschwitz: Radical Theology and Contemporary Judaism*, pp. 153, 152; cf. pp. 224 f.
[10] Merleau-Ponty, *Sens et Non-Sens*, pp. 192 f.; *Éloge de la philosophie*, pp. 64 f.

The unity of the world, which was not achieved with God, will henceforth be attempted in defiance of God.[11]

To the brutality of men must be added the evils rooted in physical nature. "The order of the world," asserts Camus, "is shaped by death." Hence the best way open to us is to reject belief in God and struggle with all our might against death and the other evils that lead to it, even though we know we are doomed to defeat. Though confronted by insuperable odds, we can still be absurd, tragic heroes.[12]

Antony Flew deals with natural evil in the perspective of linguistic philosophy, indicating that theists are guilty of Orwellian "double-think" in their effort to preserve faith in a loving God in spite of "a heartless and indifferent world." "Someone tells us that God loves us as a father loves his children. We are reassured. But then we see a child dying of inoperable cancer of the throat. His earthly father is driven frantic in his efforts to help, but his Heavenly Father reveals no obvious sign of concern."[13] Flew regards as evasive the qualifications often offered by the theist: God's love is "not merely a human love"; it is "inscrutable"; God disciplines those he loves for the sake of their spiritual growth. Instead, he suggests, might it not be more forthright to conclude that God does not love us or that he does not exist? Nor can the religious believer escape his dilemma by claiming that God would like to help but cannot, or that he would help if he only knew, for traditional theism affirms that God is both omnipotent and omniscient. Likewise it will not avail to allege that God is not responsible for the wickedness of men, since he created them. "Indeed an omnipotent, omniscient God must be an accessory before (and during) the fact to

[11] *The Rebel*, p. 61.
[12] *The Plague*, pp. 147 f., 117 f.
[13] Flew and MacIntyre (eds.), *New Essays in Philosophical Theology*, pp. 108, 98 f.

every human misdeed; as well as being responsible for every non-moral defect in the universe." [14]

Perhaps none of the searching queries we have cited state the problem any better than the simple question of a six-year-old child in Newtonville. Returning home from church school, she asked her mother: "Why are little girls in Africa starving while I have plenty to eat? Doesn't God love them as much as he does me?"

5. The argument for atheism based on suffering focuses attention on the human situation, and thus leads naturally to a further objection, the judgment that *belief in the sovereignty of God is inconsistent with recognition of the worth, freedom, and full responsibility of man*. Indeed, many atheists today may be said to reject theology for the sake of anthropology. Our culture is anthropocentric rather than cosmocentric or theocentric, immanentist and this-worldly rather than transcendental, horizontal rather than vertical in its perspective.

When Karl Marx called for the *"positive* abolition" of religion, he meant that his primary aim was the affirmation of man rather than simply the denial of God. The same is true of Roger Garaudy's "post-atheistic humanism." For Marxism man is the highest expression of nature, hence centrally important. He is responsible for fulfilling or "producing" himself through his own work. Sartre reaches similar conclusions from existentialistic premises: Man is his own law-maker, who must make his own decisions with no essential structure to guide or determine him. Each individual fulfills himself by seeking a goal outside himself in a human universe. Each man is responsible for his own existence—and also for that of other men, since the freedom of each depends on that of others.

Obviously implicit in this humanism is at least a methodic,

[14] *Ibid.*, p. 107.

limited atheism which leaves God out of consideration in all activities controlled by man. A highly technological culture, for example, tends to be atheistic in practice. Men committed centrally to the values of such a culture are simply not concerned with what may lie beyond the reality comprehensible to and controllable by man. What relevant function could God have within our manipulable, predictable existence?

However, much more than this tacit ignoring of God is apparent in the utterances of the most outspoken antitheistic humanists. They make plain their conviction that the priority which they give to the dignity of man can be guaranteed only by the absence of God. We confront here what is sometimes called "postulatory" atheism, since it is the condition or postulate of a positive humanism, the presupposition of a basic emphasis on the centrality of man. In Nietzsche's thought Superman can exist only through the death of all belief in a supersensory order above man. Nicolai Hartmann postulates atheism as the condition of ethical freedom: Man can rearrange his ethical principles, but he cannot restructure a higher person; therefore he cannot admit a higher person than himself.[15] Similarly, a major influence in Sartre's atheism is his persuasion that the existence of God would imperil human freedom. If God existed, values would be given in advance of human choices, and men could not then be wholly free. Prominent in scientific humanism likewise is the assumption that theism shifts to God the responsibility which belongs to man alone, and to another realm the achievements which should be sought in this world of time and space.

The same attitude finds militant expression in Marxism. Though Marx's own critique of religion is mainly positive concerning man rather than negative regarding God, his view that man is the highest being produced by nature makes im-

[15] *Ethik* (Berlin and Leipzig: W. de Gruyter, 1926), pp. 604-14, 741 f.; *Theologisches Denken* (Berlin: W. de Gruyter, 1951), pp. 35 ff., 107 ff., 119 ff.

perative the overthrow of all ideas, structures, and practices in which man is debased. Similarly, Helmut Dressler no doubt voices the opinion of many other contemporary Marxists when he states that God cannot be allowed to exist, since if he did he would replace man as the highest being by making man dependent on him. A major ground of the atheism of Ernst Bloch is his assumption of the mutual exclusiveness of the omnipotent, timeless Absolute of traditional theism and the freedom and responsibility of man. "Where the great Lord of the world is," writes Bloch, "there is no room for freedom, not even the freedom of the 'children of God' "; hence human activity can be liberated "only through atheism." [16] The same concern was manifest in a conversation in Tübingen in September, 1966, when in commenting on the present theological situation Bloch said that he was more interested in detheocratizing than demythologizing!

Olof Klohr, professor of scientific atheism at the University of Jena, cites specific statements of Lutheran theologians to support his opinion that Christian belief in God undercuts free human action. In his book *Conversation with Atheists*, Aurel von Jüchen states: "To confess God as Creator means to confess him in all conceivable temporal forms, to confess him in the perfect, present, and future tenses as him through whose will I and the whole world have our life." [17] In Klohr's view this assertion of a transcendent power rules out any understanding of historical events as functioning according to law and any possibility of historical prediction; hence it condemns man to passivity. In the same context Klohr cites two statements of Heinz Zahrnt of Hamburg. In an address in 1962 Zahrnt declared: "According to everything taught by the history of mankind down to the most recent past, there is no cause for faith in man." [18] In a paper presented at the

---

[16] Bloch, *Das Prinzip Hoffnung*, p. 1413.
[17] *Gespräch mit Atheisten* (Gütersloh: Verlag "Kirche und Mann," 1962), p. 106.
[18] "Der Atheismus als Frage an die Kirche." Handreichung vom 27.

Kirchentag in Dortmund in 1963, Zahrnt said: "We shall not presume that we are able to transform this world and to establish a perfect order among men." [19]

Such utterances, writes Klohr, encourage the assumption that since man and his social arrangements are alike imperfect, there can be no progress from capitalism to socialism, and the struggle for a socialistic society is useless. They therefore tend to restrain workers in West Germany from fighting imperialism and undermine the readiness of Christians in East Germany to accept socialism. Thus Christian faith, by orienting man toward a transcendent power, decreases his responsible action in society and hinders human progress. Even when Christians look positively at the possibility of improving conditions, they still see the world as broken and man as unable to free himself from himself. Therefore, instead of accepting their human responsibility they turn to Jesus Christ for strength to endure the circumstances which confront them.[20] What Christians regard as divine grace must be recognized as a potentiality inherent in man himself.

6. The objection just considered leads almost imperceptibly to another—that *theistic belief produces passivity in the presence of injustice and opposition to social change.* Sometimes this criticism deals mainly with the logical implications or consequences of theism; more frequently it simply points to the historic attitudes or actions of Christians and churches as proof of the reactionary influence, hence the unacceptability of religious faith. The theistic tree is judged by its social fruits, which are found to be unpalatable. As represented by its adherents, belief in God is condemned as (a) productive

---

Juli 1962. *Amtsblatt der VELKD* (Hannover), 15. Oktober 1962, Zitat 138.

[19] Address at 11th Evangelischer Kirchentag, Dortmund, 1963, reported in *Christ und Welt,* July 28, 1963.

[20] Klohr, "Probleme des wissenschaftlichen Atheismus und der atheistischen Propaganda," *Deutsche Zeitschrift für Philosophie,* 2(1964), 135-37.

of indifference toward social evil and the struggle for a just society, (b) irrelevant to concrete human concerns here and now, and (c) supportive of the political and economic status quo. These motifs will be interwoven in the examples which I now cite.

Much atheistic humanism in Holland springs from the judgment that the church is not concerned about ethical and social questions, and that Christian faith is oriented toward another and future world rather than this one. The attitude is less one of antagonism than simply the assumption that the beliefs of the church are irrelevant to the real interests of modern man. Bertrand Russell, writing also from a humanistic standpoint, is openly hostile. Maintaining that the organized churches have "consistently opposed" every movement toward more humane treatment of criminals, the diminution of war, the abolition of slavery, better race relations, and other forms of ethical advance, he concludes categorically: "The Christian religion, as organized in its churches, has been and still is the principal enemy of moral progress in the world." [21] Walter Kaufmann feels that Christianity has betrayed its original vocation: "What is so ironical is that in the Gospels and the Epistles there is such a radical streak, while Christianity is, and has been for centuries, a religion of compromise." [22]

The historical influence of Christian indifference to human exploitation in the elevation of atheism to the status of a Communist dogma should be too well known to require emphasis here. The *de facto* alliances of throne and altar in Germany and of Czarism and Russian orthodoxy in the nineteenth century can be readily documented, as can the impact on Marx of the efforts of Anglican churches to prevent the enactment in England of legislation reducing child labor to twelve hours a day. Helmut Gollwitzer believes—I think rightly—that it

[21] Russell, *Why I Am Not a Christian*, p. 21.
[22] *The Faith of a Heretic*, p. 415.

was empirical factors like these, not logical or philosophical considerations, which played the decisive role in the acceptance as party doctrine of Marx's rejection of religion.[23] But instead of reviewing this record, I should like to look at contemporary Marxist attitudes, particularly as revealed in a few personal conversations which I was able to hold in the fall of 1966.

Milan Machovec told me that a major reason for his atheism was his experience as a youth in 1948, when the Communists came to power in Czechoslovakia. He had been raised in a Protestant Christian home, but when he spoke of wanting to help change the world his parents told him this was impossible. They and most other Christians did not believe in human improvement. Pointing to the sinfulness of man, they held that social differences would always remain as they were; hence Christians should learn to accept and endure this world while preparing for another. In sharp contrast, the Communists called for the humanization of society and the transformation of the world. Said Machovec: "The Christians forgot the promise of Revelation 21:5: 'Behold, I make all things new,' but the Marxists talked and acted as the Christians should have." Machovec recognizes that millions of Christians today, motivated by their concern for the kingdom of God on earth, neighbor-love, and brotherly solidarity, are struggling actively for social righteousness. But, he asks, what difference has been made by the preaching of these principles for two thousand years? In any event, he cannot accept a belief in God which so often has left the believer content with the status quo.[24]

Similar views were expressed in various ways by several East German Marxists. Martin Robbe's reaction upon visiting a number of Christian worship services has already been

[23] *Die marxistische Religionskritik und der christliche Glaube* (München, Hamburg: Siebenstern Taschenbuch Verlag, 1965), p. 89.
[24] Machovec, *Marxismus und dialektische Theologie*, pp. 186 f.

noted.[25] Hans-Joachim Seidowski of East Berlin, after giving as one major ground of his unbelief the church's historical alignment with the exploiters and suppressors of the common people, concluded, "The church has had its chance for two thousand years. Now it's our turn!"

Concerns like these are eloquently articulated in Ernst Bloch's philosophy of the "not-yet." From the perspective of his conception of reality as a dynamic movement toward an open-ended future offering ever new possibilities which men are summoned to realize, he attacks all static theisms. Where God is the most real or perfect being, the fixed, enthroned Absolute who demands and guarantees the fulfillment of his arbitrary will, men are seen as his subjects who have no initiative of their own, but are called on to trust and obey while awaiting the already determined outcome of the divine plan. Such notions, thinks Bloch, have led traditional Christianity quite consistently to resist change and acquiesce in injustice. Hence a world view which stresses futurity, novelty, and hope, and which assigns to man an active role in the forward movement of history, is for Bloch inevitably atheistic.[26]

7. Finally, mention should be made of a basis of unbelief which is quite practical in nature. *Multitudes of persons, including many who are seriously committed to the highest human values, have no personal awareness of God.* The world of physical things and other human beings is to them unmistakably, sometimes painfully, real, but God remains at best vague and shadowy. They listen to the accounts of others who tell of "experiencing a divine Presence" or "encountering God," but since in their own lives they know nothing of such experiences they conclude that those who report them are deluded. Since such people have no sense of God, they are

[25] See above, p. 53.
[26] *Tübinger Einleitung in die Philosophie,* II, 175-77; *Das Prinzip Hoffnung,* pp. 17, 1524, 1527-29; *Erbschaft dieser Zeit,* pp. 407 f.

described by Karl Rahner as "unmusical in religion." However, unlike persons who, in spite of their lack of musical appreciation, admit that musicians and concerts exist, the religiously "unmusical" see their own situation as normative, or at best regard religious belief as purely subjective.

In November, 1966, I talked with Julius Tomin, a young Marxist teacher of philosophy in Prague, concerning his attitude toward religion. He made plain that he was not impressed by the traditional Marxist claim that religious belief is unscientific. "I am an atheist," he said, "not because I am sure there is no God, but because I cannot believe in God. I cannot say that I know on a strictly scientific basis that there is no God. But I have not found any occasion or cause for belief in God." No doubt many people who are not Marxists are characterized by a mild atheism of this kind.

Anything but mild is the atheism of William Hamilton and other writers who today proclaim the death of God. Hamilton declares, "We do not know, do not adore, do not possess, do not believe in God. . . . We are not talking about the absence of the experience of God, but about the experience of the absence of God." [27] That this experience need not be depressing is shown by the fact that Thomas Altizer can entitle his recent collection of essays on the death of God *The Gospel of Christian Atheism*. Ten years earlier Susan Anima Taubes identified a certain mystical, religious quality in atheism of this kind, which she called "a theology of divine absence and nonbeing, of divine impotence, divine non-intervention, and divine indifference." Paradoxically, the very exclusion of the presence and providence of God from the natural world may invest that world with religious meaning for him who accepts it in all its absurd reality.[28] Samuel H. Miller even finds an exultant quality in this atheism.[29]

[27] "The Death-of-God Theology," *The Christian Scholar*, 48 (1965), 31.
[28] Taubes, "The Absent God," *Journal of Religion*, 35 (1955), 6.
[29] *The Dilemma of Modern Belief*, p. 41.

For many, however, and perhaps for most, the absence of any personal experience of God occasions not exultation, but sorrow and regret, or simple acceptance. Moreover, there can be no doubt that large numbers of professing Christians find themselves in this state. They echo the cry of Job (23:3), "Oh, that I knew where I might find him!" or say merely, matter-of-factly or a bit defiantly, "I haven't found him."

A year ago a discussion group in theology was considering the meaning of reconciliation or atonement. Attention was called to man's self-centeredness, his alienation from God, and his need for restoration of his relationship with God which had been broken by sin. At first various intellectual objections were raised to the notion of a broken relationship. A little later, however, one student admitted that his problem with this idea was that he had experienced only twice in his life what he could call a real relationship with God. Others agreed that this was their difficulty too. Obviously it is meaningless to talk of either breaking or restoring a relationship which has never existed.

Some among us are living through what St. John of the Cross called "the dark night of the soul." For others, perhaps, the night seems less dark, mainly because they have rarely if ever seen the day. For some the experience is rightly described, in the words of Martin Buber, as an "eclipse of God"; if for others this term is inappropriate, it is only because they have never seen the sun. For some the darkness has come because they, like the young Augustine, have turned their backs to the light. For others it has crept in because physical things, technological achievements, or human suffering have blocked their vision. But whatever the reason, the hiddenness of God is for many religiously inclined people today a pervasive experience.

These seven objections I believe to be the major bases of atheism in our time. Our purpose in these pages has been to summarize them rather than to examine their weaknesses or their strengths. In the next chapter some incidental weighing of the merits and demerits of these criticisms will be unavoidable. However, our primary concern will be to rethink the meaning of God in the perspective of the atheistic critique, in the hope that his living reality, more clearly discerned, may become in truth a lamp to our feet and a light to our path.

part two
Exploring Afresh the Meaning of God

IV. Signposts

"The I-Thou relation," writes Martin Buber, "has gone into the catacombs—who can say with how much greater power it will step forth! Who can say when the I-It relation will be directed anew to its assisting place and activity! . . . The eclipse of the light of God is no extinction; even tomorrow that which has stepped in between may give way." [1]

In the preceding chapters we have looked realistically at the intellectual problems and the baffling experiences which have "stepped in between" God and men in our time. If we are honest, we shall admit that these difficulties affect not only avowed atheists, but also many within the community of faith. Obviously, more than intellectual clarity will be required to bring the eclipse to an end. Nevertheless, if we can remove the misunderstandings which have obscured our vision, we may be exposed anew to the light of the real God and enabled to enter into a truer relation with him. It should therefore prove beneficial to undertake a fresh exploration of the meaning of God, with particular reference to the atheistic criticisms. What can we learn from them? What modifications in our traditional conceptions do they make desirable? If we can satisfactorily answer questions like these, we may find not only a defensible referent for the word *God*, but an authentic encounter with his living Presence.

As a police artist uses the descriptions of witnesses to piece together a picture of an accused criminal, we can use the

---

[1] *The Eclipse of God; Studies in the Relation Between Religion and Philosophy* (New York: Harper & Brothers, [1952] Torchbook 1957), p. 129.

statements of various atheists to form a composite portrait of the God whom they have found guilty and sentenced to death—and whom they identify with the God of historic Christian faith. The emerging conception is somewhat as follows. God is the omnipotent, omniscient, timeless, changeless, perfectly good Absolute on whom all being depends for its creation and continuing existence. He is the transcendent supernatural being whose external action explains the otherwise inexplicable and mysterious processes of the natural order, but who miraculously suspends natural laws in order to demonstrate his power or to save from harm those whom he favors. He sends sickness and natural calamities to discipline his human creatures. He is the providential ruler of human history, the events of which are ordained by his arbitrary will and contributory to the ultimate accomplishment of his preconceived and predetermined ends. He supposedly loves men, yet unheedingly permits them to suffer agony and death at the hands of enemies, presumably to punish them for their sins or to fulfill other purposes which remain hidden to them. As sovereign Lord, he demands from his human subjects unquestioning trust and obedience as they await the outcome of his fixed plan in a heavenly realm beyond history, but he grants them no initiative, no real freedom, and no opportunity to contribute responsibly to his grand design. Sanctifying divisions between men such as those between rulers and ruled, owners and workers, he opposes human action to change society, and thus supports the injustice and exploitation of the status quo. He places men and women on this earth to prepare them for their true home in the life to come, where they will be punished or compensated for their earthly experiences according to their deserts. The evils of the present transitory existence are to be endured in the knowledge that they cannot affect men's ultimate relation to God or their eternal destiny. God saves from fear, guilt, finitude, and death all who serve him, and rewards them with final blessedness.

Obviously, some features of this composite image of God would and should be upheld, in spite of atheistic opposition, by intelligent Christians. Some represent a false parody of the views endorsed by the most thoughtful believers, or reflect conceptions accepted in past generations but no longer widely held. But some of the most questionable and repugnant aspects of this notion of deity find unmistakable support in the biblical writings and in the works of such revered theologians as Augustine, Thomas Aquinas, Martin Luther, and John Wesley. Many of the same ideas are deeply embedded in the traditions, liturgies, and hymns of the churches, and in the belief and practice of millions of devout Christians today. It is therefore imperative that Christians take a new look at the understanding of God which they have somehow communicated to unbelievers, and similarly at their own understanding. What modifications are in order? What weaknesses, inadequacies, or errors, either in our real beliefs or in our communication of them, are uncovered by the atheistic critique? Which truths in the biblical witness or in historic Christian thought have become obscured and now need to be brought to light and emphasized anew? Are there some assumptions which should now be rejected? In response to questions like these we shall consider eight proposals. The first will be mainly formal and epistemological, while those that follow will deal directly with the content of our conception of God.

1. *Our thought of God must be related intelligibly to all relevant knowledge gained from secular sources.* This does not mean that science or philosophy should become the norm of Christian belief. It does assume that talk of God which wants to be taken seriously must somehow make connection with the total life and thought of men, and particularly with their search for truth. The gospel is addressed to men and

women as whole persons, or as persons who need to become whole, and we render a disservice to them and to it if we suggest in any way that religious faith concerns a separate compartment of their lives. In this regard two needs are especially urgent today: that of relating God to the natural order; and that of relating revelation to other avenues leading to religious truth.

a. With respect to the action of God in nature, we must carefully guard against the temptation to use God to explain phenomena which remain unexplained by known principles. Isaac Newton and other scientists have themselves sometimes invoked God as a hypothesis to fill gaps in their explanations; and theologians have frequently found in such lacunae in scientific knowledge important support for religious belief. But thus to introduce God when men reach the boundaries of their understanding is scientifically inhibitive and theologically precarious. It allows no place for God in natural processes where causes are known, and it involves a steadily declining scope for divine action as gap after gap is closed by advancing understanding. Ample illustration is provided by changing views of the causation of rainbows, earthquakes, eclipses, and pestilences. We dare not reduce God to the status of what Père Dubarle has called "the pocket supplement to our intellectual inadequacies."[2] It is this practice which explains at least in part Bonhoeffer's assertion that God "lets us live in the world without the working hypothesis of God."[3] The thoughtful Christian will avoid using theological ideas to answer scientific questions. As C. A. Coulson has declared, "When we come to the scientifically unknown, our correct policy is not to rejoice because we have found God; it is to become better scientists."[4]

Actually, any conception of God which interprets him pri-

[2] Quoted by Roger Garaudy, *From Anathema to Dialogue*, p. 105.
[3] *Letters and Papers from Prison*, p. 196; cf. pp. 154 f., 178, 195, 197.
[4] *Science and Religion: A Changing Relationship* (Cambridge: Cambridge University Press, 1955), p. 2.

marily in causal terms, as an objective explanation of the world or any of its parts, misses the central reality in authentic faith. Such faith is above all a matter of personal relations, in which God makes himself known to men in such varied experiences as creatureliness, guilt, reconciliation, renewal, the call to fulfill one's highest potentialities as a person, and the impulsion toward beauty, righteousness, and love of God and neighbor. It is chiefly our trustful response to him who in holy love creates and redeems us and summons us to personal commitment and mission in the world.

However, this recognition gives us no warrant whatever for disparaging the natural order or assuming its insignificance for faith. Unfortunately, such tendencies are widespread in contemporary theology. Karl Barth was so averse to metaphysics and all natural theology, and so intent on interpreting everything in terms of the redemptive grace disclosed in Jesus Christ, that the world which for him was the scene of God's providential action seems completely unrelated to nature as seen by the scientist. The physical world is simply the unredeemed theater in which the drama of human redemption is performed. For Christian existentialists, nature is the impersonal setting of man's personal existence, and as such it is no concern of faith. Many theologians oriented toward linguistic analysis seem to find nothing in common between discourse about God and discourse about natural phenomena. Thus in various ways a wedge is driven between nature and grace, creation and redemption, the impersonal and the personal, and language applicable to nature and to God.

In my judgment such a dichotomy cannot long be maintained if faith is to be biblical, open-eyed, and healthy. The dominant witness of the biblical writers is affirmative regarding the natural order, portraying it as the creation of God and the instrument of his purpose. The God who redeems men through Christ is the same God who brings the world into being, pronounces it good, and gives man dominion over it.

He with whom men are summoned to enter into a covenant relation is the God on whom all things depend.[5] The early church recognized no gulf between God and nature. The Apostles' Creed opens with a confession of faith in the Creator of heaven and earth, and the church rejected as heretical the Marcionite separation between the Redeemer-God of the New Testament and the Creator-God of the Old Testament. The material order which these Christians saw as the locus of man's history, including his all-important salvation-history, was clearly the same physical world as that investigated today by the natural sciences. Thus the theologian who claims to interpret the biblical revelation cannot soundly ignore the relation of nature to faith in God.

Existentially, moreover, the life of faith is not lived in a vacuum. Much of the anxiety to which man is exposed springs from the impact of natural events which can so quickly shatter his fragile existence. He cannot forever evade the question of the relation between the reality which addresses him, and which calls for his trustful response, to the physical world which so often threatens that trust. Carl Friedrich von Weizsäcker has written discerningly: "A splitting of existence and nature, according to which existence would be the sphere of Christian faith and nature that of exact science, assigns to faith as well as to science a too narrow field, indeed one which is completely non-existent."[6] The existence in which we meet God is bodily existence, and our personal engagement includes inextricable involvement in the natural world. That world cannot be totally unrelated to the nature which is the object of scientific research. As already noted, even Martin Buber, with his strong emphasis on the I-Thou encounter, attributes to the I-It relation an assisting rather than an opposing role.

[5] Gen. 1; Pss. 8; 33; 89; 90; 104; 136; 139; 146; 147; 148; Job 38; Isa. 40:28-31; 44:24-26; John 1:1-3; Col. 1:15-20; Heb. 1:2.
[6] *Zum Weltbild der Physik* (Zürich: Hirzel Verlag, [1949] 1963), pp. 243 ff., 263.

The bearing of scientific research on religious belief was convincingly illustrated by a telecast in the winter of 1968, "The Beginning of Life." This film made clear that the potentialities for the whole future existence of the person are in the original cell formed by the fertilized ovum. The DNA (deoxyribose nucleic acid) in the genes, though completely invisible, programs all future characteristics, spiritual as well as physical. For Christian faith such information not only discloses the marvelous ways in which God operates in the creation of human life; it also opens to man staggering possibilities of playing God, if he will, by exercising genetic control over the characteristics of future generations—producing superior persons, submissive workers, or whatever may be desired!

Some linguistic analysts attempt to solve the problem of the relation between science and faith by assigning to religious language and scientific language two different spheres or functions. According to this disposition the former refers to purely personal attitudes and experiences regarded by men as significant for their lives, while the latter describes the objective world. On this view religious language cannot be said to be *true* about anything, but it is a useful guide to life and a helpful expression of human experiences like those of dependence, gratitude, worship, and commitment. Actually, however, the language of faith does not make this separation; it purports to refer cognitively and truly to a real state of affairs, and the God confessed and worshiped is seen as acting creatively in physical nature no less than in personal life. If God is relevant only to man's existence, what was he doing, or where was he, before man appeared in cosmic history? Clearly he was either a quiescent, irrelevant observer or he was nonexistent, waiting to be born. Thus the God who some claim has died in the nineteenth or twentieth century might be said to have been born with the emergence of man early in the Pleistocene period, perhaps a million years ago! But such a God has no connection with the God affirmed by

Christian faith. Difficult though the task may be, theology must interpret the divine activity which man encounters in his personal existence within the context of the reality ultimately at work in his cosmic environment. Only when belief in God is thus related to the world in which God is asserted to act can it command the respect of critical minds committed to the scientific investigation of truth.

b. Another questionable dichotomy is that which separates God's self-revelation from man's own futile search for religious truth. Some theologians answer the atheistic critique by distinguishing sharply between theistic belief and faith in the God disclosed in Jesus Christ, who is not open to human discovery. Helmut Gollwitzer asserts, for example, that "the God accessible to anyone on the basis of human nature" is nothing more than "man accessible to himself," a deity who is only a product of human reason. Conclusions reached through man's own resources "always lack ultimate certainty and the bindingness claimed for them," whereas men who are confronted by the Word as Person are given a certainty which cannot be questioned or refuted. The God whom Nietzsche pronounced dead was only a metaphysical concept, a "conceptual idol" which had never been alive; Nietzsche's criticism is therefore irrelevant to faith in the living God who reveals himself.[7] In similar vein Hendrikus Berkhof holds that the divinity rejected by atheism is a God "up there" who is outside our comprehensible world, a metaphysical entity whose existence we try to establish through argument, the divine image of natural theology, the highest being of scholasticism. But Christianity affirms an entirely different God, who announces himself, whom we meet in his deeds and words, in the realm of concrete history, in Jesus Christ. Faith in this God is thus not vulnerable to the atheistic criticism. Actually, says Berkhof, the Christian and the positivistic atheist are at home in the same dimension of reality. The Christian, em-

[7] *The Existence of God as Confessed by Faith*, pp. 141, 193, 240, 244.

phasizing the unmetaphysical, this-worldly, historical character of the God made known in the event of Jesus Christ, may be closer to the atheist than to the classical theist.[8]

One frequent expression of this point of view is the assumption of a complete disjunction between faith as a response to the gospel and religion as a human activity. Thus Karl Barth accepts as justified the criticisms of Feuerbach and others of religion as a product of man's longings, while insisting that Christian faith is untouched by such arguments, since it is not religion, but a unique occurrence wrought by God rather than man. The real opposition, says Gollwitzer, is between a religion of law and the gospel; between all possible religions, theistic or atheistic, and a life called forth by God's own deed of love and forgiveness. The gospel message does not depend on antennae already present in man; it is based rather on a wholly other Word with its own unique power.[9] On this basis Berkhof declares that the God of Israel and of Christian faith "stands no nearer to the religions than to atheism." In the struggle between religion and atheism, therefore, Christianity takes no part. It is as it were above the battle.[10]

It seems to me that this attempt to carve out a privileged position for Christian faith based on revelation is doomed to failure, for two reasons. First, the moment divine revelation is received by man it becomes a part of his experience, understood in terms of his rational capacities, influenced by all his conscious and unconscious attitudes, feelings, and volitions, and thus inevitably subject to error and distortion. Genuine revelation involves not only the Revealer, but the human recipient, who cannot help interpreting its content in accord with his wholly human psychic equipment. Note well the

[8] "Theologiseren in een a-theistisch tijdperk," katern 2, Katernen 2000, cahiers van werk-groep 2000, Oct., 1965.
[9] "Die christliche Kirche und der kommunistische Atheismus," *Evangelische Theologie*, 19 (1959), 296; *Die marxistische Religionskritik und christlicher Glaube*, pp. 31 f.
[10] Berkhof, *op. cit.*

wide differences in the conceptions of God, man, Jesus Christ, and salvation held by Christians who claim to have received the authentic revelation! It is therefore only by arbitrary fiat that we can claim to occupy an impregnable fortress where we are secure against the questions and objections which are put to those outside.

Secondly, no insistence that Christian belief in God is something completely different from all world views and religions, however satisfying it may be to the Christian, is likely to impress the atheist. Western atheists from Feuerbach to the present have directed their criticisms primarily at Christianity, and they are not prone to separate the pure gospel from its empirical expressions. To the atheist, as to most students of religion, Christian faith is one form of religion, historically conditioned like others, and it involves a view of reality which claims to be true. It is therefore subject to examination, discussion, and questioning within the same frame of reference, and with the same kind of language, as other belief systems. In the words of Howard E. Root, "Whenever theologians use the word God they are doing metaphysics. The only question is whether they are doing it well or badly." [11] In the dialogue with atheists we should of course confess our faith, but we cannot escape the responsibility also for critically examining with our dialogue partner the truth of our understanding of reality, in the same language which he uses to discuss other truth claims.

Positively, this means a continuing effort to show the extent to which the whole of human life is illuminated by the gospel. We cannot demonstrate scientifically or prove philosophically the truths we cherish, but we can make plain their relation to other truth and their significance for human existence—the degree to which man in the light of the revelation in Christ gains a new understanding of himself and his world.

[11] *Soundings: Essays Concerning Christian Understanding,* ed. A. R. Vidler (New York: Cambridge University Press, 1962), p. 14.

H. Richard Niebuhr writes of the "special occasion" of Jesus Christ as the "intelligible event which makes all other events intelligible," [12] and Walter Marshall Horton finds this revelation "confirmed by its power to unify and crown all other truth." [13] In similar fashion Wolfhart Pannenberg argues that the revelation of God himself discloses in man and his world the circumstances and relationships which in turn manifest its truth. Thus Christian affirmations concerning God involve much more than assurances. When human existence is seen in the light of the biblical witness, and found to be really perceivable in that light, it can be reasonably claimed as evidence for the reality of the biblical God.[14] This procedure makes possible genuine communication with the open-minded atheist in terms intelligible to him, as well as a kind of verification of Christian theism which is worthy of his full respect.

2. *Christian thought should affirm unmistakably the intimate relationship of God to his world, which finds in him the ground and source of its unity, its manifold activity, and its ultimate meaning.* The God rejected by many atheists has been a deity conceived as a being or an order existing above or beyond the realm of natural and human existence, yet ruling that realm by his arbitrary will. Critical Christian theism shares this rejection, stressing God's immanence no less than his transcendence. God does not act on the world from outside it, like a carpenter constructing a desk or a watchmaker a watch; rather he informs and interpenetrates his creation from within, so that its existence depends moment by moment on his energizing activity. Many philosophers of religion and theologians who in other respects differ widely are one in stressing the inwardness of the relationship be-

[12] *The Meaning of Revelation* (New York: The Macmillan Co., 1941), p. 93.
[13] John Baillie and Hugh Martin (eds.), *Revelation* (London: Macmillan & Co., 1937), pp. 260 f., 258, n. 2.
[14] "Die Frage nach Gott," *Evangelische Theologie*, 25 (1965), 242.

tween God as Spirit and the spheres of nature and human history.

The panpsychist Gustav Theodor Fechner (1801-87) treats the world as "the other side of the divine existence, as something belonging to God." Thus the Spirit of God does not stand "in a dead, external fashion above the bodily world, but manifests itself, rather, as a living essence immanent in it, or else . . . nature itself is an expression of God which remains immanent in him." [15]

In like manner the personal idealist Edgar Sheffield Brightman, in his posthumously published metaphysics, speaks of "the immanence of natural processes in God"—rather than in more traditional fashion of the immanence of God in nature.[16]

Martin Buber's central emphasis on the I-Thou relation leads him to a similar view. "To step into pure relation," he writes, is "to see everything in the *Thou*, not to renounce the world but to establish it on its true basis." We do not reach God by looking away from the world. Rather, "he who sees the world in Him stands in His presence. . . . To include nothing beside God but everything in Him—this is full and complete relation." Therefore he who hallows life in this world meets the living God.[17] Rudolf Bultmann likewise seeks to abolish the opposition between the here and the beyond, the natural and the supernatural. In his judgment the only idea of God possible for modern man is one which recognizes *"the unconditional in the conditional,* the beyond in the here, the transcendent in the present at hand, as possi-

---

[15] *Zend-Avesta: Oder über die Dinge des Himmels und des Jenseits, vom Standpunkte der Naturbeschreibung,* 5th ed. (Leipzig: Leopold Voss, 1922), I, 200-202.

[16] *Person and Reality,* ed. Peter Anthony Bertocci (New York: Ronald Press, 1958), p. 295.

[17] *I and Thou,* tr. Ronald Gregor Smith (Edinburgh: T. & T. Clark, 1937), p. 79.

bility of encounter." [18] Bultmann applies this conception to his interpretation of the psalmist's affirmation of the presence of God "before the mountains were brought forth." The meaning of *before* here is not merely chronological; it refers to God as "creative superiority," "creative origin." "This origin did not occur once as prima causa, out of which world history then unfolded in time; on the contrary, this origin is always present." [19]

Albert C. Outler is equally concerned to avoid anything approaching a deistic notion of God's relation to the world. In his view God is not *a* motion, *a* cause, or *a* being, but the ground of *all* motions, causes, and beings, and of "the entire 'cosmos' in which they co-exist." The God of Christian faith is "the Provider of all the possibilities and meanings in human history as well as all the forms and processes of nature." [20]

Recently John A. T. Robinson has popularized Bonhoeffer's notion of God as "the beyond in the midst" [21] in his reiterated insistence that the divine is to be located not "up there" or "out there" but in the center of man's life in the world. The term *God* "denotes the ultimate depth of all our being, the creative ground and meaning of all our existence," and the world is the "field" of his being and activity. "The eternal *Thou* is met only *in, with and under* the finite *Thou*, whether in the encounter with other persons or in the response to the natural order." [22]

---

[18] "The Idea of God and Modern Man," *Journal for Theology and Church*, II, ed. Robert M. Funk (New York: Harper & Row, 1965), 91-94.

[19] *Ibid.*, p. 93.

[20] *Who Trusts in God* (New York: Oxford University Press, 1968), pp. 40, 47, 109.

[21] *Letters and Papers from Prison*, p. 155. It should be noted that there is nothing novel in the conception of "the beyond in the midst." Such formulations, combining immanence with transcendence, appear frequently in twentieth-century liberal theology.

[22] *Honest to God* (Philadelphia: Westminster Press, 1963), pp. 47, 53; *Exploration into God* (Stanford: Stanford University Press, 1967), pp. 81, 96.

In the late nineteen-sixties, no theologians have emphasized the closeness of the God-world relation more than those who have been strongly influenced by the process philosophy of Alfred North Whitehead. Whitehead himself conceives God as having two polar aspects, his primordial and consequent natures. Seen as primordial, God is the abstract, conceptual (though not conscious) realization or "envisagement" of the potentialities implicit in the "eternal objects," and hence the source of all novelty in the world. As such, "he is not *before* all creation, but *with* all creation." God's consequent nature, his physical pole, is derived from his participation in the world's creative advance. Since all things are related to one another, the world reacts on God and is objectified in him. Thus all events are received into God's conscious experience, becoming occasions for new and richer concretions.[23] On the one hand, "the world lives by its incarnation of God in itself." On the other, "he is the binding element in the world" who in fact makes the world possible through "adjusting" its individual aspects to one another.[24] In a classic statement Whitehead summarizes his conception of the relation in a series of paradoxes which assert the permanence and fluidity of both God and the world, the unity and the multiplicity of both, the transcendence of each over the other, the immanence of each in the other, and the creation of each by the other.[25]

The interactionism of Whitehead's thought finds effective expression today in the writing and teaching of a number of able Christian theologians, like Charles Hartshorne, W. Norman Pittenger, Daniel Day Williams, Schubert M. Ogden, and John B. Cobb, Jr.[26] The panentheism of Hartshorne pro-

[23] *Process and Reality* (New York: The Macmillan Co., 1929), pp. 521-24.
[24] *Religion in the Making* (New York: The Macmillan Co., 1926), pp. 156, 158 f.
[25] *Process and Reality*, pp. 527 f.
[26] Hartshorne, *The Divine Relativity; A Social Conception of God* (New Haven: Yale University Press, 1948); *A Natural Theology for Our Time* (LaSalle, Ill.: Open Court Publishing Co., 1967); Pittenger,

vides a particularly good example of the way in which process theology seeks to overcome any disjunction between God and the world. According to Hartshorne God is "surrelative," or supremely relative; he is in fact "constituted by relationships." God is absolute, even immutable, in the sense that in all his relations he can be counted on to act unfailingly in accord with his supreme excellence. As absolute, he is Being itself, essence but not existence, in abstraction from all particular determinations. But as actual, concrete reality he is supereminently relative, sensitive to all beings, related to all as he alone can be, and literally all-inclusive. Logically he is "distinguishable from and independent of" all relative items, but taken as an actual whole he includes them all. He is "the wholeness of the world," "the Life in which all things live." Thus reality is panentheistic. Ultimately there is only one sphere of action, "this-world-in-God." [27]

In spite of significant differences, the theologians just surveyed are fundamentally agreed in regarding God as in some sense the matrix of all cosmic reality who is intimately involved in its ongoing life. In this emphasis they are in harmony with a recurrent theme of the New Testament. The Fourth Evangelist suggests a close relation between the Creator and his creation when he declares that all things were made *through* the Word (John 1:1-3), and this impression is heightened when we remember that the gospel which follows identifies the Word made flesh with the Redeemer-God who acts in Jesus Christ to save the world he has created. Something like panentheism seems implied in Paul's reminder to his Athenian audience, in the words of a Greek poet, that in

---

"Toward a More Christian Theology," *Religion in Life*, 36 (1967), 498-505; Williams, "The New Theological Situation," *Theology Today*, 24 (1967-68), 444-63; Ogden, *The Reality of God and Other Essays* (New York: Harper & Row, [1963] 1966); Cobb, *A Christian Natural Theology* (Philadelphia: Westminster Press, 1965).

[27] *The Divine Relativity*, pp. vii f., xv, 11, 76, 88-90, 152; *A Natural Theology for Our Time*, pp. 6 f., 12; *The Logic of Perfection and Other Essays* (LaSalle, Ill.: Open Court Publishing Co., 1962), p. 297.

God "we live and move and have our being" (Acts 17:28). A comparable idea is interpreted christologically when the author of Ephesians proclaims the plan for the fullness of time which God has disclosed in Christ: "to unite all things in him, things in heaven and things on earth" (Eph. 1:9-10). By taking such conceptions seriously and grounding nature and history in the dynamic, interpenetrating life of God, theology may correct a fateful error of much traditional theism and cut the nerve of a major atheistic objection.

3. *Our conception of the relation of God to man must maintain the real freedom and responsibility of man and the importance of his contribution to cosmic and historic processes.* We have noted as a central feature of most atheistic thought a humanism which assumes that the full dignity and mature growth of man requires the denial of God. An all-powerful determiner of destiny, it is held, condemns man to insignificance and passivity. This atheistic assumption reflects misunderstanding of the gospel, and it often expresses more arrogance and presumption than concern for truth. Yet when due allowance is made for these factors, we must admit that the Augustinian, Calvinistic, and Lutheran traditions which have dominated Protestant theology have in various ways excluded, jeopardized, or made problematic the reality of free human agency. One recent example of this tendency is provided by Karl Barth. He does assert that God acts in the freedom of his love for man, and he tries valiantly to conserve the freedom of man's response to the divine mercy. Nevertheless, he still regards God as absolute sovereign, and he fails to confront squarely the question as to whether man can contribute anything to the work of God. At one point he states, "If we ask why creation or each of us or everything has to be as it is, the only answer is that it must be so by God's free will." [28]

[28] *Church Dogmatics,* II/1 (Edinburgh: T. and T. Clark, 1957), 561.

Similar ambiguity appears frequently in popular religious thought. On the last day of the 1967 baseball season, the Minnesota Twins lost the American League pennant to the Boston Red Sox. On returning to Minneapolis, Cal Ermer, the Twins' manager, told fans at the airport: "I really feel that they're not as good as us. They may be the third or fourth best club in the league, but they won it and you've got to give them credit. The good Lord saw fit for it to go the other way." Many ordinary Christians, in equal confusion, attempt to transfer to God responsibilities which actually belong to them and other men.

This is of course a very old and profound problem—the respective roles of God and man in human life. Struggling with it, many able and devout minds, among them various biblical writers, have chosen to circumscribe or abolish the freedom of men rather than limit God's control over history. But there is weighty biblical and empirical support for a Christian humanism which assigns to man full responsibility for his acts, and which sees no necessity for God to die in order that man might live.

According to the Genesis narrative of creation, when God made man "in his own image" he gave him dominion over the earth and all the lower animals, and called on him to "fill the earth and subdue it." This broad grant of freedom and authority was further embodied in the commissioning of man to give names to the animals. The same basic conception of man's status and function appears in Jesus' assurance that the Sabbath—and by inference all other institutions—is made for man, not man for the Sabbath. In all these instances man is given power as a trust from God and expected to exercise it in stewardship to God. But the freedom to use it for good or ill is his, and the responsibility for making decisions is fully his own. In this sense freedom is as inescapable for the Christian as it is for the Sartrian existentialist.

Since historically a pronounced stress on the divine immanence, like the opposite emphasis on God's absolute sovereignty, has tended to eliminate or drastically to limit human freedom, it is significant that the theologians who today ground human life most intimately in the indwelling life of God see this relationship as supportive of the free agency of man. Whitehead's God acts by "persuasion"; his power is "the worship he inspires." He is "the poet of the world, tenderly leading it by his vision of truth, beauty, and goodness." [29] Hartshorne points out that God's consequent nature is multiple as well as one, thus providing for the full individual reality of the creatures in him. Not even "the supreme orderer" reduces the members of the world to "mere subjects with the sole function of obedience." [30] Johannes B. Metz, writing from a modified Thomistic perspective, agrees that God is not a cause competing with human agency, but the freedom which underlies human freedom, making it possible or "letting it be," and thus supporting rather than hindering man's self-fulfillment.[31] Another progressive Roman Catholic, Leslie Dewart, maintains similarly that the reality of God must be found in his *"presence to history"* as the context of man's striving. However, man's freedom in history does not mean that he alone freely creates history. He works in a *given* situation, a situation of grace. "History is made by man, but in the presence of God." God and man are mutually present and active in "the conscious creation of the world." [32]

[29] *Process and Reality*, p. 526.

[30] *The Divine Relativity*, p. xv; Charles Hartshorne and William L. Reese (eds.), *Philosophers Speak of God* (Chicago: University of Chicago Press, 1953), p. 283; Whitehead, *Science and the Modern World* (New York: The Macmillan Co., 1926), p. 276.

[31] "Freiheit als philosophisch-theologisches Grenzproblem," Johannes B. Metz and others, *Gott in Welt; Festgabe für Karl Rahner* (Freiburg: Herder und Herder, 1964), I, 310 f.

[32] *The Future of Belief; Theism in a World Come of Age* (New York: Herder and Herder, 1966), pp. 195, 197; *Initiative in History: A Christian-Marxist Exchange* (Cambridge, Mass.: The Church Society for College Work, 1967), pp. 6, 9. Dewart regards his interpretation as a Christian counterpart of Engels' statement: "Men themselves make their history, only they do so in a given environment which conditions it, and on the

In general harmony with this position is the view of Albert C. Outler, who from an Augustinian background writes of man's freedom as "the power to act in the presence of the Provident Mystery that encompasses our lives." [33]

Such freedom calls man to active cooperation with God. In the earliest biblical book God discloses his will to Amos and summons him to aid in its realization. But the man thus commissioned is not a blind, passive instrument; he is free in relation to both God and men. "To God's sovereign address," writes Buber, "man gives his autonomous answer." [34] In modern times this means the faithful acceptance of responsibility for scientific research, technical invention, and all the work needed for the sustenance of human life and the richest fulfillment of human values. Man is a free subject responsible to God and to himself before God. It is in and through the uniting of his efforts with those of God that he and the world can become what his Creator intends them to be. Man's relation to God thus involves not the suffocation of human energies, but their emancipation.

Had Christians understood and practiced better the gospel they are called to proclaim, atheists would have had scant justification for their claim that religious faith exalts God at the expense of man and so depreciates human worth. In the words of Vatican II, "The recognition of God is in no way hostile to man's dignity, since this dignity is rooted and perfected in God." [35] According to the New Testament, men who respond in trust and love to the love of God become sons and heirs of God, creatures of eternal worth; and their relation to God is one not of childish dependence but of mature, re-

---
basis of actual relations already existing." (Letter to Starkenburg, Jan. 25, 1894.)

[33] *Who Trusts in God*, pp. 51 f.

[34] *To Hallow This Life*, p. 12.

[35] "Pastoral Constitution on the Church in the Modern World," Sec. 21; *The Documents of Vatican II* (New York: Association Press, 1966), p. 218.

sponsible sonship in which they become God's fellow workmen.[36] Nicolas Berdyaev reports that he turned from Communism to Christianity not because he ceased to believe in the worth, high destiny, and creative freedom of man, but because he sought and found a firmer ground for that faith. His resultant faith in man, he writes, cannot be shaken even by human meanness, "for it is not based on what man thinks of man, but what God thinks of man."[37] Likewise the later Barth, seeing man in the light of the Incarnation, asserts that even sinful man cannot negate God's covenant relation with him or cease to be a man whose nature is freedom for God.[38]

Actually, the deepest roots of western atheistic humanism are to be found in Christian humanism, though the atheist is usually ignorant of, or unwilling to, acknowledge the fact. All the more valuable, therefore, is the recognition of Ernst Bloch that the idea of the "kingdom of freedom" which Marx took over from Hegel is derived from "the freedom of the children of God" in the apostle Paul. Though the reference to the children of God disappeared, the theme and much of the substance remained.[39] Christians need to remind both themselves and their atheistic partners-in-dialogue of the biblical basis of belief in the intrinsic personal worth of all men.

If we affirm that God has appointed man to dominion and sonship, we should be ready to take the further step of recognizing that man's actions make a difference to God. His relation to his Creator and Redeemer is one of interaction, and hence two-directional. His positive efforts, though limited, add something to the work of God and help to fulfill the divine purpose. He may also subtract something from God's action, obstructing the realization of divine ends. Under the

[36] Rom. 8:14-17, 21; Gal. 3:29; I John 3:1, 2; I Cor. 3:9.
[37] *Self-knowledge; Attempt at a Philosophical Autobiography*, tr. Katharine Lampert (London: Geoffrey Bles, 1950), p. 191.
[38] Barth, *Church Dogmatics*, III/2 (Edinburgh: T. and T. Clark, 1960), 274 f.; IV/1 (Edinburgh: T. and T. Clark, 1956), 46-49.
[39] "Der Mensch des utopischen Realismus," *Dokumente der Paulus-Gesellschaft*, XII, 102 f.

spell of an extreme version of the Reformation doctrine of *sola gratia*, we shrink from suggesting that human deeds contribute anything. For example, Eberhard Jüngel has recently written that the deeds of men of faith add nothing whatever to what God has already done in Jesus Christ. The Christian in his ethical life expects everything from God, nothing from himself. To claim that men contribute even the smallest fraction would imply an ethic of works or self-justification.[40] However, if human choices and actions bring to pass events which would not otherwise occur, and which fulfill the intention of God, must we not consistently conclude that men do augment God's action? Moreover, to recognize this is not equivalent to an arrogant effort to install man in the place of God. As Karl Rahner has said, ultimately the grace of God is everything. But men empowered by him can respond to his love with acts acceptable in his sight and contributory to his ends.

Men are constantly changing the course of nature and of human life—by developing hybrid corn, performing surgical operations, writing poems, composing and producing symphonies, or inventing automobiles, airplanes, television, or the means of exploring space. In our present era of scientific technology this capacity has been immeasurably increased. Defective human organs are being replaced through the transplanting of healthy organs or the use of plastic or metal parts. Effective control of world populations is now a real possibility through the wide dissemination of contraceptive information. The discovery of the role of deoxyribose nucleic acid (DNA) in genetics opens up the possibility of preventing congenital abnormalities and even of influencing the future direction of human evolution.

The granting of such powers to man entails great risks, yet risks which God has apparently been willing to take for the

[40] "Erwägungen zur Grundlegung evangelischer Ethik im Anschluss an die Theologie des Paulus," *Zeitschrift für Theologie und Kirche*, 63 (1966), 386-88.

sake of the goals sought. Repeatedly man proves himself unworthy, yet he is allowed to try again. He remains a creature, subject to his Creator and Lord. He uses resources which are given to him, and he must operate within a system of law which he finds and cannot change. Yet he is an actor as well as a recipient, and his status before God is not that of a slave, a serf, or an abject subject, but that of a mature son and coworker entrusted with responsible freedom. God's address to him, as to Ezekiel, is, "Son of man, stand upon your feet" (Ezek. 2:1).

Implicit in this understanding of the God-man relation is the responsibility of men of faith to participate in the struggle for a just society. We have noted how devastating has been the atheistic criticism of Christian passivity in the face of social evil. Here American Christians, with their history of social concern, may be tempted to plead not guilty. It was the churches of Germany, we say, and not we, who remained silent under Hitler. But as long as we accept two widely different standards of life for black and white in America, acquiesce in the barbarities perpetrated in our name in Vietnam, and remain unengaged in the costly quest for world peace, we do not rightly understand the claim on our lives of the God we claim to worship. The reconciling and transforming Spirit disclosed in Jesus Christ is the Lord of all earthly life, and nothing will demonstrate his reality more effectively to the atheist than the living witness of those who manifest his righteousness in the world.

4. *God should be understood as other than and transcendent to all finite reality.* With this assertion we move in a different direction from that followed thus far, since our discussion of God's relation to nature and man has dealt chiefly with his immanence. Furthermore, whereas we were concerned before to conserve the truth found in atheistic criticisms, we now seek to point out a serious defect in atheistic

thought, as well as to guard against errors in Christian thinking about God which have been reinforced or partly produced by atheistic arguments. Currently fashionable is a tendency to interpret Christian faith predominantly or wholly in horizontal, this-worldly, human terms, while repudiating or devaluing its vertical, transcendent, metaphysical reference. As with Feuerbach, theology is again reduced to anthropology.

According to Altizer the distant primordial God, after first emptying himself in Jesus, has become fully embodied in the totality of human experience. The sacred has been replaced by the profane, the God of grace by the gracious neighbor. God is dead, and man is freed from his subordination to the transcendent Creator. For the German lay theologian Dorothee Sölle, Christ identified himself with the now absent God and became his representative; likewise, men who identify themselves with Christ represent God in the world. For the present at least God appears only in such mediation or representation. The enthroned God has disappeared from view, but we can play God's role for one another as we devote ourselves in love to our fellows.

In the view of Herbert Braun of Mainz, the constant element in the New Testament is its teaching concerning man. God becomes here "my God," the ground of my self-understanding, the source of my "I should" and my "I may." Man as man implies God, but objectifying metaphysical statements about God are to be avoided. Hence Braun is unwilling to say that "God is love," but finds no problem with "Love is God," where God becomes predicate rather than subject. God may be spoken of, however, as a particular kind of fellow humanity. With a similar accent William Robert Miller writes that "the prophetic idea of God . . . is an expression of man's longing for unity and for rescue from his own inner duality." [41]

[41] Review of *On Judaism*, by Martin Buber, *Saturday Review*, Feb. 10, 1968, p. 34.

Some of the prophets of secular Christianity, though they are not so extreme as Christian existentialists like Braun, are as sweeping as he in their rejection of metaphysics. John A. T. Robinson holds that the "beyondness" of God must be sought in the midst of man's relations with his fellows in worldly activities. For Paul van Buren the language of faith can speak intelligibly to our time only if it eliminates talk of God or anything transcendent and restricts itself to "men's experience of each other and of things." Christian faith connotes a way of life in which man becomes free for his neighbor, a man for others, released for acts of reconciliation. For Harvey Cox our talk of God must be severed from all metaphysical connotations. In the era of the secular city "politics replaces metaphysics as the language of theology." God is met less as a *thou* than as the plural *you* of other human beings. "God wants man to be interested not in Him but in his fellow man." [42] Inevitably this concentration on the life of men in the world has found expression in various patterns of liturgical renewal. One recently produced ritual, for example, describes the goal of Christian revolutionary action as "the full realization of twentieth-century humanness."

Thus on all sides today is evident a tendency to interpret man's relation to God entirely or chiefly in terms of his relations with his fellowmen. I hope that the discussion thus far has made unmistakably clear my own agreement with the central *intent* of this movement—to destroy the dualism of sacred and profane, to demonstrate the relevance of faith to life, and to involve Christians in creative and redemptive action in society. Yet it seems to me equally clear that Christian theology should resist the temptation to make God wholly secular or human. We shall offer no effective answer to atheism by succumbing to its central postulate—the supremacy and adequacy of man. The so-called "mood of contemporary

---

[42] *The Secular City* (New York: The Macmillan Co., 1965), pp. 1-4, 17-37, 60-62, 123, 129, 190, 247 f., 255, 263-68.

man" may seem to call for such humanism. But who is contemporary man, and why should we accept him as our chief norm and guide in interpreting the gospel? We have heard much of the disastrous consequences of the culture Protestantism of the late nineteenth and early twentieth centuries. Yet we are in danger of falling victim to a culture Protestantism or a cultural subjectivism of our own. As we examine anew the meaning of God we must be careful lest the necessary use of the thought-forms of our own day lead to the loss or distortion of abiding realities of our Christian faith. Pannenberg is fully justified in his warning that the dissolution of the divine other in existential relations, consistently thought through, involves also the end of theology.[43]

A centrally humanistic, this-worldly understanding of God gets caught in unnecessary and restrictive either-or choices. Metaphysics need not reduce God to static being or some abstract principle of causation. To affirm God's objective, independent reality is not tantamount to treating him as a thinglike object at man's disposal. To find a vertical dimension in God's relation to man does not mean ruling out the horizontal. Attention to the center does not require forgetfulness of the orbit of man's daily existence—though if he forgets the center his journey may lose direction and meaning.

As Ian Barbour has asserted, in all theological discussion "metaphysical categories are inescapably present, whether recognized or not; even the personalistic language of scripture has ontological implications."[44] Biblical faith is nonacademic and existential, but at every point it reflects metaphysical convictions or presuppositions. The declarations that God is Lord of the world and active in it, that man has sinned and needs forgiveness, that the deepest direction of the universe is disclosed in Jesus Christ, that God loves men, suffers for them,

---

[43] "Die Frage nach Gott," p. 241.
[44] *Issues in Science and Religion* (Englewood Cliffs, N. J.: Prentice-Hall, 1968), p. 459.

and seeks them for fellowship with himself, and that he can be experienced in prayer and worship—these are all statements about reality. Moreover, they purport to speak of one who is not a mere predicate of man or a complex of human relations, but the eternal Subject on whom men ultimately depend for their existence and fulfillment. Conceivably such statements may be mistaken, but we need stronger reason for dismissing their objective reference than the opinion that they are unacceptable to some abstract, hypothetical modern man or that they reflect only man's own understanding of himself.

Normative Christian faith, in the light of and partially because of atheistic objections, finds in the divine reality a more-than-human dimension. However, the self-transcending quality of human experience, our awareness of receiving our existence from beyond ourselves, our sense of accountability for what we become, may prove to be an open bridge between the man of faith and his agnostic or atheistic neighbor. Possibly the questions we raise regarding our own meaning point to a reality greater than ourselves that poses the questions.

What, then, do we mean by the divine transcendence? At least four basic emphases are suggested by the term:

a. God is other than and distinct from the world and man. He is deeply involved in the life of the world, and its laws are his ways of acting, but he is not identical with it, nor is he merely a constituent of it as one element among many. He is present in and with his finite creatures, but not exhausted by them or circumscribed by the processes which mark their behavior. In accord with Karl Heim's "dimensional transcendence," we may conceive the spheres of nature, human life, and God as correlative yet different dimensions of reality, with God alone providing the answer to the questions of the other spheres concerning the why and the whither of their being.[45]

[45] *God Transcendent; Foundation for a Christian Metaphysic*, 3rd ed., tr. Edgar Primrose Dickie (New York: Charles Scribner's Sons, 1936).

b. As noted above in the discussion of immanence, God is the ultimate ground of all finite reality, on whom all existence depends. More particularly, he is the ground of our being as persons, and of the meaning of our existence. As Wolfhart Pannenberg suggests, he is the power which determines the fundamental structure of all reality; hence he transcends what we know as objectively or externally real; and he is the ground which supports man in "the openness of his existence." [46]

c. God immeasurably surpasses his creatures in power, wisdom, and goodness, calling forth our experiences of mystery, awe, and reverence as well as of inadequacy and limitation. Gordon D. Kaufman finds in the limits we experience in our knowledge of other finite selves in ordinary social relations a clue to the meaning of divine transcendence. The persons with whom we interact transcend the physical manifestations which are directly accessible to us. Similarly, we are aware of an ultimate Limit which conditions us on all sides, and this implies an active reality beyond it which faith interprets as God. We know the true reality of other human selves and of God to the extent that they reveal themselves in word and deed.[47] In somewhat similar fashion John A. T. Robinson, though he rejects all disjunctive transcendence, still speaks of a "beyond" which is active "in the midst of" earthly life, and of "the unconditional" who "forms the living frontier, inside and out, of every aspect of man's being, of every particle in the universe." In certain situations we meet "a claim, a mystery, a grace, whose overriding, transcendent, unconditional character can only be expressed by responding with the prophet, 'Thus saith the Lord.'" [48] Such experiences reach their climax for the Christian when he feels grasped by a love

[46] "The Question of God," *Interpretation*, 21 (1967), 306, 309.
[47] "On the Meaning of 'God': Transcendence Without Mythology," *New Theology No. 4*, ed. Martin E. Marty and Dean G. Peerman (New York: The Macmillan Co., 1967), pp. 91-97.
[48] *Exploration into God*, pp. 11, 68 f.

which far exceeds both his comprehension and his merit, and through which he receives healing and renewal which he could never attain in his own strength alone.

d. A further meaning of transcendence centers in the idea of God as the ground of hope and the promise of the future. He is as it were horizontally rather than vertically beyond us. We encounter him in our awareness of the prospective character of human existence, and particularly in the goals he places before us and the support he offers us as we move forward. Since a heightened understanding of this conception among Christians has been stimulated by the atheistic critique, it will be discussed more fully in our fifth proposal.

5. *God should be conceived eschatologically, as he who opens before men a future, gives them a hope which outruns every present, and leads them toward the fulfillment of ever new possibilities.* For an increasing awareness of this dimension of Christian faith, theologians are indebted in part to the revolutionary atheistic humanism of Ernst Bloch. This unorthodox Marxist rejects all belief in God as the static, omnipotent, timeless absolute. Instead he sees reality, which is ultimately nature itself, as a dynamic, open-ended process advancing constantly toward the "not-yet" which can through cosmic and human striving become real. Looking ahead instead of above, Bloch affirms "a transcending without heavenly transcendence." He repudiates any "finished transcendence," an already built castle to which travelers come, but accepts transcendence as the possibility which exceeds anything so far attained. In one of his many biblical allusions, he points out that "Moses did not proclaim God in Canaan, but Canaan in God." Instead of locating God in a settled land, the author of Exodus relates a land of promise to a God leading the way.[49] In vivid imagery Bloch describes the ground of all possibility as "wanderer and compass and land together

[49] *Das Prinzip Hoffnung*, pp. 1522, 1456.

at the front. That is grace." [50] In view of such utterances we can feel the force of Jürgen Moltmann's assertion that a dialogue with the humanists "who are seeking a 'future without God'" can persuade Christians to "leave off seeking 'God without his future.'" [51]

Hope in and movement toward a promised future are clearly basic emphases of the biblical writings. From Abraham to Second Isaiah the God of the Old Testament is always on the way, leading his pilgrim people into new and untrodden paths toward goals only dimly perceived in advance. He appears to Moses in the burning bush as "I will be who I will be," "I will be there as he who is there," or "I will do what I will do" (Exod. 3:14). He makes covenants with his people oriented toward the future, and through Jeremiah (31:31-34) promises a new covenant: "I will be their God, and they shall be my people." The prophets announce the coming of his messianic Kingdom. Aware that the journey into the unknown will involve risks and dangers, he assures those who undertake it, "When you pass through the waters, I will be with you. . . . I will bring. . . . I will gather you" (Isa. 43:2, 5).

The revelatory events proclaimed in the New Testament are also eschatologically oriented, as are the people of the new covenant thus called into being. The God disclosed in Jesus Christ is the God of the coming Kingdom. The resurrection of Christ points forward; in it, writes Moltmann, we discern "the future of God for the world" and the future opened to men by God's acts. The Easter appearances are experiences of promise and mission, "beckoning us on to his future and the future of his lordship." [52] According to Paul, God "gives

---

[50] "Der Mensch des utopischen Realismus," *Dokumente der Paulus-Gesellschaft*, XII, 114 f. At one point Bloch states explicitly that through the Bible "the utopian conscience" came into the world.

[51] "Hope Without Faith: An Eschatological Humanism Without God," *Is God Dead?* (*Concilium*, Vol. 16 [New York: Paulist Press, 1966]).

[52] Jürgen Moltmann, *Theology of Hope; On the Ground and the Implications of a Christian Eschatology*, tr. James W. Leitch (New York: Harper & Row, 1967), pp. 194, 195 f.

life to the dead and calls into existence the things that do not exist" (Rom. 4:17). The passages describing the institution of the Lord's Supper give prominent place to future fulfillment in the coming of the Lord and the kingdom of God (I Cor. 11:23-26; Luke 22:16, 18). The author of Hebrews sees man's life as a pilgrimage of faith, struggle, and hope: "We do not yet see everything in subjection to him. But we see Jesus." "Here we have no lasting city, but we seek the city which is to come" (Heb. 2:8, 9; 13:14). A recurrent theme of apostolic preaching is the new creation, the new man, the new heart, newness of life (Rom. 8:19-21; Eph. 2:15, 4:22-24). In the book of Revelation he who makes all things new promises the coming of a "New Jerusalem," "a new heaven and a new earth" (Rev. 3:12; 21:1, 5).

The hope in the future voiced by the biblical writers relates much more closely to man's earthly, historical life than is generally understood today. Unfortunately, Christian eschatology through the centuries has often suffered from a predominantly otherworldly and static view of the future, with a passive role assigned to man. Under the influence of Augustine and Thomas Aquinas, the end of history has been conceived as the happiness of eternal repose in the heavenly city, or the perfect vision of the divine essence in a timeless eternity.[53] God himself has frequently been portrayed as somehow comprising past, present, and future in an eternal now of perfect fulfillment. Only a year ago I heard an Easter sermon in which the preacher declared, "God cannot be the God of unfinished business." Unfortunately, the dominance of an otherworldly eschatology has led many twentieth-century Christians, convinced of the importance of the here and now, to neglect eschatology almost completely, to the great impoverishment of their faith. The attention now being devoted

---

[53] Augustine, *The City of God*, XXII, 30; XIX, 17; X, 14; Thomas Aquinas, *Summa Contra Gentiles*, XLVIII, LI.

to a theology of hope may help us to recover the wholeness of our own biblical heritage.

Regarding biblical faith as normative, Wolfhart Pannenberg understands God as the Power of the Future, since only such a God can be an adequate object of hope and trust.[54] Similarly, Karl Rahner describes Christianity as "the religion of the absolute future," insisting that this is the self-interpretation of Christianity on the basis of its own nature and concrete historical situation, and is not stimulated by any external factor such as Marxism. The absolute future, of course, is God, conceived as the ground of man's projection or planning of a future. He is essentially transcendent, "the inexpressible mystery," since the wholeness of man's future cannot be expressed in this-worldly terms. God is the transcendent condition of human possibility.[55]

Johannes Baptist Metz is in basic agreement with Pannenberg and Rahner, but uses more concrete language. He insists that divine transcendence and the future, traditionally separated in Christian theology, should be brought together. Transcendence is best conceived as the pull of the future. God comes to us from ahead more than from above. He is the promise of our future which always outruns our own best plans. He leads us forward as he led the children of Israel through the wilderness into the promised land. Christian faith is therefore first of all a hoping faith. Hope must be lifted out of a parenthesis or a subordinate clause to become the main theme in our understanding of faith, the essence of Christian existence.[56]

Broadly similar convictions are expressed by thinkers not ordinarily associated with a theology of hope as such, and

[54] "Der Gott der Hoffnung," *Ernst Bloch zu ehren*, pp. 217-19.
[55] *Christentum und Marxismus—heute*, ed. Erich Kellner, pp. 206 f.; Rahner, *Schriften zur Theologie*, VI (Einsiedeln: Benziger Verlag, 1965), 80 f.
[56] *Christentum und Marxismus—heute*, pp. 221-28; "Gott vor uns," *Ernst Bloch zu ehren*, p. 232.

representing varied philosophical and theological orientations. Bultmann, for example, declares that God is not comprehensible as a static now, but only as the one who is always calling on me for new decisions; "He stands ever before me as the coming one, and this his continuing futurity is his beyondness."[57] John Cobb mentions with approval that for Whitehead novelty is the decisive factor of life, while God is its ground and organ.[58] All the process theologians stress the fluidity and open-endedness of the creative movement related to God's consequent nature, as well as the responsibility of men to share in bringing the new to birth. The "essentialization" which for Paul Tillich constitutes the goal of history is not merely a return to essential being, the reunification of existence and essence; it includes the actualization of the new, which adds to essential being something not originally involved.[59]

This type of thought opens the way to deeper understanding of the meaning of God, and particularly of his transcendence. In the words of the poet Rainer Maria Rilke, "God is the guest who is always going on." When we speak of him, the verb *to be* needs to be supplemented with verbs of action, especially action pointed ahead. Moreover, his activity provides the possibility of our future and leads the way into it.

To conceive God as the power of the future has far-reaching implications for the Christian and his relation to society. Really to believe in God means to face forward in trust, expectation, and active hope—to reach out for that newness of life which he seeks to realize in us. In contrast, as Peter Hebblethwaite shows in his interpretation of Vatican II, "an atheist is not so much a man who does not recognize where

[57] *Glauben und Verstehen*, III (Tübingen: J. C. B. Mohr [Paul Siebeck], 1960), 121.
[58] *A Christian Natural Theology*, pp. 74, 161.
[59] *Systematic Theology*, III (Chicago: University of Chicago Press, 1963), 400 f.; *The Eternal Now* (New York: Charles Scribner's Sons, 1963), p. 126.

he comes from as one who does not know where he is going; he is unaware of the divine vocation to which he is invited." [60] Repentance means much more than regret for what one has been. To repent does include turning away from one's misdirected past, but even more it means turning toward the future, the decision to accept redirection forward in openness to the purpose of God. Likewise, salvation is not simply the restoration of a lost condition. It is rather a process of becoming in which, delivered from bondage to the sins and errors of our past, we are enabled to move toward fulfillment of our real potentialities in relation to God and our fellows. It is the mature life of "straining forward to what lies ahead," in accord with "the upward call of God in Christ Jesus" (Phil. 3:13-14).

Faith in a God who is himself "on the way" also affects radically our relation to society. Unlike Marxist eschatology, Christian hope is not limited to man's earthly history. However, if truly understood it is just as relevant as Marxism to the historical future. Christian eschatology also differs radically from Marxist hope in its ultimate point of reference. The ground of our hope is not an unconscious dialectical process, but the living God of transforming love who awakens and strengthens us and sets us on the way as co-workers with him. His long-range goals are normative here and now, and we share responsibility for their implementation. In the vivid metaphor of Ernst Bloch, our hope gives us not only something to drink, but something to cook! That is, we ourselves have tasks to perform in behalf of his promised Kingdom, the heavenly-earthly Jerusalem.

Therefore Christians are not authorized to defend the status quo, with its misery and injustice. They are committed rather to the world transformation sought by God himself. Christian hope is not "conformed to this world." As Metz suggests, it

[60] *The Council Fathers and Atheism* (Glen Rock, N.J.: Paulist Press Deus Books, 1967), p. 56.

rejects the orthodoxy of faith in the existing order in favor of "the orthopraxy of changing the world within the horizon of the promised future of God." [61] Thus the new creation proclaimed by the gospel involves a revolutionary ethic. The early Christians, thoroughgoing monotheists, were called atheists because in repudiating the Roman deities they disturbed the peace of the religiously supported social order of their time. But in singing what Moltmann calls the first "International," they also overthrew the nationalistic political system of Rome.[62] The task of the Christian theologian, therefore, is not merely "to supply a different *interpretation* of the world, of history and of human nature, but to *transform* them in expectation of a divine transformation." [63] A Christianity which allows full scope for hope and the future will no longer be a handmaid who plods behind society; it will be instead a torchbearer leading the march.[64] Its role is to serve the world by preparing for God's coming Kingdom.

6. *Christian thought of God should now add to its historic affirmation of his eternity a frank acknowledgment of his temporality.* Such a recognition seems implicit in the conception of God as the promise of the future, but it is supported also by other weighty considerations.

Much traditional theology, taking its cue from Aristotle and thinking in substantialistic terms, has stressed the permanence and absoluteness of God and ascribed to him a stationary, timeless perfection. In the divine life, it has been assumed, there can be no before or after; God's omniscience enables him to grasp past, present, and future in one nontemporal now. Nor is it difficult to find biblical passages which appear to justify such a view. A familiar theme in the Psalms is the

---

[61] *Christentum und Marxismus—heute*, p. 223.
[62] "Die Kategorie *Novum* in der christlichen Theologie," *Ernst Bloch zu ehren*, pp. 259 f.
[63] Moltmann, *Theology of Hope*, p. 84.
[64] Moltmann, "Hope Without Faith: An Eschatological Humanism Without God," p. 20.

contrast between the transitoriness of created things and the eternity of the Creator:

> They will perish, but thou dost endure;
> they will all wear out like a garment.
> Thou changest them like raiment, and they pass away;
> but thou art the same, and thy years have no end.
> (Ps. 102:26-27.)

"I the Lord do not change," declares the prophet Malachi (3:6). The author of the Letter to the Hebrews strikes the same note in the familiar assurance that "Jesus Christ is the same yesterday and today and for ever" (13:8). Likewise the Letter of James asserts that with "the Father of lights," that is, the Creator of the heavenly bodies, "there is no variation or shadow due to change" (1:17).

However, passages like these are primarily concerned to emphasize that God is not subject to the perishability and evanescence which characterize all finite things, and that he is utterly dependable. Unlike human beings who are born, grow old, and die, and who throughout their lives vacillate and fluctuate in their commitments or lack of them, God can always be counted on. Sun, moon, and stars may change, but not the Lord of all! His good will toward men never varies. His steadfast love abides forever. He has neither beginning nor end, and his Word is true at all times. That is, he is eternal.

However, equally clear throughout the biblical writings is the assumption of the temporal character of the divine activity. Historicality, time, and development are understood as basic categories of existence. The God who creates and redeems his people is deeply involved in temporal events. Terms like covenant, promise, and providence applied to God's relations with men are meaningless unless a time-spanning action of God is assumed. Trust and hope in him who leads men toward his Kingdom likewise imply that God himself seeks to realize in later time ends not yet attained. The God of the Bible requires time for the fulfillment of his purposes. Here it is important to note the interpretation of two notions of time: *chronos*—quantitative, measurable, repetitive, or clock time; and *kairos*—qualitative, significant, or fulfilled time. The New Testament assumes the reality of the chronological process, but it is especially interested in the *kairoi,* the creative moments of special or unique meaning, and above all in the *kairos* of Jesus Christ. God's self-revelation in history culminates "in the fullness of time" in the momentous event which makes all things new.

The sciences, of course, take the temporal process for granted. In the physical world, says Ian Barbour, "time is constitutive rather than incidental." In quantum physics the atom is "a sequence of vibratory patterns," and vibration obviously requires time.[65] Both cosmic and biological evolution involve movement, becoming, and therefore temporality. But the natural order also exhibits something not unlike the *kairotic* time of the New Testament. Nature is a dynamic process. The patterns of vibration in the atom do not simply repeat themselves forever, but offer alternative potentialities for future realization. Evolution discloses again and again the emergence of real novelties, new phenomena which could not have been expected on the basis of their antecedents. As Barbour expresses it, in the actual world of our experience time is not the "unrolling of a previously written scroll, but passage into a novel and indeterminate future," "a spontaneous and novel coming-into-being of the unpredictable in an unrepeatable history." [66] If we regard this natural, temporal order as an expression of the creative activity of God, it is hard to avoid the conclusion that time has real meaning for God himself, and that the initiation and guidance of change, movement forward into the new, and the meeting of new situations

[65] *Issues in Science and Religion,* pp. 455, 273, 129 f.
[66] *Ibid.,* pp. 457, 298.

produced in part by finite persons created for freedom, are ingredient to the divine life. The notion of God as changeless, static substance is inconsistent with both the biblical witness and the dynamic movement of the empirical world.

It is therefore not surprising that many eminent religious thinkers of the twentieth century have rejected the divine immutability of classical theism and asserted God's real involvement in time and history.[67] Hartshorne applauds earlier thinkers like Socinus, Gustav Theodor Fechner, and Jules Lequier for their costly willingness to oppose tradition in declaring that the eternity and worshipful perfection of God do not require his changelessness. "Thus God is not pure being, there is a divine form of becoming." To assert that "God exists eternally means that he could not *not* exist; it does not mean that he exists always in the same state, incapable of additional values."[68] Schubert M. Ogden aligns himself with Whitehead's view that "the ultimate metaphysical reality is not timeless and unrelated being, but the temporal and social process known to us in our own existence."[69] Metaphysical personalists like Brightman and Bertocci uphold an equally temporalist view of God.[70] Thomas W. Ogletree has good grounds for maintaining that such conceptions are more compatible with concrete religious experience than those which conceive God wholly as absolute, timeless, unchanging Being.[71] As Leslie Dewart puts it, God is not a Greek *theos*

[67] E. g., Nicolas Berdyaev, Henri Bergson, Hastings Rashdall, James Ward, Samuel Alexander, A. N. Whitehead, John E. Boodin, William Ernest Hocking, Edgar S. Brightman, William P. Montague, Pierre Teilhard de Chardin, Charles Hartshorne.

[68] *A Natural Theology for Our Time*, p. vii; "Process Philosophy as a Resource for Christian Thought," *Philosophical Resources for Christian Thought*, ed. Perry LeFevre (Nashville: Abingdon Press, 1968), pp. 64 f.

[69] "The Christian Proclamation of God to Men of the So-called 'Atheistic Age,'" *Is God Dead?* (*Concilium*, Vol. 16), p. 50.

[70] Brightman, *Person and Reality*, pp. 323-31; Peter A. Bertocci, *Introduction to the Philosophy of Religion* (Englewood Cliffs, N. J.: Prentice-Hall, 1951), pp. 309-15, 445-47.

[71] "A Christological Assessment of Dipolar Theism," *Journal of Religion*, 47 (1967), 92.

who from his heavenly abode beyond history makes occasional forays into time. In Christian experience,

> God does not dip his finger into history; he totally immerses himself in it. When he visits the world he does not come slumming. He comes to stay. He arrives most concretely and decisively of all in the person of the Word in order to make earth and history his home, his permanent residence.[72]

Thus we are led to affirm both the eternity and the temporality of God, and without any basic contradiction. The God who works in the temporal, changing processes of nature and history is he who has no beginning or end, who endures and remains himself through all change, who provides the uniform structure of reality which men find rather than make, and who can always be depended on to act according to the unchanging wisdom, love, and righteous purpose which are integral to his life. He not only embraces time but transcends and fulfills it. But the converse is equally true. He whose abiding Presence provides unity, continuity, and stability in human existence is also the Pilgrim, Pioneer, and Explorer who is continually *en route,* working in the ever-changing temporal order to achieve his ends. Human existence itself offers at least a hint of the synthesis suggested. The finite person experiences succession, but is not bound to the passing moment; he endures as a unified self through all his changing activities. In broadly similar fashion we may think of God as combining permanence and change, being and becoming, stability and dynamism, eternity and time.

7. *Christian thought should maintain the conception of God as Creator, with emphasis on his continuing creative activity, and recognition of human responsibility to share in creation.* Creativity is presupposed in what we have already said regarding the immanence of the world in God and the

[72] *The Future of Belief,* p. 194.

eschatological and temporal character of the divine action. However, further clarification is needed. On the one hand, theology cannot be content with an atheistic orientation toward the future which, however hopeful, takes existence for granted and ignores the question of creation. On the other, it must avoid the concentration on a finished past creation which has marked traditional theistic doctrines.

Jews and Christians have always worshiped God as the sovereign Lord and hence Creator of all things. Thus the psalmist exclaims:

> O Lord, how manifold are thy works!
> In wisdom hast thou made them all;
> the earth is full of thy creatures. (Ps. 104:24.)

"Thou didst create all things," declares the author of the book of Revelation, "and by thy will they existed and were created" (Rev. 4:11). The same faith is expressed in the Apostles' Creed when "God, the Father Almighty" is identified as "the Maker of heaven and earth." At an early date the church found itself confronted by various dualistic views, particularly the Gnostic conception of matter as evil or as the work of a subordinate but competing power. It was therefore forced to think through and formulate what it meant by creation. This it did by way of the concept of *creatio ex nihilo* (creation from nothing), which though not a biblical term was felt to conserve the biblical truth. As Langdon Gilkey points out, this formula served negatively to deny the three specific implications of dualism: preexistent matter, the restriction of God by an antithetical principle or principles with power equal to his, and the necessity of evil. Positively, the doctrine asserted two significant truths, both of which were implied in faith in God as sovereign Lord of all things: (a) existence has its source in God alone, and (b) it is essentially good and, though distorted by man's misuse of freedom, capable of being redeemed by God's transforming power.[73]

Though much of the basic meaning of the ancient formula remains relevant today, it is hardly an adequate interpretation of creation for the twentieth century. God's creativity relates to present and future as well as past time, hence is manifest in sustaining and directing as well as originating creation. But until the mid-nineteenth century it was conceived overwhelmingly if not wholly as God's origination of the world. God was declared to be the initiator of both human life and the physical order which provides its setting. Nature and man were conceived as springing full-blown and complete from the hand of God at the beginning of time, much as a finely carved cuckoo clock emerges from an artisan's shop in the Black Forest. But evolutionary science has produced a radical change. We now take for granted that the world has been coming into being through eons of time. Furthermore, it is not a finished, closed system of cause and effect, but still in process. It exhibits regularity and uniformity, but also dynamic movement, flexibility, and openness to novelty. Hence creation is best understood as continuous and continuing, and it includes origination of the genuinely new, preservation of the old, and action toward later fulfillment. Christian faith affirms that God is creatively active in every moment of time.

Such a view is amply supported by the Bible. Indeed, the biblical account of creation in Genesis should be seen not as an explanation of the origin of the world, but as an extension of the belief in the sovereignty of God which had already reached expression in faith in his abiding covenant with Israel and in his providential direction of his people. He is consistently portrayed as at work throughout the history of Israel; and in some of the prophets—most emphatically in Second Isaiah—and in the New Testament his activity in

[73] *Maker of Heaven and Earth* (Garden City, N. Y.: Doubleday & Co., Anchor Books, [1959] 1965), pp. 49-51.

history is broadened to include all mankind. A recurring theme of the Psalms is God's continuing creative action in the forces of nature and in plant and animal life: "When thou sendest forth thy Spirit, they are created" (Ps. 104:30; cf. Ps. 147:8-19; Job 34:14-15). The Statement of Faith of the United Church of Christ shares this understanding when it uses the present tense to describe the deeds of God as Creator: "We believe in God. . . . He calls the worlds into being, creates man in his own image, and sets before him the ways of life and death."

Essentially, the doctrine of creation has to do with the basic relation of the finite world to God as its source and ground. In dramatic, mythical, analogical language, faith declares that all finite reality depends ultimately for its existence on the divine will. However or whenever it may have originated, it is rooted in the power and love of God. Yet we miss the deepest meaning of creation if we do not interpret it in terms of our own relation to God. This is a further reason why any view is inadequate which locates it in a remote past, which does not directly involve us. The God affirmed to be the transcendent ground of all existence is encountered as the deepest dimension of my own present existence. Langdon Gilkey writes perceptively:

It is only when we can say "Lord" to our Creator that we really understand Him as the Maker of heaven and earth. And it is only when in our own existence we can affirm the meaning of our life in obedience and commitment to Him that we understand what is to be created by God.[74]

Implicit in everything I have said about creation, but now needing to be stressed, is faith in the freedom and goodness of the Creator. He does not act out of external compulsion, but in the freedom of his gracious, righteous purpose. In Genesis (1:10, 12, 18, 21, 25, 31) the Lord pronounces his

[74] *Maker of Heaven and Earth,* p. 349.

work good. When the author of the Fourth Gospel declares that "all things were made through" the Word (John 1:1-3), he roots creation in the love which is disclosed in Jesus Christ. Christians affirm that the God whom they know in Christ as self-giving, reconciling, transforming love is the same as he who has acted in love to give them life, with its opportunity for freely chosen sonship to him and fellowship with one another. Creation and redemption proceed from the same source, the agape of God.

The faith that God in creating men calls them to sonship suggests another aspect of the Christian doctrine of creation which is often overlooked—God's gift to men of the capacity to create and his expectation that they will realize it. The human responsibility which we have previously affirmed as real includes responsibility to share in the creative activity of God. Berdyaev laments the fact that the Christian call to the service of God typically concentrates on the moral commandments (mainly negative), and pays little attention to the summons to artistic and scientific creation.[75] We do not have to depreciate the avoidance of stealing and killing to recognize the religious vocation of every man, as his talents permit, to bring positive values to birth in all possible areas of human life. Berdyaev rightly underscores the imperative: Create, and encourage creativity in others!

Obviously we must create humbly, with no pretense of rivaling God, and clearly perceiving our finite limitations of time, space, and capacity. Human creation is radically different from divine. Yet by God's gift we are called to be fellow workers for him (I Cor. 3:9), lesser creative agents joining freely with their Creator in new realizations of truth, beauty, and goodness. Within limits, therefore, it is not inaccurate to speak of God's dependence on us for creation. By creating a

[75] Nicolas Berdyaev, *The Meaning of the Creative Act,* tr. Donald A. Lowrie (New York: Harper & Brothers, 1954), pp. 160-79, 246-49, 252, 335-37; cf. Hartshorne, *Philosophical Resources for Christian Thought,* ed. Perry LeFevre, pp. 59-61.

world which includes creatures with a real measure of freedom, God makes himself partly dependent on their free decisions. Every new poem or painting, every invention or scientific discovery, every deed of self-forgetful love, every enactment of justice or wisdom in human social relations brings into reality something which apart from human creativity would have remained nonexistent. God's dependence on us does not even remotely approach our dependence on him. Nevertheless, it is real, and Christian faith in God as Creator carries with it a glad and serious acceptance of our responsibility to place our own creative efforts at the disposal of his supremely creative activity.

8. *God should be thought of as participating in the pathos and tragedy of existence, nevertheless keeping men in his invincible love and through suffering fulfilling his ends.* The question of human suffering becomes urgent in the light of the claim just made that the universe is the work of a good Creator. If creation expresses a loving purpose, ask many sensitive minds, why does it contain so many factors which thwart and destroy human good? As we have already observed, the stark reality of seemingly undeserved suffering is the weightiest of all arguments for atheism. It is therefore imperative that we face head-on the implications of the evils of life for faith in God.

On this issue I find myself both agreeing and disagreeing with the atheist. Like him, I have grave difficulty with the traditional view which regards God as the all-powerful, all-knowing, and infinitely good Ruler of nature and history who ordains all for the best; and who wills or permits evils in order to discipline men, to punish them for their sins, or to achieve other purposes which remain obscure to them.

Unavoidable starvation has been for centuries a grim reality in many parts of the world. Each year innumerable persons suffer and die in consequence of natural catastrophes which they are powerless to prevent or avoid: flood, drought, earthquake, tidal wave, or hurricane. Our response as Christians to such events is ambiguous, to say the least. With Isaac Watts we praise God as "our shelter from the stormy blast," no doubt speaking figuratively, but forgetting that if God is Creator he himself is in some way causally related to the literal stormy blasts in the physical order. Reflect on this prayer in *The Book of Common Prayer*:

Almighty and most merciful Father, we humbly beseech thee of thy great goodness, to restrain those immoderate rains wherewith thou hast afflicted us. And we pray thee to send us such seasonable weather, that the earth may, in due time, yield her increase for our use and benefit, through Jesus Christ our Lord.

I must confess that I find much more defensible the question of the child described as asking in a letter to God: "Dear God, why did you make the river too small to hold all the water, so that our house got flooded and we had to move?"

Other evils involving no discernible human responsibility are familiar to all sensitive persons. I recall, for example, the girl whom I saw during a pastoral call as she was sitting on the floor playing with dolls, and who I later learned was thirty years of age, a Mongoloid. I think of a dear friend of mine, a gifted and talented minister in Baltimore, who died at the height of his powers after a six-months' illness with cancer, leaving a widow and three school-age children. And I vividly remember my grand-nephew, who died of leukemia at the age of twelve, after a valiant and painful battle of two and a half years, with all the resources of the National Institute of Health at his disposal. I cannot regard the human suffering involved in events like these as ordered by an all-powerful God according to his righteous will.

There are other evils in which human agency plays a significant part, large or small: the drowning of two small children in Lake Sunapee, New Hampshire, in 1967, when the family car in which they were playing rolled down a driveway into eighteen feet of water; the defenselessness of a Kennedy or a Martin Luther King before the assassin's bullet; the harsh social realities which contribute so powerfully to the production of the warped personality of the murderer; the mass slaughter of our century, typified in its main forms by three cities: Auschwitz, Stalingrad, and Hiroshima; the agony of hundreds of thousands of helpless, uncomprehending civilians in Vietnam.

We may attribute such events primarily to the careless or willful misuse of freedom on the part of men who without freedom would be puppets rather than men, but we cannot view them as willed by an all-loving God. Yet the idea persists that even such tragic negativities are somehow involved, as punishment, discipline, or in some other unknown fashion, in God's sovereignty over his world. One woman, interviewed on a Boston street by a radio reporter following the murder of Robert Kennedy, commented, "It must have been intended by God, or it wouldn't have happened." Within the past two years I have heard or read several statements by professing Christians who quite seriously attribute the sufferings of the Jews through the centuries, and down to the recent past, to God's judgment on Israel for her failure to accept Jesus as the Messiah. Moreover, in one of the best recent books on the problem of evil, John Hick joins many earlier theologians in regarding human pain as contributory to the primary purpose for which the world exists, that of "soul-making." [76] But souls are unmade as well as made by suffering. Adversity does not seem to be distributed according to need. Some individuals might really become greater persons if they faced more obstacles, while others confront far more hardship than they can bear, and are crushed by it. We may sing with Joachim Neander,

[76] *Evil and the Love of God* (New York: Harper & Row, 1966), p. 295.

> Hast thou not seen
> How thy desires e'er have been
> Granted in what he ordaineth?

But if we look without blinders at the facts and report honestly what we see, are we not often compelled to answer No? Many of the most laudable and unselfish desires of high-minded people are not granted, and if what occurs instead is alleged to be ordained by God, many of us will join the atheist in declaring, "That God does not exist."

Yet at this very point I also profoundly *disagree* with the atheist. To reject an untenable conception of God is not the same as rejecting God, who may be differently understood. The dark reality of human suffering does require, it seems to me, a revision of traditional theistic absolutism, but this may open the way to a more positive faith. Atheism, in the very process of facing one problem, overlooks others or deals with them inadequately. For example, in disposing of the problem of evil by denying deity it exposes itself to the problem of good in a godless universe. How reconcile with a blind, indifferent, irrational, meaningless cosmos the patent reality in human existence of the pursuit and discovery of truth, the creation and appreciation of beauty, and the power of self-sacrificial love? Moreover, atheists rarely take with full seriousness the light shed on the causation of human suffering by such factors as (a) men's need for a dependable structure of natural law, which a good God will not set aside even though hardship may ensue when orderly processes are violated; (b) the interdependence or social solidarity of men, as a result of which we suffer from the cruelty of others but also benefit immeasurably from the constructive contributions of our fellows; or (c) the implications of even limited human freedom, which is necessary if men are to be truly persons, but which may be carelessly or maliciously misused and thus inflict extreme harm on others as well as ourselves.

On the issue of freedom atheists are particularly vulnerable. As we have noted several times, most varieties of atheism are basically humanistic, rejecting God in order to make room for man. The existence of an extra-human or super-human ground of value, it is held, would destroy the autonomy, freedom, and responsibility of men. Yet the same people who argue in this way also repudiate belief in God because he does not intervene to rescue the victims of human villainy, even though such intervention would inevitably cancel human freedom. The atheist cannot have it both ways. He cannot consistently indict God for both obstructing and upholding human freedom!

If we then reject atheism as well as traditional absolutistic theism, what alternative remains? Two considerations are worthy of special attention. First, we need to take with full seriousness the suggestion already made that the freedom needed for the development of real persons entails the risk of suffering. "History is so free," writes Leslie Dewart, "that we can actually crucify God; we can actually deny Him; we can, in a way, make Him not to exist." [77] Auschwitz does thwart the immediate purpose of God for the victims of its barbarism; it also for many of us kills the belief in an absolute sovereign who wills all that occurs. But it does not exclude faith in a God who seeks to accomplish his will by persuasion and love rather than by coercion.

In a recent article Ninian Smart offers a cogent rebuttal of the claim of Antony Flew and J. L. Mackie[78] that an omnipotent God could have created men wholly good, incapable of sinning. Smart points out that the term *goodness* is applied to beings of a certain kind, who are liable to temptation and fear, capable of courage and cowardice, self-assertion and regard for others, and the like. Such concepts would have no

[77] *Initiative in History*, p. 14.
[78] Antony Flew, "Divine Omnipotence and Human Freedom," Flew and MacIntyre (eds.), *New Essays in Philosophical Theology*, 144-69; J. L. Mackie, "Evil and Omnipotence," *Mind*, 64 (1955), 200-212.

clear application if men were created entirely good. Thus if men "were to be immunized to evil they would have to be built in a different way." Then, however, the ascription of goodness to them would be unintelligible, for *good* and *bad* are characteristics connected with human nature as empirically known. Men could not be called good in a situation where it was not possible for them to be bad.[79]

The biologist L. Charles Birch joins Whitehead and Hartshorne in suggesting that a kind of freedom may extend also to subhuman and even suborganic entities.[80] At first sight this may seem to be a far-fetched notion in view of the general scientific assumption of the reign of inviolable law in nature. However, the mechanistic, deterministic view of nature has been undermined by Werner Heisenberg's Uncertainty Principle, which shows that scientific laws have a statistical character which does not allow the prediction of individual events. Biologists like A. Bachem point out the possibility that at critical neural junctions a very small number of atoms might initiate a change in pulse-conduction patterns. Likewise, one cosmic-ray particle can alone bring about an unforeseeable gene mutation and thereby, during the process of growth, produce large-scale changes in an organism.[81] In view of data like these, Birch is right in suggesting that in physical nature, within the structure of universal law, "a partly chaotic, indetermined and random element may be unavoidable." [82] This element may be directly operative in some of the events which have adverse effects on human life. Can we assert with confidence that a world which excluded this kind of dangerous indeterminacy would be better for human well-being than

[79] Smart, "Omnipotence, Evil and Supermen," *Philosophy*, 36 (1961), 188-95.
[80] Birch, "Creation and the Creator," *Science and Religion*, ed. Ian G. Barbour, pp. 204 f.
[81] Bachem, "Heisenberg's Indeterminacy Principle and Life," *Philosophy of Science*, 19 (1952), 261. See Ian Barbour, *Issues in Science and Religion*, pp. 78, 303 f., 308 f., 455.
[82] "Creation and the Creator," p. 205.

the world we actually have? Does it not appear also that in such an order God himself is affected and qualified by the undetermined actions and free choices of his creatures? To some degree contingency is then a reality for God as well as for man.

We live in a world in which innumerable creatures, subhuman as well as human, are constantly affecting one another. Not all the effects of this interaction are beneficial, since the agents are imperfect in or devoid of knowledge, wisdom, and goodness. But we cannot enjoy the values of such an order without also being exposed to its risks. Possibly the only way in which God could remove suffering would be to eliminate perilous freedom. However, this would impair rather than enrich the value of human life.

Seldom if ever has this truth been stated so forcefully as in the following passage by Charles Hartshorne:

The creaturely freedom from which evils spring, with probability in particular cases and inevitability in the general case, is also an essential aspect of all goods, so that the price of a guaranteed absence of evil would be the equally guaranteed absence of good. Thus not even the nastiest or most conceivably unhelpful evil could have anything to do with the nonexistence of God. Risk of evil and opportunity for good are two aspects of just one thing, multiple freedom; and that one thing is also the ground of all meaning and all existence. This is the sole, but sufficient, reason for evil as such and in general, while as for particular evils, by definition they have no ultimate reason. They are nonrational.[83]

Closely related to the reality of multiple freedom, and partially illuminated by it, is a second consideration which involves a modification of traditional absolutistic theism. Both the Christian gospel and human experience suggest that there is something in the depths of reality—in God himself—which

[83] *A Natural Theology for Our Time*, p. 81; cf. Hartshorne and Reese (eds.), *Philosophers Speak of God*, p. 284.

entails suffering for him as well as his creatures. Christian faith has always pointed to the cross as the highest and truest symbol of God's redemptive love. May it not be equally the profoundest representation of his creative activity? L. Charles Birch finds that evolutionary studies reveal a "cross pattern deeply woven into the very fabric of creation." For example, in reproduction harmful mutations not only occur but are preserved in the genetic makeup of the organism. The accumulation of genetically hurtful genes on the human level may produce congenital idiots. Such "accidents" and misfits "seem to be an inevitable part of . . . the cost of creation." [84] If so, the Creator at the heart of the process shares deeply in its pain. In the words of Whitehead, "God is the great companion—the fellow-sufferer who understands." [85]

The suggestion that God himself suffers in his creative work might be dismissed as a new form of the ancient patripassian heresy. But this will not do. The error of Sabellius lay in his confusion of the distinctive ministries or activities of Father and Son within the Trinity, not in his relating suffering to God. However, his opponents also erred in exaggerating the distinction to the point of denying that God as Father could suffer. As Albert Outler has indicated, it is christological heresy to interpret the suffering and death of Christ as purely human events which did not affect God the Father.[86] Only indefensible notions of immutability and impassibility carried over from an outmoded substance theology are threatened by the affirmation that the cross connotes something eternal in the nature of God himself. For Christian faith God is not a calm, detached spectator of our human trials, but himself a participant in the struggle, pain, and anguish of existence. "Up to the present," declares the apostle Paul, "the whole created universe groans in all its parts as if in the pangs of

---

[84] "Creation and the Creator," p. 214.
[85] *Process and Reality*, pp. 532 f.
[86] *Who Trusts in God*, pp. 96 f.

childbirth" (Rom. 8:22 NEB). The same conclusion was reached by Sebastian Franck in the sixteenth century. "God is not wholly other," he writes, "but he who groans unutterably at the heart of creation." The creation of a world in love is costly for both God and man.

In spite of all our pious talk about the Suffering Servant and the crucifixion on Calvary, and despite our fine hymns addressed to "the sacred Head, now wounded," have we not tended to sentimentalize the divine love and gloss over the harsh reality of its agony? The green hill remains very far away, well beyond the wall of our city, and not really a contemporary event which involves us. Herbert H. Farmer tells of preaching once on the love of God in a congregation which included an elderly Polish Jew who had become a Christian. Afterward the old man said to the preacher, "You have no right to speak of the love of God until you have seen, as I have seen, a massacre of Jews in Poland—until you have seen, as I have seen, the blood of your dearest friends running in the gutters on a gray winter morning." When asked how, having seen such a massacre, he had come to believe in the love of God, he replied that the gospel spoke convincingly to him because it called on him to see God just where he was—where he would always be in vivid memory—in those blood-stained streets on a cold gray morning. When it spoke of the blood and agony of Golgotha, it was grappling with the facts of human existence as he himself had known them. He said: "As I looked at that man upon the cross, . . . I knew I must make up my mind once and for all, and either take my stand beside him and share in his undefeated faith in God . . . or else fall finally into a bottomless pit of bitterness, hatred, and unutterable despair." [87]

When we seek to think through the meaning of God, we must try to see as clearly as does the gospel itself his involve-

---

[87] Herbert H. Farmer, *God and Men* (Nashville: Abingdon Press, Apex ed. [1947]), pp. 190 f.

ment in the travail of our world. In a perceptive interpretation of both the incarnation and the crucifixion, Albert Camus has written, "For God to be a man, he must despair." [88] Though Camus himself could never believe in such a God, he voiced a truth which believers may affirm. If God would be involved in human life and history, he must suffer. Conceivably he might have chosen not to create a world, but if he is to achieve the values of such creation he must experience the risks and negativities of a stable, interdependent order which summons men to responsible freedom in sonship to him. Why this is so we cannot fully know. Perhaps it is enough simply to see ourselves as here confronted with something ultimate, whether or not we can conceptualize it to our satisfaction. My own thinking in this respect has been influenced by the profound thought of my beloved teacher Edgar S. Brightman. I do not find necessary, or within my competence, the formulation of a detailed theory of the divine structure, like that of Brightman's Given. But I am led by the same factors which produced his conception to affirm that God, in his own deepest being, experiences and shares the hurt and sorrow of the world which he is constantly calling into existence.

However, it is precisely in and through suffering that God fulfills his purposes. The cross is followed by the resurrection, Calvary by Easter. "Death is swallowed up in victory" (I Cor. 15:54; Isa. 25:8). God is not a tragic hero who wins our admiration and pity as he goes down to courageous, glorious defeat. He is not helpless before evil. He is the Lord of all being, and the power by which his rule is maintained reaches its apex in the suffering, self-giving love which takes to itself the pain of the world and thereby heals and transforms it.

The potency of evil can be overestimated as well as underrated. Samuel H. Miller, after pointing out that nature is redeemed by the cross, adds:

[88] *The Rebel*, p. 32.

There is no redemption except by the cross. No poem is written, no picture painted, no music made, no sinner forgiven, no child born, no man loved, no truth known, no stone shaped, no peace attained, except grace took a risk, bore a burden, absorbed the evil, and suffered the pain.[89]

But grace does redeem! Poems are written, pictures painted, stones shaped, music made, sinners forgiven, children born, men and women loved; truth is being known and peace attained. In countless experiences like these persons are finding joy in the fulfillment of hopes and the attainment of cherished goals. This, too, reflects the nature of our world and the creative, life-giving and renewing activity of God.

Countless persons, moreover, have learned what it is to be kept in the love of God. Amid danger and death in Burma in World War II, Paul Geren wrote of parting from acquaintances, knowing well that death might be just ahead for any of them, with the words, "God keep you." By this he meant, as he himself interprets it,

that God will keep us from the ultimate evil. That ultimate evil is not death. If I were hit by a bomb or a shell, I as I died and they who love me must not think of it as God's failure to keep me. To be kept by God means to be in his love whether living or dying, being hit or escaping. "Neither death, nor life . . . shall be able to separate us from the love of God." The ultimate evil would be the absence of love. A life outside it would be more evil than a death in it. While we may not be delivered from evils, if God keeps us we shall be delivered from Evil.[90]

The apostle Paul voices normative Christian faith when he declares, "In *everything* God works for good with those who love him" (Rom. 8:28). This is far from the claim that everything turns out for the best. It does mean, however, that God constantly strives through persons of good will to fulfill his

[89] *The Dilemma of Modern Belief*, p. 58.
[90] *Burma Diary* (New York: Harper & Brothers, 1943), pp. 30 f.

righteous ends; and that even evil deeds, as the psalmist says, may in unexpected ways contribute to those ends. Note also that God works *with* those who love him. They too have a responsibility. What that responsibility is may be inferred in part from one of Paul Geren's sentences: "The ultimate evil would be the absence of love." No one is really outside the love of God, but many remain tragically unaware of it because they see no sign of it in the human beings who most powerfully affect their lives. For them therefore the absence of love is a numbing reality. Thus we are reminded again of the pathos of life and of the extremity of the evil which many men must endure. However we interpret suffering, we who believe in God are called to work with him in reducing and eradicating it.

Frederick Herzog has suggested that the goodness of God may be "an eschatological goodness," which can become fully manifest only in the future.[91] "We do not yet see everything in subjection to him" (Heb. 2:8). But we have the promise of his coming Kingdom, and we know he is on the way. This assurance, however, is not only the ground of our hope, but an imperative to participate in an unfinished struggle.

---

[91] "God, Evil, and Revolution," a paper read before the American Theological Society, April 21, 1968.

V. Findings

In the context of the atheistic critique of theistic belief, we have explored in Chapter IV a number of proposals designed to make the reality of God more intelligible. These suggestions seek to modify traditional conceptions of God by removing weaknesses and errors, to bring to light truths which sometimes have been obscured, and to elucidate certain emphases especially needed today. However, something more is needed if we are to profit most from listening to the critics. The eight propositions offered are all interconnected, but they still do not add up of themselves to a unified conception of God. A neat definition, even if attained, would have little or no value in itself, but the effort to see the various suggestions as a whole and to ask what kind of total view they point to should deepen our understanding of God and also facilitate our practical relationship with him. This chapter will therefore attempt to bring the whole investigation to a focus. In the light of both criticisms and positive proposals, what do we really mean by God?

A constructive answer to this question is most likely to be attained if we keep within guidelines like the following: (1) The view arrived at should embody the truths disclosed by the atheistic criticisms. (2) It should be true to the basic meanings and intentions of historic Christian faith. (3) It should interpret illuminatingly the data of experience—what we actually find there rather than what we are supposed to find—in the natural order, history, and present-day existence. (4) For the sake of understanding and relevance, it should utilize thought forms familiar to contemporary man.

It is not difficult to describe what is ordinarily meant by God in broad, more or less formal terms. Philosophically, the term customarily refers to the self-dependent reality thought to impart intelligibility to the totality of things. Religiously, it denotes the reality regarded as the ground and fulfillment of our existence, and particularly as our ultimate answer to the threats of finitude, anxiety, guilt, and meaninglessness. However, when the effort is made to characterize the divine reality more concretely, knotty problems arise, and the resulting conceptions differ widely. As finite minds attempting to deal with ultimates, we cannot avoid using symbols and analogies drawn from thought concerning more limited aspects of our experience, as well as terms employed in the philosophical quest for truth. In the process we need to recognize that our best thought-models are constantly subject to correction and combination, and that God far transcends our best human ideas of him.

Any serious theological inquiry into the meaning of God inevitably overlaps on metaphysical investigation of the nature of the real. (Even the philosophy which renounces the metaphysical quest or the theology which interprets faith purely in secular terms is a form of metaphysics, making its own judgments about what reality is.) It is therefore not surprising that theologians have often related their work quite self-consciously to philosophical inquiry, or that they have sometimes formed alliances with metaphysical systems or supposedly anti-metaphysical philosophies regarded as especially well adapted to the expression of religious truth. For example, at various periods Platonism, Aristotelianism, Hegelianism, personal idealism, naturalism, and existentialism have provided conceptualities for Christian thinkers concerned to clarify the meaning of God and his relation to men. Today a considerable number of theologians are finding in the process philosophy of A. N. Whitehead a peculiarly valuable medium for the interpretation of Christian affirmations in a scientific era.

Much depends on the kind of use that is made of such philosophical categories. A theology of revelation which regards its truth claims as closed to examination according to the ordinary canons of critical reason cuts itself off from effective communication with multitudes of serious inquirers. The opposite danger confronts the theology which accepts as its determinative means of expression a thought system arrived at without reference to any Christian faith commitment. The theologian who embraces any metaphysical system as complete or definitive runs the risk of blurring the distinctiveness of the Christian message, erecting barriers between himself and thinkers who hold other philosophies, and identifying the gospel with a relatively temporary formulation of it. Such dangers are largely avoided if one adopts a procedure somewhat like that of Ian Barbour. "Our endeavors," he writes, "must be tentative, exploratory, and open, allowing a measure of pluralism in recognition of the variety of experience. Christianity cannot be identified with any particular metaphysical system." But we may and should "employ metaphysical categories *within* the expression of the Christian message."[1] Thus Barbour opposes starting with process philosophy as a unified and religiously neutral body of truth and formulating Christian belief in accord with it. Instead, he seeks to adapt some of the major ideas of process thought to the task of interpreting the Christian faith in our contemporary world. Philosophical categories may help to bring wholeness into diversified human experience and contribute to an intelligible and unified view of the world process, which is necessary if religious beliefs are to be credible for many persons today.

A Christian conception of God should be basically an interpretation of the meaning of God as disclosed to and experienced by the Christian community in interaction with the rest of mankind. Philosophical ideas may aid greatly in the attainment of Christian understanding, but no one con-

[1] *Issues in Science and Religion,* pp. 460 f.

cept borrowed from a particular philosophical system should play the determining role. In the nature of the case, should we expect to be able to compress the meaning of God into any one conceptual model? A reality so rich and many-faceted as the ground of all existence and meaning cannot be fully understood even when all our conceptual resources are exhausted, much less when we limit our intellectual instruments. Our best hope is to utilize a number of symbols which, taken together, may genuinely advance our understanding. In the present situation there are four concepts which seem to merit special consideration as we seek to clarify the meaning of the divine reality: being, process, love, and personality.

1. GOD AS BEING

Much atheism in our time has been a rebellion against belief in God understood as a timeless Absolute, an immutable, impassive First Cause, a personal Supreme Being whose arbitrary rule stifles free and responsible human action. Many Christian thinkers today are also dissatisfied with the prominence assigned to terms like being and substance in classical Christian expositions of the divine nature. Such terms, it is held, have no clear, specific, definable meaning. Moreover, to conceive God in terms of being risks reducing him to the status of one being among many; it tends so to stress the changeless and timeless that it makes God a static Absolute who exists in solitary splendor unrelated to the living flow of events in either nature or history; and it threatens real human freedom.

Leslie Dewart's criticism of traditional Thomism represents an extreme form of these objections. In Dewart's view the presence of human initiative in history is inconsistent with belief, such as that found in Greek philosophy, in an abiding structure in reality which is intelligible to man. Such a structure would involve a fixed state, determining events in advance. But this would rule out any real human responsibility in history, as does Greek teleology. If man is to be free there can be no predetermined pattern. "Being is not given intelligibility by God; it is given intelligibility by man." With respect to knowledge it is in itself neither intelligible nor absurd, but neutral:

There is no such original reality that man must simply respect. Man's creativity reaches up to the very intelligibility of reality. . . . We do not respectfully recognize the law of gravitation: we invent it. . . . We do not invent the facts of gravitation. It's the facts that have to be respected.[2]

The central concern of the current objections to conceiving deity as being is sound. The notion of God as a fixed, static, external Determiner of Destiny should be repudiated. But it is by no means clear why this rejection must carry with it the denial of any enduring structure in reality, or why such a structure necessarily rules out all human freedom and responsibility. Dewart's alternation between ontological and epistemological language is confusing. He is certainly right in treating the law of gravitation as a human formulation, and in distinguishing it from the facts on which it is based. But are not these facts, which he asserts we must respect, actually a part of the "original reality" to which he would deny respect? Man does create the rational descriptions by which the functioning of reality becomes intelligible to him, but he does not impart to reality the character which makes it intelligible. This is a given which he finds and seeks to understand. But it is what it is. In short, it can be truly said to *be*. Its "isness" must be recognized. There is therefore truth as well as humor in the comment of Frederick Ferré during the 1968 meeting of the American Theological Society: "Don't give up being

[2] *Initiatives in History*, pp. 9-12.

too quickly because people throw lances at you. After all, what else *is* there?"

If Christian theology is to speak of God as acting and entering into relations with men, it must also talk of him as be-ing. Some notion of being is indispensable, indeed basic, in serious discussion of the meaning of the divine reality, though it is far from sufficient. There is, however, no good reason why it must be conceived as static or unchanging. This traditional error is avoided, for example, by John Macquarrie, when he defines being as the *is-hood* in virtue of which one can say that anything is, the prior "condition that there may be any beings or properties of beings." The essence of being is "the dynamic 'letting-be' . . . of the beings." Being lets things be; it enables to be, empowers to be, or brings into being. Thus "being 'is' present-and-manifest in every being." [3] Macquarrie identifies being thus conceived with God, adding, however, the crucial qualification that God is "holy being." Whether or not one accepts this existentialist view of being as adequate, it not only clarifies the term but also makes plain that being need be no more static than the particular beings which it "lets be."

In any event, being can and must be construed in such a way as to provide for becoming, action, and novelty. It can be broadly understood as the power to act—in infinitely varied ways—which sustains itself through time. If God is thought of in these terms, then his being becomes the enduring, dependable, but dynamically functioning ground or matrix of the activity of all created beings. An abiding structure so conceived would make possible rather than exclude the exercise of a large measure of freedom on the part of men. In this connection there is virtue in the suggestion of Arthur Gibson that "participial being" be substituted for supreme

[3] *Principles of Christian Theology* (New York: Charles Scribner's Sons, 1966), pp. 100, 103, 99, 109, 105.

being substantively conceived.[4] If being is related to the verb *to be* as walking, eating, and working are related to their respective infinitives, then God is seen as the richly diversified creative life on which depend, without being inhibited, the existence, meaning, and creative possibilities of finite creatures. But the ground of being must himself be, and his being implies essence as well as existence, a *what* as well as a *that*.

In view of the distinction between existence and essence here mentioned, we say more about God, and we say it more accurately, if we speak of his being or reality than if we talk about his existence. To ascribe existence to anything is to make the abstract assertion *that* it is, while saying nothing as to *what* it is. Further, as John E. Smith has shown, since "to exist" ordinarily means to be part of a system reacting with similar things in a total environment, to state that God exists tends to treat him as a finite constituent of a system "instead of the ground and goal of all systems." But God is not in the same category as the ordinary objects of sense experience. In the case of finite beings existence and essence are disrupted; they might or might not exist. However, in God there is no intelligible distinction between the two, so that it is misleading to separate existence from God and make it a special object of discussion or demonstration.[5] This does not, of course, beg the question of whether God is real, but simply calls on us to use language appropriate to the discussion. One error of atheism has been its tendency to conceive God as a thing in the world of things, one entity among other entities. No doubt Christians have been partly responsible for this misunderstanding. Hence in all consideration of the being of God we must make plain that what is meant is not his bare

---

[4] "Dewart's Reconceptualization of Catholic Belief in God," *The Future of Belief Debate*, ed. Gregory Baum (New York: Herder and Herder, 1967), p. 154.

[5] *Experience and God*, pp. 118 f. Smith acknowledges here his indebtedness to Charles Sanders Peirce and Paul Tillich.

thatness but the rich concreteness of his total reality, not his static "thereness" but his active, dynamic "isness."

2. GOD AS CREATIVE PROCESS

While affirming the being of God, or God as being, we have held that the divine reality must not be statically conceived. If theology is to offer an intelligent account of the vitality of nature and history, and if it is to communicate with thoughtful persons today, it must provide for movement, change, and creative novelty in its understanding of God. Being must not be so construed as to exclude becoming or advance toward the "not-yet" of the future.

In the forefront of those who are now emphasizing this truth are the process theologians, who in closely related ways advocate a "dipolar theism" stimulated by Whitehead. Taking their cue from Whitehead's distinction between primordial and consequent natures of God, these Christian thinkers regard God as both abstract and concrete, eternal and temporal, infinite and finite, supremely absolute and supremely relative. God is absolute in that he exists necessarily, depending for his existence—the fact *that* he exists—on nothing but himself. He is related to others, but this very relativity is wholly nonrelative, so that no finite being or action can make any difference as far as his existence is concerned.[6] His absoluteness also concerns "the generic and universal form of his relationships, abstracting from their specific or individual content." He has an innate, immutable essence or character, in virtue of which he acts unfailingly in all his relations according to his supreme excellence.[7] Yet such assertions are meaningless apart from a recognition that God is "the eminently relative One." His absoluteness is "simply the abstract struc-

---

[6] Ogden, *The Reality of God*, pp. 47 f. Ogden makes here a distinction between existence and actuality similar to that discussed above, p. 197.

[7] Hartshorne, *The Divine Relativity*, pp. 143, 11, 76, 88 f., 129; Ogden, *op. cit.*, p. 141.

ture or identifying principle of his eminent relativity." [8] His reality is thoroughly social and temporal, so that he is the recipient of, and intimately affected by, the achievements of finite beings.

Involved as he is in the ongoing life of the world, the God of dipolar theism is a God of unending creative becoming or self-creation, who is constantly bringing forth new realizations of value. "Life is process," declares Hartshorne, "divinity itself is process, nothing matters but the kinds of processes which occur or can be made to occur. . . . And all process brings new values into existence." [9] For Pittenger, likewise, God is no changeless essence; he is rather

a living, active, constantly creative, infinitely related, ceaselessly operative reality; the universe at its core is movement, dynamism, activity, and not sheer and unrelated abstraction. Whitehead's view, that the cosmos is "alive," is basic to the whole enterprise of process-thought; and this carries with it a conviction that the only reasonable explanation of the living cosmos is in fact "the living God." [10]

Process theology has contributed notably to the increasing recognition among Christians of both the mutual relatedness of God and the world and the importance of dynamic creativity in the divine life. These emphases are either explicit or implicit in most of the proposals made in Chapter IV. They are likewise strongly affirmed or assumed again and again in the biblical writings. The God proclaimed in the Old and the New Testament is a God who acts in nature and history to fulfill his creative and redemptive purposes. He is praised for his mighty deeds in the worship of both Israel and the

[8] Ogden, *op. cit.*, p. 65.
[9] Perry LeFevre (ed.), *Philosophical Resources for Christian Thought*, pp. 65 f.; cf. *Philosophers Speak of God*, Hartshorne and Reese (eds.), p. 6.
[10] "A Contemporary Trend in North American Theology: Process-Thought and Christian Faith," *Religion in Life*, 34 (1965), 502.

Christian community, with the latter gratefully acknowledging in particular the living embodiment of his forgiving, reconciling love in Jesus Christ and the life-giving, renewing, transforming action of his Holy Spirit throughout history. The God of the Bible and of authentic Christian faith is unmistakably the *living* God.

It is not clear, however, that the panentheism of process thought provides the best conceptuality for the expression of these truths. For example, serious questions arise regarding the role of finite persons in the creative advance. Process theologians stress the freedom and responsibility of men, regarding God himself as dependent on their contributions. Yet the genuineness of this freedom seems to be jeopardized by the way in which the relations between God and men are conceived. For Ogden, these relations are wholly internal. Man's action, he writes, "actually *is* God's action." Moreover, God's boundless love is "the one essential *cause* of each moment" and equally its "one essential effect." [11] What, then, does man really contribute to the effectiveness or the actuality of God?

The same problem appears in Hartshorne. He insists that God as supreme Being must be all-inclusive. He is independent of and distinguishable from all relative entities, yet "as an actual whole" he includes them. Here Hartshorne seems to mean not merely that God is related to or aware of all and affected by all, but that he literally contains all; more precisely, God is "a relative actuality of which there are constituents." Here he seeks to avoid the error of pantheism by treating the individual essence of God—what makes him God—as completely independent of the All, yet he holds nevertheless that deity is the All in the sense that there is nothing outside itself.[12] However, such an All can hardly avoid sharing the defects of its constituents, while at the same

[11] *The Reality of God,* pp. 181, 214.
[12] *The Divine Relativity,* pp. 76, 88 f.

time it threatens their full individuality, which Hartshorne is so concerned to preserve.

With respect to human beings, this judgment is supported by Hartshorne's view that values are permanent only as divine possessions. The world is constantly adding to the sum of realities and goods, but this ever-growing total of actualized values is ultimately enjoyed by God alone.

In the long run—so I believe—we are nothing, except as God inherits reality and value from our lives and actions. In ultimate perspective all life other than divine is purely contributory. We serve God is the last word, not, God serves us. And our reward? Our reward for serving God is simply that service itself. The essential reward of virtue . . . is intrinsic and present, not extrinsic and future. Eventual future gains are for God, not for creatures.[13]

These are noble sentiments. Hartshorne is right in holding that the realization of values and the service of God are inherently worthful, quite apart from the possibility of continued life for the individual after physical death. He is also sound in his rejection of the whole theology of rewards and punishments as motivation for the good life. But this does not justify his failure even to consider the possibility that the permanence of values may apply also to the individuals who actualize them. If finite beings are so important that they really make lasting contributions to God which he would otherwise lack, may they not be worthful enough to continue as constituents of the divine life? If not, the intrinsic value which Hartshorne elsewhere ascribes to them seems to be undermined. "Purely contributory" sounds like a synonym for "solely instrumental." Critically examined, Hartshorne's view of human individuals is hardly different in principle from that upheld by the Puritan Calvinism which demanded from men a willingness to be damned for the glory of God!

[13] *Philosophical Resources for Christian Thought*, ed. Perry LeFevre, pp. 52 f.; cf. pp. 48-51.

Moreover, if the finite beings who constitute God are constantly coming and going, what is really permanent even in God other than his purely abstract absolute pole? The never-ceasing flux of the world process threatens the real unity and self-identity of God himself.

Hartshorne lists three possibilities respecting the relation between God and the system of things: (1) the two are inseparable (pantheism); (2) God is both the system and something independent of it (panentheism); (3) he is not the system, but is in every respect independent of it (absolutistic theism). There seems to be a fourth possibility: God is not the system, but in intimate relatedness creatively sustains it and is affected by it. He is not given his being by the process or the finite participants in it, but his activity can be either hindered or advanced by their deeds. He is constantly undertaking new forms of creation, but in accord with his eternal character as dynamic ground of the whole. Such a view appears to conserve both the priority, integrity, and creative involvement of God and the worth and free responsibility of men.

Valuable complementation of process thought, with its evolutionary scientific and metaphysical perspectives, is provided by other theologians who likewise stress the relational and dynamic activity of God, but from a more biblical orientation. Contrary to the initial impression made by the title, Eberhard Jüngel's work *Gottes Sein ist im Werden (God's Being Is in Becoming)* does not reduce God's being to becoming, but maintains that divine being by its very nature acts in human history. For Jüngel this means primarily the action of the trinitarian God, in the coming of Jesus Christ and in his ongoing work as Holy Spirit, to disclose himself to men in history. "The becoming in which God's being is, is a becoming out of the Word in which God affirms himself." God creates his world, acts in its life redemptively through Jesus Christ, and *remains* a being in becoming by continuing to act in creation as Spirit.[14] Obviously Jüngel's largely Barthian understanding of the being and becoming of God differs greatly from that of the process thinkers, and it lacks their scientific outlook. However, it can contribute specifically Christian elements to a conception of God which relates him concretely to the current of events in nature and history.

Much closer to the central motif of process thought is the theology of hope now being developed by Jürgen Moltmann, Wolfhart Pannenberg, Johannes B. Metz, and others. Stimulated in part by Ernst Bloch's philosophy of the "not-yet," but deeply rooted in the biblical witness, they are expounding an eschatology which is this-worldly as well as trans-earthly. God is for these theologians the promise or power of the future. In Moltmann's words, we cannot have him "in us or over us but always only before us."[15] He is the God of the Exodus and of promise, who makes all things new and calls into existence that which is not (Rev. 21:5; Rom. 4:17). The sphere of his promise is the ceaselessly moving horizons of history.

For Moltmann Christian hope is grounded in the resurrection of Jesus Christ. The radical opposition of cross and resurrection discloses the contradiction between God's promise and present reality, but the risen Lord reveals God's power and potentiality and arouses hope. Christ's parousia means not the return of one who has departed, but an arriving future which involves the coming of the new.[16] In the light of the "history-making event" of the resurrection, all other history is "illumined, called in question and transformed." Since the God who is coming promises a new world of righteousness and truth, he calls the currently real into question because it

---

[14] *Gottes Sein ist im Werden; Verantwortliche Rede vom Sein Gottes bei Karl Barth. Eine Paraphrase* (Tübingen: J. C. B. Mohr [Paul Siebeck], 1965), pp. 117-19.
[15] *Theology of Hope*, pp. 16, 30, 106.
[16] *Ibid.*, pp. 198, 210 f., 224-29.

is not yet what it can become. "Thus 'history' arises in the light of its end," and its driving force is the promise of God.[17] Moreover, such a God calls his people to mission in the world. The church which celebrates the Exodus of Israel and the exodus of Christ from death must be an exodus church, released like an arrow into history to point to God's future by working for his coming Kingdom. The Christian task therefore includes social transformation: the realization of justice, humanization, socialization, and peace.[18]

The theology of hope is sometimes led by its eschatological enthusiasm to neglect the past and present action of God. If assertions regarding God's future are to be more than romantic hopes they must be rooted to some degree in past and present experience. The God who is coming must be in some measure already here; divine promise implies a Promiser—someone who makes the promise to us now. Questionable also is Moltmann's thesis that the sole ground of Christian hope is the resurrection of Christ or the assurance of its future consummation. Somehow the future affirmed by a resurrection faith must be related to man's total experience of reality. At points like these Moltmann's understanding of God could well find correction in process thought. However, the theology of hope brings strengths of its own to the conception of God as dynamic, life-transforming activity: the convincing evidence it offers of the biblical witness to a God who is constantly working to create the new; its clear espousal of an eschatology closely related to man's earthly history; its interpretation of divine transcendence in terms of God's going before men, leading his pilgrim people into untrodden paths; and its stress on the involvement of God in the struggle for social justice.[19]

Process thought and the theology of hope are important contemporary interpreters of long-recognized but often-over-

[17] *Ibid.*, pp. 180, 164 f., 260 f.
[18] *Ibid.*, pp. 194-96, 202 f., 333, 329.
[19] See my review of Moltmann, *Theology of Hope*, in *Interpretation*, 22 (1968), 480-83.

looked aspects of the Christian understanding of God. No conception deserves the support of Christians today if it does not relate the divine life to the empirical realities of dynamic change and movement toward the new. "To have faith in God," writes Samuel H. Miller, is "to believe in becoming, in the limitless possibilities of becoming, in the kind of becoming that transfigures men and transforms the world." [20]

3. GOD AS LOVE

If we synthesize being and process and regard God as the dynamic processual be-ing or "isness" which enables the world to be and to become, we move far toward an intelligible idea of the divine reality. However, at this stage we are still short of an adequate conceptualization of the meaning of God as known to faith and encountered in worship. The relation of God to our human experiences of value, though implicit in much that has been said, must now be made explicit.

Being and process might be indifferent or inimical to human well-being. Power could be tyrannical or demonic, frustrating rather than enhancing the values cherished by men. As Hegel said, "God must do more than thunder." If the term *God* is to be applied to the ground of our existence, that ground must also be conceived as the source and sustainer of value, and as itself supremely worthful. Fact and value, though often in tension with each other, belong together, and no interpretation can render either intelligible if it ignores the other. Thus Christian thought is led to understand the whole of reality in terms of the righteousness, the fatherly goodness, or the love of God. Macquarrie, for example, asserts that "being which gives being is also gracious being," or "holy being." [21]

The importance of this dimension appears with particular clarity when we recall that God for Christian faith is centrally

[20] *The Dilemma of Modern Belief*, p. 56.
[21] *Principles of Christian Theology*, pp. 110, 105, 108.

the object of men's worship, trust, and personal commitment. He is worshiped primarily not because he is regarded as the creator and preserver of nature, or even of human life, but because he is encountered in faith as superlatively worthy of worship and trust. Experienced as the wholly righteous one and as the self-giving love which will not let us go, he is adored as the ultimate source and support of all that is good. No concept is better qualified to gather together and express the various elements of this fundamental experience of faith than that of love.

There can be no question about the centrality of the divine love in the biblical writings. It is important to note, however, that the love of God proclaimed by the Hebrews prophets and the New Testament evangelists is never an abstract quality. Rather it is God himself acting in history to create, redeem, and renew his creatures for fellowship with himself. In love he calls Israel to become a covenant community, and in love he leads his people out of bondage in Egypt. But in love also, operating as discipline, he permits them to be carried into captivity in Babylon because they have persistently broken the covenant. In the New Testament it is above all God's redemptive action in Jesus Christ which reveals his character as love. "God shows his love for us," declares Paul, "in that while we were yet sinners Christ died for us" (Rom. 5:8). The same affirmation appears repeatedly in the Johannine writings (cf. John 3:16; I John 4:8-10). Though the apostolic witnesses do not work out a detailed theology, they clearly ground their empirical awareness of transforming love in the reality of God himself: "Love is of God, and he who loves is born of God and knows God. . . . God is love" (I John 4:7-9).

Nels F. S. Ferré finds in agape both the essential content of the divine nature and the determinative motif and norm of the whole of theology. Agape he defines as the outgoing, unconditional, and inclusive love of God; its function is to create a fellowship which is found uniquely in Christian faith. Few theologians are inclined to make love so all-encompassing; however, most assign to it an important if not a central place in their thought of God. The views of Macquarrie and Hartshorne are worthy of special attention here, since they illustrate how love can be synthesized with the two motifs—being and relational process—which we have so far found to be indispensable in our attempt to conceive the reality of God.

Macquarrie provides for love in God by interpreting love as ontologically equivalent to the "letting-be" which defines being. To *let* means to empower or enable, while to *be* means to enjoy the maximum range of being which is possible for a particular being. Hence loving or "letting-be" a person means helping him to realize his fullest potentialities; since this involves the expenditure of one's own being, it is costly. With reference to God, therefore, love denotes his "self-giving and letting-be"; his very essence "as Being is to let-be, to confer, sustain, and perfect the being of the creatures." The model of love for the Christian is the absolute letting-be of the love disclosed in Jesus Christ.[22]

In process thought, the love of God is interpreted mainly in terms of the activity by which God draws together and sustains in mutually supportive relationships the parts of the interconnected whole which contribute to and find their fulfillment in his life. In Hartshorne's view, when we speak of God as love we focus attention on his social character. To love is to share deeply in the joys and sorrows of others, hence to be influenced by those loved; it means to give oneself rather than to receive. Love asks above all for an opportunity to contribute to the being of others. However, in men this relationship is limited, partial, mixed with indifference and self-centeredness. As Charles Wesley saw, the divine love which excels all others is "pure" and "unbounded." Love is basically

[22] *Principles of Christian Theology*, pp. 310 f., 452; cf. pp. 193, 200, 235, 247; *God-Talk*, p. 227.

social awareness; taken without qualification, and literally rather than merely metaphorically, love so conceived is God. The highest kind of love is the ideal form of social interdependence, and both are ultimate. Deity, then, can be described as "the unsurpassably interacting, loving, presiding genius and companion of all existence." [23]

Both these interpretations help to illuminate the meaning of divine love. Moreover, they complement each other: Hartshorne stresses the multidirectional, social character of love which is not developed in Macquarrie's concentration on God's letting-be of each finite being, while Macquarrie's existentialist analysis discloses implications for love in the meaning of being itself which remain unexplored in Hartshorne. Both approaches enrich our understanding of God as love, and they can be utilized without threatening the divine unity. However, it is important to avoid subordinating love to either being or process, as would occur if love were treated simply as an attribute of either. The fact that both can be interpreted in terms of love suggests that it is as ultimate as they, so that God might be referred to as enduring or dynamic love no less fittingly than as loving being or socially aware becoming. The Christian gospel proclaims the transforming power of the self-giving agape which frees persons from the bonds of their fears and self-centeredness. Such love cares so much for the true good of others that it willingly suffers in their behalf. Our thinking must provide for the distinctiveness of such love, which in Jesus Christ is disclosed as integral to the deepest reality of God.

Admittedly, to interpret the value dimension of our relation to God wholly in terms of love is to run the risk of oversimplification if not distortion. However, for the sake of brevity love is here conceived broadly to include the righteousness or justice of God as well as his character as the source and ground of

[23] *The Divine Relativity*, pp. 26, 55 f., 36; *A Natural Theology for Our Time*, pp. 75, 45, 137.

all of men's experiences of true worth. One expression of God's concern for those he loves is his provision of an order in which their practice of such concern contributes to the fullest welfare of all, and in which therefore an outgoing, self-giving regard for all other persons becomes an imperative —the righteous, holy will of God. The same imperative applies to the pursuit of truth, the creation and enjoyment of beauty, and the richest possible realization of the whole range of value. The opening to men of infinite possibilities for such experiences and the summons to actualize them are alike the work of divine love.

4. GOD AS PERSONAL LIFE

A favorite target of atheistic hostility is the personal, supernatural, omnipotent God of traditional theism. Belief in a personal deity is rejected in part because it is thought to enthrone above the world an absolute monarch whose arbitrary will leaves no room for any exercise of responsible freedom by men. We have found weighty reasons for sharing the atheistic rejection of this conception.

However, dissatisfaction with personalistic notions of God is not limited to atheists. The naturalistic theism of Henry Nelson Wieman and the "ecstatic naturalism" of Paul Tillich find personality an inappropriate and inadequate symbol to designate the source of human good or the ground of being, even though these thinkers admit that worship and prayer are impossible unless God is imagined to be personal. Leslie Dewart holds that personality could be ascribed to God as long as it could be regarded, as it was by Thomas Aquinas, as "what is most perfect in all nature," [24] but our present understanding of personality no longer permits this. Dewart recognizes that the relations between man and God are inevitably personal, since *we* are personal. Nevertheless, he believes, we

---

[24] *Summa Theologica,* I, 29, 3.

should give up conceiving of God as a personal center of being to which we are drawn, and think of him instead as "an expansive force which impels persons to go out from and beyond themselves." [25]

However, the abolutistic suppression of human freedom to which the atheists object is not inherent in every conception of God as personal. Moreover, the admission of Wieman, Tillich, and Dewart that we cannot avoid thinking of the deepest relations between God and man in personal terms should warn us against a too easy dismissal of the personal analogy. Our thought of God should offer the most coherent interpretation of our total human experience; hence it must ask seriously what experiences like encounter, trust, prayer, acceptance, and commitment say to us regarding the God to whom they refer.

Each of the main lines of thought stimulated by the atheistic critique, and discussed in Chapter IV, points toward an activity at the heart of things which is more closely akin to personality as we know it than to anything else. We have spoken of God in terms of a relationship to the world grounding its unity, manifold activity, and ultimate meaning; of free creativity making possible both order and novelty; of a synthesis of change and identity; of movement in hope and promise toward attainment of a future Kingdom which is not yet realized; of temporality linking past, present, and future and implying both memory and anticipation; of dynamic participation in history; of self-giving love; of redemptive purpose; of victory through suffering; of self-revelation, incomparably in Jesus Christ; of interpersonal relations in worship and the whole of life; of a call to men to accept freedom and responsibility as God's fellow workers. Such activities remain incomprehensible if they are regarded as functions of timeless being or static substance, or if they are ascribed to an unconscious

---

[25] *The Future of Belief*, p. 189.

force or an unknowing process, but they become intelligible on the personal plane.

Such an interpretation, moreover, is completely in harmony with the three conceptual models so far considered in this chapter. Although none of them makes personality central, being, process, and love as we have presented them imply some kind of self-consciousness, and these concepts are most illuminating if this implication becomes explicit. Since the term love originates peculiarly in human social relations, its personal connotations are evident. This appears immediately if we simply list some of the terms used in the foregoing exposition: care, concern for others, righteous will, self-giving regard, sharing of joys and sorrows, fatherly goodness, social awareness. Such language becomes practically meaningless if it is not interpreted in terms of personal relations.

With regard to being and process, a few of the theologians who regard these concepts as definitive may speak for themselves. Macquarrie, for example, in interpreting God as being or letting-be, makes much of the divine *initiative*—in eliciting worship, giving himself to men in revelation and grace, making himself known, and calling and choosing man.[26] Neither initiative as such nor these forms of it would make sense if conceived impersonally. But Macquarrie does not leave us dependent on such inferences. He states quite explicitly that the holy being which he identifies with God is best represented as personal being.

Personal being is the most appropriate symbol for Being itself; for personal being stands highest in the hierarchy of beings which all seek to be like God, and personal being, as showing the richest diversity in unity and the highest possibilities for creativity and love, gives to our minds the fullest disclosure of the mystery of Being that we can receive.[27]

[26] *Principles of Christian Theology*, pp. 6, 46, 134, 303, 433 f.
[27] *Ibid.*, p. 250.

The process theologians are equally clear in asserting the consciousness of God. Whitehead himself declares that the consequent nature of God is conscious. Viewing personality as a "personally ordered" sequence of experiences with certain traits which characterize all its stages, he conceives God as divine personality, with the qualification that God does not share the imperfection involved in finite forgetting. Hartshorne, in effect equating *social* and *personal* in his conception of God, asks,

What is a person if not a being qualified and conditioned by social relations, relations to other persons? . . . Either God really does love all beings, that is, is related to them by a sympathetic union surpassing any human sympathy, or religion seems a vast fraud.[28]

Similarly, Ogden asserts that "the first (and last!) thing to be said about God is that He is the supreme Self or Thou, whose absolute relativity or all-embracing love is the beginning and end of man and, indeed, of the whole creation." [29]

Thinkers who interpret God as personal being or personal relational processs are joined by a host of others who conceive God in personal terms. Their numbers include all those contemporary theologians who with Martin Buber regard the relation between God and man primarily as an I-Thou encounter between subjects, liberal evangelicals (whether personal idealists or realists in philosophy), Protestant conservatives, and most Roman Catholic and Eastern Orthodox thinkers. Often personalistic language is mixed with and even submerged in other terms, as when the Trinity is still interpreted as one substance in three hypostases or "persons." Also, all too frequently this admixture results, as we have seen, in static, absolutistic, deterministic notions of God which separate him from a living relation to events in the world and

[28] *The Divine Relativity*, p. 25.
[29] *The Reality of God*, p. 66. Here Ogden refers to Rom. 8.

unduly limit human responsibility. However, these ideas are not integral to the personal analogy, and they can be purged from it. If they are, the conception of God as personal may greatly advance rather than hinder our understanding of his living reality.

Such a conception is clearly supported by the biblical witness. In both the Old and the New Testaments God addresses men and expects a response. He loves men to the uttermost and hopes for an answering love. He gathers together a community of faith and mission. He acts purposively in history. He is referred to by a variety of titles taken from human relations: King, good Shepherd, Lord of the vineyard, Father, Servant, Spirit. Most importantly, to the community of the new covenant he discloses himself supremely in a historical person, Jesus Christ. John E. Smith suggests that this climactic event taken as a whole "points to an individual reality, spiritual in character, and including within its own nature capacities that are analogous to a self as known to us in human experience." [30] In the light of the Incarnation, terms like selfhood, personality, or conscious individuality are the most appropriate means of expressing in words the Christian understanding of God.

The differentiated unity of God affirmed by the doctrine of the Trinity is also better expressed when God in his wholeness is conceived as personal rather than when he is regarded as tri-personal. When the Latin Fathers spoke of God as three *personae* sharing one substance they did not mean three individual centers of awareness, as the recent meaning of *person* would suggest. We shall probably be closest to the original intent of the doctrine, and to its abiding truth, if we think of God not as three persons, but in terms of three fundamental manifestations or aspects, three interrelated modes of activity or forms of expression of one personal life, correspond-

[30] *Experience and God,* p. 93.

ing to the main fashions in which God has manifested himself in Christian experience. To the Christian, one divine personality is eternally active and known preeminently in three ways. He is Father—Creator and Sustainer of all existence and Conserver and Advancer of all values. He is Son—Savior, Redeemer, self-giving, suffering, reconciling Love. He is Holy Spirit—sanctifying, empowering, life-giving, and renewing Spiritual Presence.

In thinking of God in these terms we must of course beware of reducing him to the level of finite personality, and thus creating God in our own frail image. God must far transcend the limitations of knowledge, power, and goodness which characterize human persons. As the ground of all that is or may become, he cannot be restricted to particular times and spaces; omnipresent and eternal, he is capable of acting everywhere and at all times. Whereas human selves are related to only a few others, the divine Self is intimately related to all finite selves as the source and continuing basis of their dynamic interconnectedness. These and other decisive differences between God and men must be fully recognized. Nevertheless, our understanding is enriched and clarified if we conceive him as possessing characteristics somewhat akin to what we experience as self-consciousness, reason, purposiveness, discrimination among and ability to realize values, and capacity to enter into and sustain relations with other persons. Personality at its highest provides the best conceptuality available as we attempt to grasp something of the meaning of the divine.

Such thinking is admittedly and necessarily analogical, and in a double sense. It seeks to move from our knowledge of the ideas, words, and deeds of human persons to an understanding of their Creator and Redeemer. But it also moves from an extra-human activity which confronts men to a better comprehension of the meaning of human life. Martin Buber writes, "The real God is the God who can be spoken to, because He is the one who speaks to men." [31]

Two further words of caution are needed. First, we must use the personal analogy in close relation to the other three previously discussed. Each supplies something essential to our thought of God, and none is sufficient by itself. Taken together, they provide a diversified yet integrated conceptuality that expresses the major positive proposals which were stimulated by the atheistic critique of theistic belief. We are thus led to think of God as the dynamic personal love at the heart of reality, as the creative, energizing actuality of the personal life who in love animates and interpenetrates all that is and seeks to realize what ought to be, or as the loving personality in process who is the ultimate ground of all being and becoming, and who is supremely manifest in Jesus Christ. Some such concept may contribute to deepened understanding by Christians of the meaning of their faith, while at the same time providing a useful basis for constructive conversation between Christians and atheists.

The other caution concerns the need for humility. Hebrew-Christian thought has always recognized that God is hidden as well as revealed; paradoxically, his very self-disclosure makes us more acutely aware of his hiddenness. We dare never imagine that we can box him into a neat formula. The *mysterium tremendum fascinans* analyzed in Rudolf Otto's classic study of the numinous points to a presence which cannot be contained in even our most sophisticated concepts. Though our relation to God is marked by nearness as well as otherness, by fascination as well as awesome mystery, the mystery remains profound. Nevertheless, this acknowledgment is not an invitation to stop thinking, but rather a summons to use our God-given capacities to understand as fully as possible. God's own revelatory activity sends shafts of light into the dimness of our existence. By facing toward the light

[31] *To Hallow This Life*, p. 5.

with eyes of faith and active, receptive minds we give to God the response he needs to show us who he is and what he calls on us to do. Our theologizing is our effort to do what we can to make his self-disclosure intelligible. We can engage in the task fully conscious of our limitations yet confident that truth is attainable. In relation to God we know only in part, but we do know. We see through a glass darkly, but we do see, and what we see illumines our way as we seek to contribute responsibly to the ongoing life of the community of love which God is ever seeking to create anew.

bibliography

I. DISCUSSIONS OF ATHEISM IN GENERAL

Beckett, Samuel. *Waiting for Godot.* London: Faber & Faber, 1956.
Blackham, H. J. (ed.). *Objections to Humanism.* Philadelphia: J. B. Lippincott, 1963.
Borne, Etienne. *Modern Atheism.* London: Burns & Oates, 1961.
Buckley, George T. *Atheism in the English Renaissance.* New York: Russell & Russell, 1965.
Burkle, Howard R. *The Non-existence of God; Antitheism from Hegel to Dumery.* New York: Herder and Herder, 1969.
Fabro, Cornelio. *God in Exile: Modern Atheism; A Study of the Internal Dynamics of Modern Atheism from Its Roots in the Cartesian Cogito to the Present Day,* tr. and ed. Arthur Gibson. Glen Rock, N. J.: Newman Press, 1968.
Gibson, Arthur. *The Faith of the Atheist.* New York: Harper & Row, 1968.
Girardi, Giulio (ed.). *Contemporary Atheism.* Four volumes. Torino: Societa Editrice Internazionale, 1968-69.
Hartshorne, M. Holmes. *The Faith to Doubt; A Protestant Response to Criticisms of Religion.* Englewood Cliffs, N. J.: Prentice-Hall, 1963.
Hebblethwaite, Peter. *The Council Fathers and Atheism.* Glen Rock, N. J.: Paulist Press, 1967.
Is God Dead? (Concilium, Vol. 16). Glen Rock, N. J.: Paulist Press, 1966.
Kasch, Wilhelm F. *Atheistischer Humanismus und christliche Existenz in der Gegenwart.* Tübingen: J. C. B. Mohr (Paul Siebeck), 1964.
Kaufmann, Walter. *Critique of Religion and Philosophy.* New York: Harper & Brothers, 1958.
―――. *The Faith of a Heretic.* Garden City, N. Y.: Doubleday & Co., 1961.
―――(ed.). *Religion from Tolstoy to Camus.* New York: Harper & Brothers, 1961.
Klijn, G. P. "Schiet niet op de Atheist," *De Open Deur,* Vol. 30, No. 992 (March 18, 1966).

Lacroix, Jean. *The Meaning of Modern Atheism,* tr. Garret Barden. New York: The Macmillan Co., 1965.

———. "The Meaning and Value of Atheism Today," *Cross Currents,* 10 (1955), 203-19.

Lepp, Ignace. *Atheism in Our Time,* tr. Bernard Murchland. New York: The Macmillan Co., 1963.

Lilje, Hanns. *Atheism, Humanism and Christianity,* tr. Clifford Davis. Minneapolis: Augsburg Publishing House, 1964.

Lochman, Jan M. "Der Atheismus—Frage an die Kirche," *Evangelische Theologie,* 18 (1958), 112-22.

———. "Evangelium für Atheisten," *Internationale Dialog Zeitschrift,* 1 (1968), 221-29.

Loen, Arnoldus Ewout. *Secularization; Science Without God?* tr. Margaret Kohl. Philadelphia: Westminster Press, 1967.

Lubac, Henri de. *The Drama of Atheist Humanism,* tr. Edith M. Riley. Cleveland: World Publishing Co., (1951) 1963.

Luijpen, William A. *Phenomenology and Atheism.* Pittsburgh: Duquesne University Press, 1964.

MacKinnon, D. M., et al. *Objections to Christian Belief.* Philadelphia: J. B. Lippincott, 1963.

Marquardt, Friedrich Wilhelm. " 'Solidarität mit den Gottlosen'; Zur Geschichte und Bedeutung eines Theologumenons," *Evangelische Theologie,* 20 (1960), 533-52.

Marty, Martin E. *Varieties of Unbelief.* New York: Holt, Rinehart & Winston, 1964.

Mehl, Roger. *Images of Man.* Richmond: John Knox Press, 1965.

Miller, J. Hillis. *The Disappearance of God; Five Nineteenth-century Writers.* Cambridge, Mass.: Harvard University Press, 1966.

Miller, Samuel M. *The Dilemma of Modern Belief.* New York: Harper & Row, 1963.

Müller-Schwefe, Hans-Rudolf. *Atheismus.* Stuttgart: Kreuz-Verlag, 1962.

Ogden, Schubert M. "The Christian and Unbelievers," *motive,* Vol. 25, No. 8 (May, 1965), pp. 21-23.

Pannenberg, Wolfhart, "Typen des Atheismus und ihre theologische Bedeutung," *Zeitwende,* 34 (1963), 597-608.

Paul, Jean. *Rede des toten Christus vom Weltgebäude herab, dass kein Gott sei.* Tübingen: Rainer Wunderlich Verlag (Hermann Leins), 1947. (This essay from Paul's *Siebenkäs* appears also in Günther Bornkamm, *Studien zu Antike und Urchristentum; Gesammelte Aufsätze,* II [München: Chr. Kaiser Verlag, 1959], pp. 245-52.)

Paul, Leslie. *Alternatives to Christian Belief.* Garden City, N. Y.: Doubleday & Co., 1967.

Pfeil, Hans. *Der atheistische Humanismus der Gegenwart.* Aschaffenburg: Pattloch, 1959.
Rahner, Karl (ed.). *The Pastoral Approach to Atheism,* tr. Theodore L. Westow and others (*Concilium,* Vol. 23). Glen Rock, N. J.: Paulist Press, 1967.
Rich, Arthur. "Glaube und Unglaube in unserer Zeit," *Evangelische Theologie,* 19 (1959), 52-65.
Strunk, Orlo, Jr. *The Choice Called Atheism.* Nashville: Abingdon Press, 1968.
Stürmer, Karl. *Atheistischer Humanismus.* Göttingen: Vandenhoeck & Ruprecht, 1964.
Thielicke, Helmut. *Nihilism; Its Origin and Nature with Christian Answer.* New York: Harper & Row, 1961.
———. "Studie zum Atheismus-Problem," *Spannungsfelder der Evangelischen Soziallehre,* ed. Friedrich Karrenberg and Wolfgang Schweitzer. Hamburg: Furche Verlag, 1961. Pp. 202-10.
Tillich, Paul. *Perspectives on 19th and 20th Century Protestant Theology.* New York: Harper & Row, 1967.
Wyneken, Gustav. *Abschied vom Christentum.* München: Szczesny Verlag, 1963.

II. THE ATHEISTIC CRITIQUE OF RELIGIOUS BELIEF

A. николаиNETEENTH-CENTURY SOURCES

1. Ludwig Feuerbach

Feuerbach, Ludwig. *The Essence of Christianity.* London: Chapman, 1854; New York: Harper & Brothers (Torchbook), 1957.
———. *Lectures on the Essence of Religion,* tr. Ralph Manheim. New York: Harper & Row, 1967.

2. Marxist-Leninist Atheism

Marx, Karl. *Capital; A Critical Analysis of Capitalist Production,* tr. from 3rd Ger. ed. by Samuel Moore and Edward Aveling and ed. by Frederick Engels. London: William Glaisher, 1920.
———. *Early Writings,* tr. and ed. T. B. Bottomore. New York: McGraw-Hill, 1964.
———. *Selected Essays.* London: Leonard Persons, 1926.
———. *Werke,* III. Berlin: Dietz Verlag, 1962.
———, and Engels, Friedrich. *On Religion.* New York: Schocken Books, 1967. (References in the text refer to the Moscow ed. of 1957.)
Lenin, V. I. *Collected Works.* Moscow: Foreign Language Book House; London: Lawrence and Wishart, 1960-66:

"The Attitude of the Workers' Party to Religion" (1909), XV, 402-13.

"Classes and Parties in Their Attitude to Religion and the Church" (1909), XV, 414-23.

"Socialism and Religion" (1905), X, 83-87.

Two letters to Maxim Gorky (1913), XXXV, 121-24, 127-29.

———. *Religion*. New York: International Publishers, 1933.

Schachnowitsch, M. I. *Lenin und die Fragen des Atheismus*. Berlin: Dietz Verlag, 1966.

3. Friedrich Nietzsche

Biser, Eugen. *"Gott ist tot," Nietzsches Destruktion des christlichen Bewusstseins*. München: Kösel-Verlag, 1962.

Grau, Gerd-Günther. *Christlicher Glaube und intellektuelle Redlichkeit; Eine religionsphilosophische Studie über Nietzsche*. Frankfurt am Main: Schulte-Bulmke, 1958.

Heidegger, Martin. "Nietzsches Wort 'Gott ist tot,'" *Holzwege*. Frankfurt am Main: Vittorio Klostermann, 1950. Pp. 193-247.

Kaufmann, Walter (ed.). *The Portable Nietzsche*. New York: Viking Press, 1954.

Löwith, Karl. *From Hegel to Nietzsche; The Revolution in Nineteenth-century Thought*, tr. David E. Green. New York: Holt, Rinehart & Winston, 1964.

Nietzsche, Friedrich. *Complete Works of Friedrich Nietzsche*, ed. Oscar Levy. New York: Russell & Russell, 1964.

XII. Beyond Good and Evil.
XIV. The Will to Power.
XVI. The Antichrist.

———. *The Gay Science*, in *The Portable Nietzsche*, ed. Walter Kaufmann.

———. *Thus Spake Zarathustra*, tr. Thomas Coleman. New York: Modern Library, n. d.

B. Varieties of Atheistic Humanism

1. Freudian Psychoanalysis

Bamberger, John. "Religion as Illusion? Freud's Challenge to Theology," *Is God Dead?* (*Concilium*, Vol. 16) Glen Rock, N. J.: Paulist Press, 1966. Pp. 73-88.

Freud, Sigmund. *The Future of an Illusion*. London: Hogarth Press, 1928. Also in *The Complete Psychological Works of Sigmund Freud*. New York: Liveright; London: Hogarth Press, 1961. XXI, 5-56.

———. *Moses and Monotheism*, tr. Katherine Jones. New York: Alfred A. Knopf, 1939.

———. *Totem and Taboo*, tr. A. A. Brill. New York: New Republic, 1927.
———, and Pfister, Oskar. *Psychoanalysis and Faith: The Letters of Sigmund Freud and Oskar Pfister*, ed. Heinrich Meng and Ernst L. Freud, tr. Erich Mosbacher. New York: Basic Books, 1963.
Fromm, Erich. *The Dogma of Christ, and Other Essays on Religion, Psychology, and Culture*, tr. James Luther Adams. New York: Holt, Rinehart & Winston, 1963.
Guirdham, Arthur. *Christ and Freud; A Study of Religious Experience and Observance*. London: Allen & Unwin, 1959.
Jones, Ernest. *The Life and Work of Sigmund Freud*, III. New York: Basic Books, 1953-57.
Lee, Roy Stuart. *Freud and Christianity*. New York: A. A. Wyn, 1949.
Ostow, M., and Scharfstein, B. *The Need to Believe*. New York: International Universities Press, 1954.
Philip, H. L. *Freud and Religious Belief*. London: Rockliff, 1956.
Reik, Theodor. *Dogma and Compulsion; Psychoanalytic Studies of Religion and Myths*, tr. Bernard Miall. New York: International Universities Press, 1951.
Ricoeur, Paul. "The Atheism of Freudian Psychoanalysis," *Is God Dead?* (*Concilium*, Vol. 16) Glen Rock, N. J.: Paulist Press, 1966. Pp. 59-72.

2. Marxism

Bloch, Ernst. *Atheismus im Christentum*. Frankfurt am Main: Suhrkamp Verlag, 1968.
———. *Erbschaft dieser Zeit*. Frankfurt am Main: Suhrkamp Verlag, (1935) 1962.
———. *Geist der Utopie*. Frankfurt am Main: Suhrkamp Verlag, (1918) 1964.
———. "Man as Possibility," *Cross Currents*, 18 (1968), 273-83.
———. "Der Mensch des utopischen Realismus," *Dokumente der Paulus-Gesellschaft*, XII. München: Paulus-Gesellschaft, 1965. Pp. 98-119.
———. *Philosophische Grundfragen*. I. *Zur Ontologie des Nochnicht-seins*. Frankfurt am Main: Suhrkamp Verlag, 1961.
———. *Das Prinzip Hoffnung*. 2 volumes. Frankfurt am Main: Suhrkamp Verlag, (1953) 1959.
———. *Thomas Münzer als Theologe der Revolution*. Frankfurt am Main: Suhrkamp Verlag, (1921) 1962.
———. *Tübinger Einleitung in die Philosophie*. 2 volumes. Frankfurt am Main: Suhrkamp Verlag, 1963-64.
Cox, Harvey. "The Christian-Marxist Dialogue—What Next?" *Dialog*, 7 (1968), 18-26.

———. "Ernst Bloch and 'The Pull of the Future,'" *New Theology No. 5,* ed. Martin E. Marty and Dean G. Peerman. New York: The Macmillan Co., 1968. Pp. 191-203.

Fetscher, Iring. "Die bolschewistische Religionskritik und die Wissenschaft," *Zeitwende; Die neue Furche,* 32 (1961), 798-807.

Fiorenza, Francis P. "Dialectical Theology and Hope," I-III. *The Heythrop Journal,* 9 (1968), 143-63, 384-99; 10 (1969), 26-42.

Fischer, Gerhard, et al. *Fruchtbares Gespräch; Der Christ und die moderne Wissenschaft.* Berlin: Union Verlag, n. d. (1966).

Flügel, Heinz. *Zwischen Gott und Gottlosigkeit.* Stuttgart: Evangelisches Verlagswerk, 1957.

Garaudy, Roger. *From Anathema to Dialogue; A Marxist Challenge to the Christian Churches,* tr. Luke O'Neill. New York: Herder and Herder, 1966.

———, Metz, J. B., and Rahner, Karl. *Der Dialog, oder ändert sich das Verhältnis zwischen Katholizismus und Marxismus?* Hamburg: Rowohlt Taschenbuch Verlag, 1966.

Gardavský, Vítězslav. *Gott ist nicht ganz tot.* München: Chr. Kaiser Verlag, 1968.

Girardi, Giulio. *Marxism and Christianity,* tr. Kevin Traynor. New York: The Macmillan Co., 1968.

Gollwitzer, Helmut. "The Christian Church and Communistic Atheism," *Dialog,* 7 (1968), 27-33.

———. *Die marxistische Religionskritik und der christliche Glaube.* München, Hamburg: Siebenstern Taschenbuch Verlag, 1965.

———, and Lehnbruch, Gerhard. *Kleiner Wegweiser zum Studium des Marxismus-Leninismus.* Bonn: Publikationsstelle des Bundesministeriums für gesamtdeutsche Fragen, 1956.

Heidtmann, Günter, et al. (eds.). *Protestantische Texte aus dem Jahre 1965.* Stuttgart: Kreuz-Verlag, 1966.

Heim, Theodor. "Blochs Atheismus," *Ernst Bloch zu ehren; Beiträge zu seinem Werk,* ed. Siegfried Unseld. Frankfurt am Main: Suhrkamp Verlag. Pp. 157-79.

Heise, Wolfgang. *Aufbruch in die Illusion; Zur Kritik der bürgerlichen Philosophie in Deutschland.* Berlin: VEB Deutscher Verlag der Wissenschaften, 1964.

Hromádka, Josef L. *An der Schwelle des Dialogs zwischen Christen und Marxisten.* Frankfurt am Main: Stimme-Verlag, 1965.

Initiative in History: a Christian-Marxist Exchange. Cambridge, Mass.: The Church Society for College Work, 1967.

Jüchen, Aurel von. *Gespräch mit Atheisten.* Gütersloh: Verlag "Kirche und Mann," 1962.

Kellner, Erich (ed.). *Christentum und Marxismus—heute.* Wien, Frankfurt, Zürich: Europa Verlag, 1966.

Klaus, Georg. *Jesuiten, Gott, Materie; Des Jesuitenpaters Wetter*

Revolte wider Vernunft und Wissenschaft. Berlin: VEB Deutscher Verlag der Wissenschaften, 1957.

Klohr, Olof. "Probleme des wissenschaftlichen Atheismus und der atheistischen Propaganda," *Deutsche Zeitschrift für Philosophie,* 12 (1964), 133-48.

―――― (ed.). *Moderne Naturwissenschaft und Atheismus.* Berlin: VEB Deutscher Verlag der Wissenschaften, 1964.

―――― (ed.). *Religion und Atheismus heute; Ergebnisse und Aufgaben marxistischer Religionssoziologie.* Berlin: VEB Deutscher Verlag der Wissenschaften, 1966.

Koch, Hans-Gerhard. *The Abolition of God; Materialistic Atheism and Christian Religion,* tr. Robert W. Fenn. Philadelphia: Fortress Press, 1963.

Lukács, Georg. *Geschichte und Klassenbewusstsein; Studien über marxistische Dialektik.* Berlin: Der Malik-Verlag, 1923.

――――. *Die Zerstörung der Vernunft; Der Weg des Irrationalismus von Schelling zu Hitler.* Berlin: Aufbau-Verlag, 1955.

Machovec, Milan. *Marxismus und dialektische Theologie; Barth, Bonhoeffer, und Hromádka in atheistischer-kommunistischer Sicht.* Zürich: EVZ Verlag, 1965.

Marsch, Wolf-Dieter. *Hoffen worauf? Auseinandersetzung mit Ernst Bloch.* Hamburg: Furche-Verlag, 1963.

――――. "Wie revolutionär sind Christen? Christlicher Glaube und das Problem der Revolution." *Information* Nr. 31. Stuttgart: Evangelische Zentralstelle für Weltanschauungsfragen, April, 1968.

"Marxistischer Atheismus und Christentum." *Information* Nr. 14. Stuttgart: Evangelische Zentralstelle für Weltanschauungsfragen, Juni, 1965.

Moltmann, Jürgen. "Hope and Confidence: A Conversation with Ernst Bloch," *Dialog,* 7 (1968), 42-55.

――――. "Hope Without Faith: An Eschatological Humanism Without God," *Is God Dead? (Concilium,* No. 16) Glen Rock, N. J.: Paulist Press, 1966. Pp. 25-40.

Ogletree, Thomas W. (ed.). *Openings for Marxist-Christian Dialogue.* Nashville: Abingdon Press, 1969.

Pawjolkin, Paul. *Der religiöse Aberglaube und seine Schädlichkeit.* Berlin: Dietz Verlag, 1954.

Rahner, Karl. *Marxistische Utopie und christliche Zukunft des Menschen.* Einsiedeln: Benziger Verlag, 1965.

Reding, Marcel. "Atheistische Ethik," *Lexikon für Theologie und Kirche,* I, 990-94.

――――. *Der politische Atheismus.* Graz: Verlag Styria, 1957.

Robbe, Martin. *Der Ursprung des Christentums.* Leipzig, Jena, Berlin: Urania-Verlag, 1967.

Schilling, S. Paul. "Ernst Bloch: Philosopher of the Not-Yet," *The Christian Century*, 84 (1967), 1455-58.

Schrey, Heinz-Horst. *Auseinandersetzung mit dem Marximus*. Stuttgart: Kreuz-Verlag, 1963.

Stöhr, Martin (ed.). *Disputation zwischen Christen und Marxisten*. München: Chr. Kaiser Verlag, 1966.

Walser, Martin (ed.). *Ueber Ernst Bloch*. Frankfurt am Main: Suhrkamp Verlag, 1968.

Wetter, Gustav A. *Dialektischer und historischer Materialismus*. Frankfurt am Main: Fischer Bücherei, 1962.

Zimmermann, Wolf-Dieter. *Die Welt soll unser Himmel sein; Atheistische Propaganda in der DDR*. Stuttgart: Kreuz-Verlag, 1963.

3. Existentialism

Camus, Albert. *The Fall*, tr. Justin O'Brien. New York: Alfred A. Knopf, 1957.

———. *The Myth of Sisyphus, and Other Essays*, tr. Justin O'Brien. New York: Vintage Books, 1959.

———. *The Plague*, tr. Stuart Gilbert. New York: Modern Library, 1948.

———. *The Rebel; An Essay on Man in Revolt*, tr. Anthony Bower. New York: Vintage Books, 1956.

———. *The Stranger*, tr. Stuart Gilbert. New York: Alfred A. Knopf, 1960.

———. "Der Ungläubige und die Christen," *Fragen der Zeit*. Hamburg: Rowohlt Verlag, 1960.

Dostoevski, Fëdor Mikhailovich. *The Brothers Karamazov*. New York: Harper & Brothers, 1960. (Also available in Modern Library edition.)

Heidegger, Martin. *Being and Time*, tr. John Macquarrie and Edward Robinson. London: SCM Press, 1962.

———. *Holzwege*. Frankfurt am Main: Vittorio Klostermann, 1950.

———. "'Über den Humanismus'; Brief an Jean Beaufret, Paris," *Platons Lehre von der Wahrheit; Mit einem Brief über den "Humanismus."* Bern: Verlag A. Francke, 1947.

Kafka, Franz. *The Castle*, tr. Willa and Edwin Muir. New York: Alfred A. Knopf, 1954.

———. *The Trial*, tr. Willa and Edwin Muir. New York: Alfred A. Knopf, (1956) 1960.

Kaufmann, Walter (ed.). *Existentialism from Dostoevsky to Sartre*. New York: Meridian Books, 1957.

Merleau-Ponty, Maurice. *Éloge de la Philosophie*. Paris: Gallimard, 1953.

———. *Sens et Non-Sens*. Paris: Gallimard, 1948.

Sartre, Jean Paul. *Being and Nothingness,* tr. Hazel E. Barnes. New York: Citadel Press, 1965.
———. *The Devil and the Good Lord and Two Other Plays.* New York: Vintage Books, 1962.
———. *Existentialism,* tr. Bernard Frechtman. New York: Philosophical Library, 1947.
———. *Of Human Freedom,* ed. Wade Baskin. New York: Philosophical Library, 1967.
———. *Les mouches.* Paris: Gallimard, 1943.
———. *Le mur.* Paris: Gallimard, 1959.
———. *Nausea,* tr. Lloyd Alexander. Norfolk, Conn.: New Directions, 1964.
———. *No Exit, and Three Other Plays.* New York: Vintage Books, 1956.

4. Scientific Humanism

Fromm, Erich. *You Shall Be as Gods.* New York: Holt, Rinehart & Winston, 1966.
———. *Psychoanalysis and Religion.* New Haven: Yale University Press, 1950.
Huxley, Julian. *Essays of a Humanist.* London: Chatto and Windus, 1964.
———. "The New Divinity," *Classical and Contemporary Readings in the Philosophy of Religion,* ed. John Hick. Englewood Cliffs, N. J.: Prentice-Hall, 1963. Pp. 357-63.
———. *Religion Without Revelation.* Rev. ed. New York: Harper & Brothers, (1927) 1957.
——— (ed.). *The Humanist Frame.* New York: Harper & Brothers, 1961.
Lamont, Corliss. *Humanism as a Philosophy.* New York: Philosophical Library, 1949.
Leppin, Eberhard. *Glaubt ihr nicht, so bleibt ihr nicht.* Tübingen: J. C. B. Mohr (Paul Siebeck), 1966.
van Praag, J. P. *Humanism.* Utrecht: International Humanist and Ethical Union, 1957.
Religious Humanism; A Quarterly Journal of Religious and Scientific Humanism. Yellow Springs, Ohio: Fellowship of Religious Humanists, 1 (1967)—
Russell, Bertrand. "A Free Man's Worship," *Mysticism and Logic and Other Essays.* London: Longmans, Green & Co., 1921.
———. *Religion and Science.* New York: Henry Holt & Co., 1935.
———. *What I Believe.* New York: E. P. Dutton & Co., 1925.
———. *Why I am not a Christian.* New York: Simon and Schuster, 1957.
———. *The Will to Doubt.* New York: Philosophical Library, 1958.

Szczesny, Gerhard. *The Future of Unbelief,* tr. Edward B. Garside. London: Heinemann, 1962.
──── (ed.). *Club Voltaire I.* München: Szczesny Verlag, 1964.
Weinstock, Heinrich. *Die Tragödie des Humanismus.* Heidelberg: Quelle & Meyer, 1953.

5. Linguistic Philosophy

Ayer, Alfred J. *The Concept of a Person.* New York: St. Martin's Press, 1963.
────. *The Foundations of Empirical Knowledge.* London: The Macmillan Co., 1940.
────. *Language, Truth and Logic.* New York: Dover Publications, 1950.
van Buren, Paul M. *The Secular Meaning of the Gospel.* New York: The Macmillan Co., 1966.
────. *Theological Explorations.* New York: The Macmillan Co., 1968.
Charlesworth, Maxwell J. *Philosophy and Linguistic Analysis.* Pittsburgh: Duquesne University Press, 1959.
Ferré, Frederick. *Language, Logic, and God.* New York: Harper & Row, 1961.
Flew, Antony, and MacIntyre, Alasdair (eds.). *New Essays in Philosophical Theology.* New York: The Macmillan Co.; London: SCM Press, 1955.
Gilkey, Langdon. *The Relevance of God-language.* Indianapolis: Bobbs-Merrill, 1967.
Hanson, Norwood Russell. "What I Don't Believe," *Continuum,* 5 (1967), 89-105.
Hordern, William. *Speaking of God.* New York: The Macmillan Co., 1964.
Hutchison, John H. *Language and Faith.* Philadelphia: Westminster Press, 1963.
Wisdom, John. *Logic and Language* (First Series). Oxford: B. H. Blackwell, 1953.
────. *Philosophy and Psycho-analysis.* New York: Philosophical Library, 1953.
Wittgenstein, Ludwig. *Lectures and Conversations on Aesthetics, Psychology, and Religious Belief,* ed. Cyril Barrett. Oxford: Basil Blackwell & Mott, 1966.
────. *Philosophical Investigations.* Oxford: Basil Blackwell & Mott, (1953) 1958.
────. *Tractatus Logico-Philosophicus,* tr. C. K. Ogden. London: Kegan Paul, 1922.

6. "Christian Atheism" of the Death of God

Altizer, Thomas J. J. "Creative Negation in Theology," *The Christian Century*, 82 (1965), 864-67.
———. *The Gospel of Christian Atheism*. Philadelphia: Westminster Press, 1966.
———. *Mircea Eliade and the Dialectic of the Sacred*. Philadelphia: Westminster Press, 1963.
——— (ed). *Toward a New Christianity; Readings in the Death of God Theology*. New York: Harcourt, Brace & World, 1967.
———, and Hamilton, William. *Radical Theology and the Death of God*. Indianapolis: Bobbs-Merrill, 1966.
Bent, Charles N. *The Death-of-God Movement*. Glen Rock, N. J.: Paulist Press, 1967.
Casserley, Julian Victor Langmead. *The Death of Man; A Critique of Christian Atheism*. New York: Morehouse-Barlow, 1967.
Christian, C. W., and Wittig, Glenn R. (eds.). *Radical Theology: Phase Two*. Philadelphia: J. B. Lippincott, 1967.
Cooper, John Charles. *The Roots of the Radical Theology*. Philadelphia: Westminster Press, 1967.
Gollwitzer, Helmut. *Von der Stellvertretung Gottes; Christlicher Glaube in der Erfahrung der Verborgenheit Gottes*. München: Chr. Kaiser Verlag, 1967.
Hamilton, Kenneth. *God Is Dead; The Anatomy of a Slogan*. Grand Rapids: Eerdmans, 1966.
Hamilton, William. "The Death of God," *Playboy*, August, 1966, pp. 79, 84, 137 f.
———. "The Death-of-God Theology," *The Christian Scholar*, 48 (1965), 27-48.
———. *The New Essence of Christianity*. New York: Association Press, 1961.
———. "A Secular Theology for a World Come of Age," *Theology Today*, 18 (1961-62), 435-59.
Ice, Jackson Lee, and Carey, John J. (eds.). *The Death of God Debate*. Philadelphia: Westminster Press, 1967.
Miller, William Robert (ed.). *The New Christianity; An Anthology of the Rise of Modern Religious Thought*. New York: Delacorte Press, 1967.
Ogletree, Thomas W. *The Death of God Controversy*. Nashville: Abingdon Press, 1966.
——— (ed.). *Radical Theology Reader*. Indianapolis: Bobbs-Merrill, 1969.
Rubenstein, Richard L. *After Auschwitz; Radical Theology and Contemporary Judaism*. Indianapolis: Bobbs-Merrill, 1966.
———. "Judaism and the Death of God," *Playboy*, July, 1967, pp. 69 f., 74, 130-32.

Sölle, Dorothee. *Christ the Representative; An Essay in Theology after the "Death of God,"* tr. David Lewis. Philadelphia: Fortress Press, 1967.
Vahanian, Gabriel. *The Death of God; The Culture of Our Post-Christian Era.* New York: George Braziller, (1961) 1966.
———. *No Other God.* New York: George Braziller, 1966.
——— (ed.). *The God Is Dead Debate.* New York: McGraw-Hill, 1967.

III. THE MEANING OF GOD

von Balthasar, Hans Urs. *Die Gottesfrage des heutigen Menschen.* Wien, München: Verlag Herold, 1956.
Barbour, Ian G. *Issues in Science and Religion.* Englewood Cliffs, N. J.: Prentice-Hall, 1966.
——— (ed.). *Science and Religion: New Perspectives on the Dialogue.* New York: Harper & Row, 1968.
Baum, Gregory (ed.). *The Future of Belief Debate.* New York: Herder and Herder, 1967.
Berkhof, Hendrikus. "On the Death of the Self-evident God." New York: Department of Youth Ministry, National Council of Churches, n. d.
Bonhoeffer, Dietrich. *Letters and Papers from Prison,* ed. Eberhard Bethge, tr. Reginald Fuller. Rev. ed. New York: The Macmillan Co., (1953) 1967.
Braun, Herbert. "Gottes Existenz und meine Geschichtlichkeit," *Zeit und Geschichte, Dankausgabe an Rudolf Bultmann.* Tübingen: J. C. B. Mohr (Paul Siebeck), 1964.
———. "The Problem of a New Testament Theology," tr. Jack Sanders, *Journal for Theology and Church,* ed. Robert M. Funk. New York: Harper & Row, 1965. Pp. 169-83.
Buber, Martin. *The Eclipse of God; Studies in the Relation between Religion and Philosophy.* New York: Harper & Brothers, (1952) 1957.
———. *I and Thou,* tr. Ronald Gregor Smith. Edinburgh: T. & T. Clark, 1937.
Bultmann, Rudolf. *Essays Philosophical and Theological.* New York: The Macmillan Co., 1955.
———. *Glauben und Verstehein; Gesammelte Aufsätze,* IV. Tübingen: J. C. B. Mohr (Paul Siebeck), 1965. Pp. 107-27.
———. "The Idea of God and Modern Man," *Journal for Theology and Church,* ed. Robert M. Funk. New York: Harper & Row, 1965.
Buri, Fritz. *How Can We Still Speak Responsibly of God?* Philadelphia: Fortress Press, 1968.

Cairns, David. *God up There? A Study in Divine Transcendence.* Philadelphia: Westminster Press, 1967.

Capps, Walter H. (ed.). "A Symposium on Hope," *Cross Currents,* 18 (1968), 257-335.

Cobb, John B., Jr. "Speaking about God," *Religion in Life,* 36 (1967), 28-39.

Dewart, Leslie. *The Foundations of Belief.* New York: Herder and Herder, 1969.

―――. *The Future of Belief; Theism in a World Come of Age.* New York: Herder and Herder, 1966.

Durandeaux, Jacques. *Living Questions to Dead Gods,* tr. William Whitman. New York: Sheed & Ward, 1968.

Ebeling, Gerhard. *God and Word,* tr. James W. Leitch. Philadelphia: Fortress Press, 1967.

―――. "The Message of God to the Age of Atheism," *Bulletin,* Oberlin College Graduate School of Theology, January, 1964, pp. 3-14.

―――. *Word and Faith,* tr. James W. Leitch. Philadelphia: Fortress Press, 1963.

Edwards, David L. (ed.). *The Honest to God Debate.* Philadelphia: Westminster Press, 1963.

Farley, Edward. *The Transcendence of God; A Study in Contemporary Philosophical Theology.* Philadelphia: Westminster Press, 1960.

Ferré, Nels F. S. *The Living God of Nowhere and Nothing.* Philadelphia: Westminster Press, 1967.

Gilkey, Langdon. *Maker of Heaven and Earth; The Christian Doctrine of Creation in the Light of Modern Knowledge.* Garden City, N. Y.: Doubleday & Co., (1959) 1965.

Gogarten, Friedrich. *Die Frage nach Gott.* Tübingen: J. C. B. Mohr (Paul Siebeck), 1968.

Gollwitzer, Helmut. *The Existence of God as Confessed by Faith,* tr. James W. Leitch. Philadelphia: Westminster Press, 1965.

―――. *Gottes Offenbarung und unsere Vorstellung von Gott.* München: Chr. Kaiser Verlag, 1964.

―――. "Das Wort 'Gott' in christlicher Theologie," *Theologische Literaturzeitung,* 92 (1967), 162-76.

Hamilton, Peter. *The Living God and the Modern World.* London: Hodder & Stoughton, 1967.

Hartshorne, Charles. *The Divine Relativity.* New Haven: Yale University Press, 1948.

―――. *A Natural Theology for Our Time.* LaSalle, Ill.: Open Court, 1967.

―――. "Process Philosophy as a Resource for Christian Thought,"

Philosophical Resources for Christian Thought, ed. Perry LeFevre. Nashville: Abingdon Press, 1968.

———, and Reese, William L. (eds.). Philosophers Speak of God. Chicago: University of Chicago Press, 1953.

Herzog, Frederick. Understanding God; The Key Issue in Present-day Protestant Thought. New York: Charles Scribner's Sons, 1966.

Hick, John. Evil and the God of Love. New York: Harper & Row, 1966.

Jenkins, Daniel. The Christian Belief in God. Philadelphia: Westminster Press, 1963.

Jüngel, Eberhard. Gottes Sein ist im Werden; Verantworliche Rede vom Sein Gottes bei Karl Barth. Eine Paraphrase. Tübingen: J. C. B. Mohr (Paul Siebeck), 1965.

Kitamori, Kazoh. Theology of the Pain of God. Richmond: John Knox Press, 1965.

Küng, Hans (ed.). The Unknown God? New York: Sheed & Ward, 1966.

Kutschki, Norbert (ed.). Gott heute; Fünfzehn Beiträge zur Gottesfrage. Mainz: Matthias-Grünewald-Verlag; München: Chr. Kaiser Verlag, 1967.

Lewis, H. D. Our Experience of God. London: Allen & Unwin, 1959.

Lubac, Henri de. The Discovery of God, tr. Alexander Dru. New York: P. J. Kenedy, 1960.

MacGregor, Geddes. God Beyond Doubt. Philadelphia: J. B. Lippincott, 1966.

———. The Sense of Absence. Philadelphia: J. B. Lippincott, 1968.

Macquarrie, John. God-Talk; An Examination of the Language and Logic of Theology. New York: Harper & Row, 1967.

———. Principles of Christian Theology. New York: Charles Scribner's Sons, 1966.

Maritain, Jacques. God and the Permission of Evil, tr. Joseph W. Evans. Milwaukee: Bruce Publishing Co., 1966.

Marty, Martin E., and Peerman, Dean G. (eds.). New Theology No. 5. New York: The Macmillan Co., 1968.

Mascall, E. L. He Who Is; A Study in Traditional Theism. London: Longmans, Green & Co., (1943) 1962.

Metz, Johannes Baptist. "Future of Faith in a Hominized World," Philosophy Today, 10 (1966), 289-99.

———. "The Responsibility of Hope," Philosophy Today, 10 (1966), 280-88.

Moltmann, Jürgen. "Hope and History," Theology Today, 25 (1968), 369-86.

———. Theology of Hope; On the Ground and the Implications of a Christian Eschatology. New York: Harper & Row, 1967.

Moore, Don Sebastian. *God Is a New Language*. Glen Rock, N. J.: Newman Press, 1967.

Murray, John Courtney. *The Problem of God: Yesterday and Today*. New Haven: Yale University Press, 1964.

Novak, Michael. *Belief and Unbelief*. New York: The Macmillan Co., 1965.

Ogden, Schubert. *The Reality of God and Other Essays*. New York: Harper & Row, (1963) 1966.

———. "What Sense Does It Make to Say, 'God Acts in History'?" *Journal of Religion*, 43 (1963), 1-18.

Ogletree, Thomas W. "A Christological Assessment of Dipolar Theism," *Journal of Religion*, 47 (1967), 87-99.

Outler, Albert C. *Who Trusts in God*. New York: Oxford University Press, 1968.

Pannenberg, Wolfhart, "The Question of God," *Interpretation*, 21 (1967), 289-314.

Pittenger, W. Norman. "A Contemporary Trend in North American Theology: Process-Thought and Christian Faith," *Religion in Life*, 34 (1965), 500-510.

———. *Process-Thought and Christian Faith*. New York: The Macmillan Co., 1968.

———. *God in Process*. London: SCM Press, 1967.

———. *Reconceptions in Christian Thinking, 1817-1967*. New York: Seabury Press, 1968.

———. "Toward a More Christian Theology," *Religion in Life*, 36 (1967), 495-505.

Rahner, Karl. *Glaubst du an Gott?* München: Verlag Ars Sacra, 1967.

Ratschow, Carl Heinz. *Gott existiert; Eine dogmatische Studie*. Berlin: Alfred Töpelmann, 1960.

Reese, William L., and Freeman, Eugene (eds.). *Process and Divinity; Philosophical Essays Presented to Charles Hartshorne*. LaSalle, Ill.: Open Court Publishing Co., 1964.

Ricoeur, Paul. *The Symbolism of Evil*, tr. Emerson Buchanan. New York: Harper & Row, 1967.

Robinson, John A. T. *Exploration into God*. Stanford: Stanford University Press, 1967.

———. *Honest to God*. Philadelphia: Westminster Press, 1963.

———. *In the End God*. New York: Harper & Row, 1968.

Sauter, Gerhard. *Zukunft und Verheissung*. Zürich: Zwingli-Verlag, 1965.

Schillebeeckx, E. *God the Future of Man*, tr. N. D. Smith. New York: Sheed & Ward, 1968.

Schweitzer, Eduard. "Was heisst 'Gott'? Gedanken zur Problematik des Gottesbegriffes in der modernen Theologie," *Evangelische Theologie,* 25 (1965), 339-49.

Simon, Ulrich E. *A Theology of Auschwitz.* London: Victor Gollancz, 1968.

Smart, Ninian. "Omnipotence, Evil and Superman," *Philosophy,* 36 (1961), 188-95.

Smith, John E. *Experience and God.* New York: Oxford University Press, 1968.

———. *Reason and God; Encounters of Philosophy with Religion.* New Haven: Yale University Press, 1961.

Teilhard de Chardin, Pierre. *The Divine Milieu; An Essay on the Interior Life.* New York: Harper & Row, 1960.

Tillich, Paul. *Systematic Theology.* 3 volumes. Chicago: University of Chicago Press, 1952-63.

Unseld, Siegfried (ed.). *Ernst Bloch zu ehren; Beiträge zu seinem Werk.* Frankfurt am Main: Suhrkamp Verlag, 1965.

Whitehead, Alfred North. *Process and Reality.* New York: The Macmillan Co., 1929.

———. *Religion in the Making.* New York: The Macmillan Co., 1926.

Williams, Daniel Day. "The New Theological Situation," *Theology Today,* 24 (1967-68), 444-63.

———. *The Spirit and the Forms of Love.* New York: Harper & Row, 1968.

———. "The Vulnerable and the Invulnerable God," *Union Seminary Quarterly Review,* 17 (1962), 223-29.

Zahrnt, Heinz. *Die Sache mit Gott; Die protestantische Theologie im 20. Jahrhundert.* München: Piper & Co., 1966.

index of persons

Abraham, 67, 165
Alexander, Samuel, 173 n.
Altizer, Thomas J. J., 101, 105-8, 111, 132, 159
Aristotle, 59, 170
Augustine, 133, 139, 166
Ayer, Alfred J., 97-98

Bachem, A., 184
Barbour, Ian G., 161, 172, 193
Barth, Karl, 141, 145, 152, 156
Bense, Max, 81, 84 n., 92 n.
Berdyaev, Nicolas, 156, 173 n., 178
Bergson, Henri, 173 n.
Berkhof, Hendrikus, 144-45
Bertocci, Peter A., 173
Birch, L. Charles, 184, 186
Blake, William, 105
Bloch, Ernst, 51, 58-64, 127, 131, 156, 164, 169, 203
Bonhoeffer, Dietrich, 16, 104, 112, 140, 149
Bonnet, Charles, 20
Boodin, John E., 173 n.
Braithwaite, R. B., 122
Braun, Herbert, 102, 112-13, 159-60
Brightman, Edgar Sheffield, 148, 173, 188
Buber, Martin, 19, 133, 137, 142, 148, 155, 212, 214
Buffon, George Louis Leclerc, 20
Bultmann, Rudolf, 148-49, 169
van Buren, Paul M., 99, 122, 160

Camus, Albert, 65, 69-78, 121, 123-24, 188
de Chirico, Giorgio, 14
Cobb, John B., Jr., 150, 168
Cohen, Morris R., 81, 83, 119
Cohen, Robert S., 9
Comte, Auguste, 20, 30
Copernicus, 55, 119
Coulson, C. A., 140
Cox, Harvey, 160
Cusanus, Nicholas, 105

Darwin, Charles, 40, 119
Descartes, René, 77,
Dressler, Helmut, 56-57, 127
Dewart, Leslie, 154, 173, 183, 194-95, 209-10
Dostoyevsky, Fedor, 64, 75, 123
Dubarle, Père, 140

Ehrenstrom, Nils, 9
Eliade, Mircea, 105
Engels, Friedrich, 26, 29-33, 57, 154 n.
Ermer, Cal, 153
Ezekiel, 158

Farmer, Herbert H., 187
Fechner, Gustav Theodor, 148, 173
Ferré, Frederick, 195
Feuerbach, Ludwig, 23-26, 33, 35, 40, 116, 145-46, 159
Flew, Antony, 124, 183
Franck, Sebastian, 187
Frank, Anne, 82

233

Freud, Sigmund, 40-47, 50-51, 117, 120
Fromm, Erich, 47, 49-51, 88-90

Galileo, 55, 119
Garaudy, Roger, 27 n., 52, 57-58, 125
Geren, Paul, 189-90
Gibson, Arthur, 196
Gilkey, Langdon, 175, 177
Gollwitzer, Helmut, 56-57, 113, 129, 144-45
Gorky, Maxim, 32
Gunsalus, Catherine L., 9

Haeckel, Ernst, 30
Hamilton, William, 101-2, 108, 111, 132
Hanzel, Lev, 53, 56
Hare, R. M., 122
Hartley, David, 20
Hartmann, Nicolai, 126
Hartshorne, Charles, 150-51, 154, 173, 184-85, 199, 200-201, 207-8, 212
Hebblethwaite, Peter, 168
Hegel, G. W. F., 23-24, 30, 59, 101, 105, 111, 156, 205
Heidegger, Martin, 16, 37
Heim, Karl, 162
Heinemann, Gustav, 16
Heisenberg, Werner, 184
Herzog, Frederick, 190
Hick, John, 181
Hitler, Adolf, 109, 158
Hocking, William Ernest, 173 n.
Horton, Walter Marshall, 147
Hume, David, 20, 116
Huxley, Julian, 80, 85-88

John the Baptist, 61
John of the Cross, 133
von Jüchen, Aurel, 127
Jüngel, Eberhard, 157, 202-3

Kaufman, Gordon D., 163
Kaufmann, Walter, 82, 121, 129
Kellner, Erich, 9, 27 n.
Kennedy, John F. and Robert F., 181
Kierkegaard, Sören, 67
King, Martin Luther, Jr., 181
Klaus, Georg, 56
Knight, Margaret, 79, 84
Korch, Helmut, 54 n., 55 n.
Klohr, Olof, 54 n., 55 n., 56 n., 127-28

de La Mettrie, Julien Offroy, 20
Lenin, V. I., 32-33, 56-57
Lequier, Jules, 173
Lukács, György, 52
Luther, Martin, 139

Machovec, Milan, 51, 122, 130
Mackie, J. L., 183
Macquarrie, John, 95, 196, 205, 207-8, 211
Malachi, 171
Marieb, Joyce, 10
Marks, Gary, 10
Martin, Kingsley, 82
Marx, Karl, 16, 26-30, 32-33, 40, 57, 116, 125-26, 129-30, 156
Merleau-Ponty, Maurice, 72, 123
Metz, Johannes Baptist, 57, 154, 167, 169, 203
Miller, Samuel H., 108, 133, 188, 205
Miller, William Robert, 159
Mitchell, Basil, 121
Moltmann, Jürgen, 165, 170, 203-4
Montague, William P., 173 n.
Moses, 42, 61, 164-65
Müller-Schwefe, Hans-Rudolf, 9
Münzer, Thomas, 59, 61

Neander, Joachim, 181

INDEX OF PERSONS

Newton, Isaac, 140
Niebuhr, H. Richard, 147
Nietzsche, Friedrich, 33-40, 63, 101, 105-6, 126, 144

Ogden, Schubert M., 150, 173, 200, 212
Ogletree, Thomas W., 173
Otto, Rudolf, 215
Outler, Albert C., 149, 155, 186
Överland, Arnulf, 83, 120

Pannenberg, Wolfhart, 147, 161, 163, 167, 203
Paul, Apostle, 123, 151, 156, 186, 189, 206
Pfister, Oskar, 46
Pittenger, W. Norman, 150, 199
Popper, Karl, 91
van Praag, J. P., 87
Priestley, J. B., 20
Prometheus, 14-15, 62

Rahner, Karl, 132, 157, 167
Rashdall, Hastings, 173 n.
Reik, Theodor, 47-49
Renan, Ernest, 48
Rilke, Rainer Maria, 168
Robbe, Martin, 51, 53, 130
Robinet, Jean Battiste, 20
Robinson, John A. T., 149, 160, 163
Root, Howard E., 146
Rubenstein, Richard L., 102, 108-10
Russell, Bertrand, 82, 129

Sabellius, 186
Sartre, Jean-Paul, 65-69, 73-74, 76-77, 125-26

Seidowski, Hans-Joachim, 55, 120, 131
Sisyphus, 14-15, 70-71
Smart, Ninian, 183
Smith, John E., 195, 213
Socinus, Faustus, 173
Sölle, Dorothee, 102, 111-12, 159
Symanowski, Horst, 120
Szczesny, Gerhard, 79, 81-84

Taubes, Susan Anima, 132
Teilhard de Chardin, Pierre, 173 n.
Theseus, 14-15
Thomas Aquinas, 59, 139, 166, 209
Thorez, Maurice, 53
Tillich, Paul, 109, 168, 209-10
Togliatti, Palmiro, 53
Tomin, Julius, 58, 132

de Vries, Josef, 54 n.
Voltaire, 20

Ward, James, 173 n.
Watts, Isaac, 180
Weil, Simone, 17
von Weizsäcker, Carl Friedrich, 142
Wesley, Charles, 207
Wesley, John, 139
Whitehead, Alfred North, 150, 154, 168, 173, 184, 192, 198, 212
Wieman, Henry Nelson, 209-10
Williams, Daniel Day, 150
Wittgenstein, Ludwig, 91-92, 95
Wootton, Barbara, 81
Wyneken, Gustav, 87, 119

Zahrnt, Heinz, 127-28

index of subjects

Absurdity, 15, 67-74, 124
Agape, 178, 206-8
Alienation, 24, 26-28, 51, 133
Anthropology, 23, 59
Atheism. See also Unbelief
  age of, 7, 14-15
  Christian, 100-114, 132, 159-60
  Christian attitude toward, 7, 16-20, 115, 134
  Feuerbachian, 23-26, 33, 35, 40, 116, 145-46, 159
  Freudian, 40-51
  Marxist. See Marxism
  Nietzschean, 30-40, 63, 101, 105-6, 126, 144
  Sartrean, 65-69, 73-74, 76-77, 125-26
  value for belief, 16-20, 191
Auschwitz, 13, 82, 109-10, 122-23, 181, 183

Being, 194-98

Change, revolutionary, 27-30, 33, 58-64. See also Creativity; Newness; Process
Christianity. See Religion
Church. See Religion
Creatio ex nihilo, 175-76
Creation. See God, creator
Creativity, 61, 87, 143, 164-66, 172, 174-79, 186, 195

Deism. See God, absoluteness
Dogma, 44-45, 47

Eschatology, 60-64, 106-7, 131, 164-70, 190, 198, 203-4
Eucharist, 43-44
Evil, 71-75, 82, 86, 121-25, 179-82, 187-90. See also God, and evil
Evolution, 85-88, 106-7, 172, 176, 186
Existentialism, 64-79, 123, 125, 141-44
Experience, religious, 173, 177, 193, 206, 215

Freedom, 62, 64-68, 71, 76-78, 109-10, 125-28, 152-58, 178-79, 182-85, 196, 200-201. See also Man, responsibility
Front, 60, 165
Future, 60-64, 106-7, 131, 164-70, 175, 190, 198, 203-4

God
  absence, 14-15, 104-5, 108-9, 111, 126, 132-33
  absoluteness, 57, 63-64, 68, 86, 108, 127, 131, 138, 149-51, 170-71, 173-74, 191, 194-95, 198
  being, 151, 173, 194-98
  and contingency, 178-79, 184-88, 200
  creative process, 149-52, 170-74, 198-205, 215
  creator, 72, 107-8, 123-25, 127, 141-42, 149, 151, 158, 174-80, 186, 189, 202-3

236

God—Cont'd
  death of, 7, 13-14, 35-39, 63, 89, 100-114, 132, 138, 159
  and evil, 71-72, 74, 82, 86, 109, 121-25, 138, 179-82, 184-90
  exalted father, 40-44, 117
  existence, 92-94, 97, 196-97
  future, 164-70, 203-4
  grace, 128, 156-57, 189
  hiddenness, 111, 192, 215-16
  as human experience, 96, 112-13, 122, 144, 159
  hypothesis of, 68, 84, 140
  immanence, 100-114, 144, 147-59, 162-63, 174, 178-79, 184-88
  irrelevance, 15, 126-27
  kingdom of, 13, 106, 130, 169-71, 190, 204
  knowledge of, 132, 141-47. See also Language, religious
  language about, 91-100, 105, 120-22, 143. See also Language, religious
  love, 205-9, 215
  and man
    basic relationship, 138, 142, 147-51, 163, 170-74, 177, 200, 202-3
    freedom and responsibility, 67, 88, 109-10, 125-28, 138, 152-58, 182-85, 208
    love for man, 121-22, 124, 138, 141, 178, 187, 189-90
  and nature, 140-44, 147-52, 170-74, 177, 202-3
  objectification of human characteristics, 23-26, 29-31, 33-34, 51-52, 115-17
  personal life, 110, 209-15,
  presence, 14, 102-4, 131-33, 137, 147-50, 154, 174

God—Cont'd
  redeemer, 138-39, 141-42, 151, 176-79
  secularization of, 99-114, 159-62
  self-revelation, 140-42, 144-47, 215
  sovereignty, 109, 138, 152-54, 158, 174-76, 181, 183, 188, 202
  suffering of, 112, 122, 185-88
  temporality, 170-74
  transcendence, 15, 28-29, 76, 84, 88, 99-100, 110, 113, 147, 158-64, 167. See also Language, religious, transcendent reference of
  word of, 144-46, 171, 174, 202
Grace. See God, grace and sovereignty

Hope, 60-64, 131, 164-70, 190, 203-5
Humanism
  atheistic, 35-38, 45, 56-58, 63-71, 76-79, 118-19, 126, 129, 164. See also Existentialism; Marxism
  Christian, 153-58
  religious, 85-90
  scientific, 79-90, 118, 126-28

Jesus Christ
  centrality, 103-4, 107, 111
  death of God, 103, 106, 108
  freedom, 100
  Incarnation, 106-8, 156,
  rebel, 63
  redeemer, 43, 141, 151-52
  representative, 111-12, 159
  resurrection, 165-66, 203-4
  revelation, 99, 144, 158, 178, 206-8, 215
  suffering of, 49-50, 186

Knowledge, religious, 139-44. See also Language, religious; Linguistic Analysis

Language, religious
 relation to totality of life, 139-47, 193, 210
 transcendent reference of, 96-100, 120-22, 144, 159-62
 verifiability of, 92-98, 143-44, 192
Linguistic Analysis
 method, 90-100, 120-22, 141, 143
 verification principle, 90-95, 121-22
Logical Positivism, 91, 96-98
Love, 206-8, 211. See also Agape; God, love, love for man

Man
 exaltation of, 15, 25, 28, 35-36, 38, 57, 65-71, 86-87, 125-27, 159-60
 finitude, 66-69, 72-73, 110, 123-24, 127-28, 158, 171
 and God. See God, and man
 interdependence of, 76-78, 182, 185, 209
 and nature, 62, 64, 123-24, 147-52
 responsibility, 34-39, 45, 57-58, 62, 64-68, 76-78, 83-84, 86-87, 89-90, 110, 125-28, 152-58, 168, 178-79, 190, 200-201
 self-definition, 65-71, 73
Marxism
 Bloch's critique of, 62-63
 contemporary, 51-64, 122-23, 127, 130-32, 164
 historic, 26-33, 51-64, 79, 84, 116, 118-19, 125-27, 130, 167, 169
 as world view, 56-58, 120

Materialism
 dialectical, 26, 30-31, 56, 61, 63
 naturalistic, 26, 30, 33, 54-56, 58, 81. See also Naturalism, atheistic
Matter, dynamism of, 61-62, 164, 172-73
Meaninglessness, 15, 66-74. See also Absurdity
Metaphysics
 necessity of, 161, 192-94
 rejection of, 37, 72, 111, 141, 160, 192

Naturalism, atheistic, 23, 80-90, 209. See also Materialism
Nature and God, 140-44, 147-52
New, the, 60-61
Newness, 60-61, 166, 168, 172, 203-4
Nihilism, 36-38, 101
Not-yet, philosophy of, 60, 62, 131, 164, 198
Novum. See New, the

Panentheism, 150-51, 200 202
Paulus-Gesellschaft, 8-9
Process
 philosophy of, 140, 173, 192
 theology of 150-51, 154, 168, 173, 192-93, 198-205, 207, 212

Rebelliousness, 71-74, 123-24
Religion
 acquiesence of in injustice, 52-53, 74-75, 83-84, 123, 128-31, 158, 169-70
 debasement of man, 24, 32, 34-36, 50-51, 57, 84, 125-28
 and economic and political forces, 26-34, 51-53, 63, 83, 116, 123, 128-29
 humanistic, 85-90

Religion—*Cont'd*
  as illusion, 24, 27, 44-48, 117
  as inhibitor of responsibility, 35, 80-81, 84, 86, 110, 128-31, 152-54, 157
  as instrument of exploitation, 26-27, 31-32, 51-52, 83-84, 131
  irrationalism of, 7, 17-18, 46-47, 82
  irrelevance of, 29-30, 53, 129
  need for criticism of, 16-19, 139, 146, 155, 161, 191
  as obsessional neurosis, 40, 48, 117
  as opium, 27, 32
  response to suffering, 26-27, 29, 34, 53, 130
  and science
    compatibility of, 55, 140-44
    incompatibility of, 30-31, 46-48, 53-55, 79-81, 84, 118-20, 132
  as wish fulfillment, 24-25, 44-46, 49-51, 115, 117
Revelation, truth of, 144-47, 193

Science. *See* Religion, and science; Unbelief, bases of, science
Secularization. *See* God, secularization of
Suffering. *See* Evil

Theism, static, 62-64, 131, 168, 170, 194-95
Time, 61, 170-74. *See also* God, temporality
Transcendence. *See* God
Trinity, 212-14
Truth, religious, 144-47

Unbelief, bases of
  absence of personal awareness of God, 131-34
  acquiescence of religion in injustice, 26-34, 51-53, 63, 74-75, 83-84, 116, 123, 128-31, 158, 169-70
  evil and suffering, 65, 71-76, 82, 86, 109, 121-25, 138, 174-82, 184-90. *See also* Evil
  freedom and responsibility, 35, 67, 80-81, 84, 86, 88, 109-10, 125-31, 182. *See also* Freedom; God, freedom; Man, responsibility
  objectification of human characteristics, 23-27, 29-34, 40-52, 115-17
  science, 46-48, 53-55, 79-81, 84, 118-20, 132
  vagueness of religious language, 92-98, 100, 120-22, 143-44, 159-62. *See also* God, knowledge of, language about

Values
  and belief, 37-38, 50, 53, 84, 88-90, 125-26, 130, 201, 205, 208-9
  creation of man, 38, 45, 65-67, 73, 84-85, 125
  transvaluation of, 35, 37, 38
Vatican II, 16-17, 155, 168